high note 5

Workbook

Pearson
KAO TWO
KAO Park
Hockham Way
Harlow, Essex
CM17 9SR
England
and Associated Companies throughout the world

www.pearsonenglish.com/highnote

First published 2021
Second impression 2021

ISBN: 978-1-292-20994-4
Set in Akko Pro
Printed in Slovakia by Neografia

Acknowledgements
The publishers would like to thank the following people for their feedback and comments during the development of this course:
Anna Bator, Ingrida Breidaka, Gordana Bujanic Tretinjak, Nida Burnekaite, Anna Czernielewska, Justyna Deja, Izabela Gojny, Ewa Goldnik-Ciok, Daniela Ille, Anita Jokic, Zrinka Juric, Justyna Kostecka, Magdalena Loska, Magdalena Marmucka, Anna Milewska, Olivera Milovanovic, Alexandra Novikova, Ivana Plockinic, Biljana Pršic, Merike Saar, Tomasz Siuta, Aleksandra Strahinic, Olga Strelchenko, Małgorzata Syc-Jedrychowska, Katarzyna Tobolska, Beata Towarnicka, Beata Trapnell, Anna Wisniewska

Image Credit(s)
The publisher would like to thank the following for their kind permission to reproduce their photographs:

123RF.com: Aleksei Glustsenko 67, lekstuntkite 40, milkos 21, netfalls 93, soleg 104, Sviatlana Barchan 55, Valentin Valkov 23; **Alamy Stock Photo**: Mariusz Szczawinski 6, PA Collection 90; **Getty Images**: aluxum/E+ 100, andresr/E+ 117, Antonio Busiello/Moment 41, Chris J Ratcliffe/Getty Images News 27, Corbis 68, Cris Cantón/Moment 40, Daly and Newton/The Image Bank 18, DanielBehmPhotography.Com/Moment Open 95, Design Pics/Ron Nickel 117, Dougal Waters/DigitalVision 102, Downunderphotos/Moment 80, Eva-Katalin/E+ 44, Filippo Monteforte/AFP 88, Flashpop/DigitalVision 75, Francis G. Mayer/Corbis Historical 47, George Rinhart/Corbis Premium Historical 77, Harold M. Lambert/Archive Photos 89, Hill Street Studios/DigitalVision 42, 64, 103, 114, Hinterhaus Productions/DigitalVision 113, hoozone/E+ 58, Horacio Villalobos/Corbis News 35, Hulton Archive 79, Image Source 19, 28, James Warwick/The Image Bank 95, JGI/Jamie Grill 4, 35, John M Lund Photography Inc/Stone 49, John Springer Collection/Corbis Premium Historical 77, Jon Feingersh/The Image Bank 20, Kevin Winter/Getty Images Entertainment 87, Kondo Photography/Cultura 5, lisegagne/E+ 29, Maarten Wouters/DigitalVision 33, Martin Barraud/OJO Images 100, Martin Puddy/Stone 10, mheim3011/iStock 57, Milan_Jovic/iStock/Getty Images Plus 93, milkjo/E+ 54, Mint Images/Mint Images RF 82, MoMo Productions/Stone 16, Monty Rakusen/Cultura 9, Nick White and Fiona Jackson-Downes/Cultura 59, Niels Busch/Cultura 13, Oscar Wong/Moment Open 47, Peathegee Inc 76, PeopleImages/E+ 106, pepifoto/E+ 40, R.Tsubin/Estonia 40, RapidEye/E+ 97, Roos Koole/Moment 30, sanjeri/E+ 115, SDI Productions/E+ 55, 56, SrdjanPav/E+ 16, Stevica Mrdja/EyeEm 116, Tara Moore/Stone 61, THEPALMER/E+ 109, Vasilina Popova/DigitalVision 7, Vlad Fishman/Moment 43, Vstock/UpperCut Images 32, 32, Westend61 8, wynnter/E+ 53, Zave Smith/Image Source 52; **Pearson Education Ltd**: Gareth Boden 119; **Shutterstock**: addkm 46, Africa Studio 39, Andrey Popov 16, Anna Kucherova 40, AnnaKostyuk 104, Daisy Daisy 67, Estrada Anton 65, fizkes 66, Gladskikh Tatiana 70, Gorynvd 71, Ian Hinchliffe 34, Jaromir Chalabala 31, M. Unal Ozmen 40, Mau Horng 40, michaeljung 94, Mikael Damkier 40, Mike Lawn 123, Nils Jorgensen 83, ravl 40, Sanjeev Gupta/EPA-EFE 69, The Faces 67, Vladyslav Danilin 40, waldru 16, WindVector 111

Cover Image: *Front:* **Getty Images**: FatCamera

All other images © Pearson Education

Text Credit(s):
Excerpt on page 81 Permission of David Higgins Associates Limited; Article on page 93 from Setting sail: one woman's year alone at sea, *The Guardian*, Susan Smillie, 4 Nov 2018 © Guardian News and Media Ltd 2018

Illustration Acknowledgements
Alyana Cazalet (IllustrationX) page 45

Every effort has been made to trace the copyright holders and we apologise in advance for any unintentional omissions. We would be pleased to insert the appropriate acknowledgement in any subsequent edition of this publication.

CONTENTS

1A VOCABULARY AND SPEAKING

Compound adjectives (personality), personality adjectives and values, fixed expressions

1 ★ Complete the fixed expressions in bold with the prepositions from the box. Some prepositions can be used more than once.

about   by   for   into   ~~out~~   with

1 I really **get a kick** <u>out</u> of renovating furniture.

2 He **is nuts** _____ remote control cars.

3 She **sets great store** _____ good table manners.

4 Their salaries should be increased **in line** _____ inflation.

5 It was a tough choice, but I finally **plumped** _____ the blue one.

6 Your results **say a lot** _____ how hard you must have worked.

7 I'm just **not that** _____ cooking, it's too much effort.

8 I **clicked** _____ her straightaway and we've been friends ever since.

2 ★★ Replace the underlined parts of the sentences with the fixed expressions from Exercise 1. Make any necessary changes.

1 He <u>was really excited to see</u> his photo in the newspaper.

really got a kick out of seeing

2 We <u>hit it off with</u> each other from the start.

_____

3 She <u>really loves</u> salsa dancing.

_____

4 The way you deal with failure really <u>indicates something about</u> your character.

_____

5 I just can't decide which cake to <u>choose</u>. They both look delicious.

_____

6 I'm <u>far from enthusiastic about</u> sport.

_____

7 I've never <u>considered money very important</u>.

_____

8 The results were <u>similar to</u> what we would expect.

_____

3 ★★ Complete the sentences with the compound adjectives from the box.

absent-minded   forward-looking   highly strung
high-spirited   kind-hearted   laid-back   like-minded
narrow-minded   streetwise   strong-willed
thin-skinned   ~~tight-fisted~~

1 She's so *tight-fisted* that when she opens her purse, moths fly out!

2 I joined this club hoping to meet _____ people I'd have something in common with.

3 She's always been really _____. Once she makes up her mind, there's no shifting her.

4 He's so _____ that some people take advantage of it.

5 Their dog is rather _____. He barks whenever anyone walks past the house.

6 I'm so _____ I can't find my glasses even when they're on top of my head!

7 Because he was brought up in a small village, he isn't very _____.

8 Be careful what you say to her. She's really _____ and can't take criticism at all.

9 She smiled as she watched her _____ daughter doing cartwheels across the grass.

10 This business is stuck in the past. They need a more _____ approach.

11 Why won't you at least try the food? You're so _____! You might actually love it.

12 He never seems to worry about anything – he's so _____.

4 ★★★ Read the definitions and complete the words with one letter in each gap.

1 S*pontaneity* is the quality of being natural and not planned in advanced.

2 C__ __ __ __ __ __ __ __ __ is a willingness to devote time and energy to something you believe in.

3 F__ __ __ __ __ __ __ __ is a kind of honesty and straightforwardness.

4 A__ __ __ __ __ __ __ __ __ __ __ is the quality of being confident and not afraid to say what you want or believe in.

5 S__ __ __ __ __ __ __ __ is a situation which you can trust will not change.

6 T__ __ __ __ __ __ __ __ __ __ is the ability to give feedback without upsetting anyone.

7 S__ __ __ __ __ __ __ __ __ is the quality of being genuine and speaking from the heart.

8 D__ __ __ __ __ __ __ __ __ __ is the ability to keep a secret.

9 M__ __ __ __ __ is being able to forgive someone who you have authority over.

10 I__ __ __ __ __ __ __ __ __ __ is the quality of including many different types of people and treating everyone fairly and equally.

11 H__ __ __ __ __ __ __ is the quality of not being too proud about yourself.

5 ★★ Complete the sentences with the correct adjectives formed from the nouns in Exercise 4.

1 I'm sorry, but we need to have a *frank* discussion about your negative attitude.

2 It wasn't very _____ to comment on the size of her feet.

3 I don't feel that you are sufficiently _____ to this job. You turn up late almost every day.

4 The King did not believe in being _____ to his enemies, and treated them harshly.

5 If I tell you this, can you be _____ and keep it to yourself?

6 I didn't realise he was famous. He's so _____ he never mentioned it.

7 Do you have to plan everything in such detail? What's wrong with being _____?

8 The government advises against travel until the political situation is more _____.

9 We need to be more _____ so that everyone has the opportunity to access the programme.

10 He sounded _____, but my instinct told me he wasn't telling the truth.

11 If you don't want to do it, just say so! You need to be more _____.

6 ★★★ USE OF ENGLISH Complete the text with the correct words formed from the words in bold.

PEOPLE DON'T CHANGE – OR DO THEY?

Have you ever had the ¹*sensation* (SENSE) while looking at a photo of your younger self that the person in the image is somehow almost a different person?

Of course, we change physically as we grow up, and as we grow older, but it seems that our personalities may also go through a ² _____ (TRANSFORM). It's not just that we're no longer nuts about collecting toy cars, or that we are perhaps a bit more ³ _____ (TACT) as we grow more aware of other people's feelings, but that, over time, we become completely different people. Psychologists call this process 'personality maturation' and it appears to begin in our teenage years and continues until we are in our seventies. By the time we retire, not only are we perhaps a bit more ⁴ _____ (ABSENT) and forgetful, but, somewhat more surprisingly, we are also likely to have become more ⁵ _____ (HEART) and generous. It seems that, on average, negative personality traits are diminished and we will probably be less ⁶ _____ (HIGH) and more ⁷ _____ (LAID) than in our younger years.

This is fascinating both because of how much more malleable personality is than we may have thought, and because it turns on its head the stereotype of the grumpy old person who becomes more ⁸ _____ (NARROW) as they age, and sets great store by doing everything 'their' way.

Despite the tendency to become more agreeable with age, how our personalities develop will, of course, be moulded by our upbringing and later life experiences. There is also some evidence that as we go into very old age, our personalities may undergo something of a reversal, and we may become more ⁹ _____ (THIN) and quick to take offence as well as less tolerant and ¹⁰ _____ (INCLUDE), as we face the greater challenges of this particular stage of life.

7 ON A HIGH NOTE Write a paragraph about your personality as a child and how you think it has changed since then.

1B SPEAKING AND VOCABULARY

1 🔊 *2* Listen and repeat the phrases. How do you say them in your language?

SPEAKING | Paraphrasing what you hear

CHECKING UNDERSTANDING

To put it another way, your personality changes over the course of adult life.

In other words, personality is the first thing that should be considered.

If I'm hearing you correctly, you can always get more qualifications, but it's hard to change who you are fundamentally.

So you're saying (that) personality is more important than qualifications?

Let me get this straight – you always start the session with some psychometric tests.

SUMMARISING

Essentially, they can't see a connection between their studies and their future career path.

Simply put, it's vital for you to understand yourself better.

In a nutshell, these tests are pretty comprehensive.

So, what it boils down to is that my job suits me, but I need to make sure I keep getting new challenges.

---

2 Match the two parts of the sentences.

1 ☐ Essentially,
2 ☐ So, what it boils
3 ☐ Let me
4 ☐ In other
5 ☐ To put it
6 ☐ Simply
7 ☐ If I'm hearing you
8 ☐ In a
9 ☐ So you're saying

a get this straight – Grandma wants to travel the world?!
b down to is that it's a personal choice.
c put, I would avoid it at all costs.
d nutshell, it's not advisable.
e words, it's a disaster.
f another way, we need to start again.
g that there's a chance.
h they are amateurs.
i correctly, you decided to drop out of school?

3 🔊 *3* Complete the conversation with the words from the box. There are two extra words. Listen and check.

boils essentially hearing nutshell ~~saying~~ simply straight

Jess I'm really nervous about this interview tomorrow. I think I'm prepared, but what if they spring something on me?

Luke So, you're **¹***saying* they might ask you something you don't know?

Jess Well, yes, they might, but it's more that they might do something I'm not expecting at all. I was reading about these interview techniques where they try and find out about you in sneaky ways. **²**_____, they test you by doing something like dropping a pen on the floor and seeing if you pick it up.

Luke Let me get this **³**_____. You're worried the interviewer might drop their pen?

Jess In a **⁴**_____, it's a way of seeing if you're a nice person, you know, kind-hearted and empathetic.

Luke Really? What else did you read about?

Jess Well, another technique was to get someone to show you around. They'd be really friendly, but secretly they'd be trying to find out what you're really like. You know, if you're actually a bit of a wet blanket or whatever.

Luke So, what it **⁵**_____ down to is that you're worried they'll find out what an awful person you are? Come on, Jess, that's ridiculous. Just be yourself and don't obsess about it. You're such a smart cookie. You'll do fine.

Jess Fingers crossed!

4 Find and correct one mistake in each sentence.

1 To put it (other) way, it's just too expensive. *another*
2 On a nutshell, we need to plump for something different. _____
3 Let me put this straight. _____
4 If I'm listening to you correctly, we have a serious problem. _____
5 Simply taken, he's just too highly strung. _____
6 So, that it boils down to, is that there's no money left. _____
7 In another words, he's nuts about her. _____
8 So you're speaking that it's impossible? _____

5 **ON A HIGH NOTE** Choose three idioms from the box. For each idiom, write a short dialogue where someone explains what they mean by using the idiom. Use the phrases from the Speaking box.

a cold fish   a dark horse   a go-getter
a mover and shaker   a smart alec   a smart cookie
a soft touch

A He's a bit of a cold fish, isn't he?
B So, you're saying that you don't like him very much?
A Not exactly, no. Essentially, he just isn't very warm and friendly.

UNIT VOCABULARY PRACTICE > page 13

1C LISTENING AND VOCABULARY

1  🔊 **4** Listen to a psychology lecturer talking about his experience of being a twin. Complete the sentences with a word or short phrase in each gap.

1 In recent years, the percentage of twins being born is around *three* percent.

2 The lecturer says that _____ of twins are identical.

3 Even identical twins are not born with the same _____.

4 According to the lecturer, it is a _____ that twins skip a generation.

5 There is no evidence that having identical twins is _____.

6 Identical twins are less _____ than other siblings who are close in age.

7 The lecturer suggests that twins may understand each other well because of their _____.

8 The lecturer implies that stories about telepathy between twins should _____.

Vocabulary extension

2 🔊 **5** Read the sentences from the recording in Exercise 1. Replace the underlined words with their synonyms from the box. Listen and check.

clashed   fluke   ~~inquisitive~~   popped   skip

1 And then maybe a little bit <u>curious</u> – they always want to ask questions. *inquisitive*

2 Now, let me see if I can guess the first question that <u>came</u> into your mind. _____

3 Many people believe that, as a rule, twins <u>miss</u> a generation. _____

4 My twin and I are both quite strong-willed, so we <u>fought</u> a fair bit as kids. _____

5 Are examples like these just a <u>coincidence</u>? _____

3 Complete the phrases with the word *rule* which you heard in the recording in Exercise 1, with one word in each gap.

1 Many people believe that, _____ a rule, twins skip a generation.

2 It seems as if twins might be an _____ to the rule.

3 Perhaps I shouldn't rule it _____.

4 Complete the sentences, which contain more phrases with the word *rule*, with the words from the box.

~~bend~~   make   petty   thumb   unwritten

1 He would never actually break the rules, but he's perfectly prepared to *bend* them if it suits him.

2 I _____ it a rule to get up the same time each day, even at the weekend.

3 A good rule of _____ is to wait until the water starts to boil before adding the pasta.

4 There's a(n) _____ rule that if you bring in biscuits, you have to share them.

5 I'm a free spirit! I don't take any notice of _____ rules and restrictions.

Pronunciation

5 Look at the extract from the recording in Exercise 1. Which word is stressed in the underlined compound adjectives, the first or the second?

My twin and I are both quite <u>strong-willed</u>, so we clashed a fair bit as kids. Of course, he's far more <u>highly strung</u> than me.

ACTIVE PRONUNCIATION
Word stress in compound adjectives

In compound adjectives, the stress is usually on the second word. However, compound adjectives with no hyphen, or which are formed with a noun + gerund or past participle are usually stressed on the first word (e.g. cárefree, éye-catching, tóngue tied).

6 🔊 **6** Decide which word is stressed in the following compound adjectives. Choose *1* for the first word or *2* for the second word. Listen, check and repeat.

a quick-witted   1 / 2
b streetwise   1 / 2
c absent-minded   1 / 2
d thought-provoking   1 / 2
e tight-fisted   1 / 2
f time-saving   1 / 2
g mouth-watering   1 / 2
h record-breaking   1 / 2
i thin-skinned   1 / 2
j world-famous   1 / 2

1D GRAMMAR

Continuous and perfect tenses

1 ★ **Match sentences 1–10 with their meanings a–j.**

1 ☐ I've been trying to work for hours now.
2 ☐ He'd been sitting there for hours. It was time to go.
3 ☐ I'm learning to ski.
4 ☐ By August, I'll have been living here for two years.
5 ☐ Next time I see you, I will have had my hair cut short.
6 ☐ I've built up a lot of muscle.
7 ☐ The water was pouring down the side of the bath.
8 ☐ This time tomorrow, I'll be flying over the Atlantic.
9 ☐ I can't exercise because I've broken my leg.
10 ☐ I had been there before.

a a temporary situation in progress now
b an action that will be in progress at a specific time in the future
c an action in progress up to the present moment
d an action in progress before a certain point in the past
e an action completed at a non-specified time before now
f a recent action with a result in the present
g an action in progress up to a certain time in the future
h an action that will be completed before a certain point in the future
i an action in progress at a certain time in the past
j a completed action which happened before a certain point in the past

2 ★ **Choose the correct options to complete the sentences.**

1 I've been trying to call you *all day / several times*.
2 You're keen! That's the third time you've *run / been running* this week.
3 Have you been eating a lot of fruit *last week / this week*?
4 How many glasses of water *had you drunk / had you been drinking* by midday today?
5 *You've been sitting / You've sat* at that desk for hours. Get up and move about a bit!
6 I couldn't believe it when I saw Jerry – *we'd just been talking / we'd just talked* about him.

3 ★★ **Complete the sentences with the correct Present Perfect Simple or Present Perfect Continuous forms of the verbs in brackets.**

1 It *'s been raining* (rain) all day. I'm fed up with it.
2 I _____ (have) a headache ever since I woke up this morning.
3 I hope you _____ (not wait) long.
4 How long _____ you _____ (be) ill?
5 How long _____ you _____ (feel) sick?
6 He's bright pink because he _____ (sit) in the sun too long.
7 Someone _____ (eat) my sandwich – they've taken a big bite out of it!
8 She's too laid-back about her work – she _____ (chat) on the phone most of the day.

4 ★★ **Choose the correct forms to complete the mini-conversations.**

Priya Are you free next Friday?
Scott What time? Not in the afternoon because I'll **¹**___ a marathon.
Priya Wow! That's impressive.
a be running   **b** run   **c** have run

Doria Do you fancy going out tonight?
Uli No, sorry, I've got to get this essay finished.
Doria Don't be such a wet blanket. You **²**___ working on it for hours. You deserve a break.
a are   **b** 've been   **c** 'll have been

Kosmo I tried to call you several times last night. Where were you?
Felix Sorry, I didn't answer the phone because I **³**___ asleep.
a was falling   **b** fell   **c** 'd fallen

Euan You're a bit of a dark horse, aren't you?
Yang What do you mean?
Euan You didn't tell anyone you **⁴**___ for plays. How are you getting on?
Yang I actually got a part in a show last night.
Euan Well done!
a 'd been auditioning
b 'll be auditioning
c 'd auditioned

Lucy I think I'm addicted to social media. So far today I **⁵**___ my phone twenty-seven times.
David You've only been awake for half an hour!
Lucy Exactly.
a 'd checked   **b** 've checked   **c** 'm checking

Leo I'm just so disorganised. I keep forgetting to hand in my work on time.
Liam I used to be like that. Let me show you this app I use. It's great. In a few weeks you **⁶**___ so organised that you won't recognise yourself!
a 'll have become   **b** 've become   **c** became

5 ★★★ Complete the sentences with no more than three words in each gap.

1 I've just *been* walking in the hills. It's gorgeous out there.

2 Next week I _____ working here for five years.

3 It _____ raining as we left the cinema, so I reached for my umbrella.

4 Don't call me at eight o'clock tonight. I _____ watching the next episode of *Glow Up*.

5 I _____ going to bed too late recently. I must get an early night tonight.

6 I _____ studying Spanish at the moment in preparation for a trip to Madrid next month.

7 I _____ seen you for ages! Where have you been hiding?!

8 I know Edinburgh pretty well, but I _____ to Glasgow before this trip. It was great.

6 ★★★ USE OF ENGLISH Complete the second sentence using the word in bold so that it means the same as the first one. Use between three and six words, including the word in bold.

1 We intended to get fit this spring, but life got in the way. **DECIDED**

We *had decided to* get fit this spring, but life got in the way.

2 You are a smart cookie. This is your best work to date. **EVER**

You are a smart cookie. This is the best work _____.

3 There is no decision from the government yet. **HAS**

The government _____.

4 I don't expect to finish until tomorrow. **FINISHED**

I probably _____ tomorrow.

5 This time tomorrow, I plan to be in conversation with all the movers and shakers at the conference. **TALKING**

This time tomorrow, _____ to all the movers and shakers at the conference.

6 Both my parents have regular piano lessons. **BEEN**

Both my parents _____ piano lessons.

7 ★★ Complete the conversation with the correct forms of the verbs in brackets.

Luke Congratulations on winning that race, Macy! That was impressive. You ¹*were running* (run) so fast you just looked like a blur! ² _____ (you/train) really hard recently?

Macy No, not really, if I'm honest. I think it was mostly a fluke. I ³ _____ (start) eating a bit better lately though.

Luke Ah, maybe that's it. You know, you are what you eat.

Macy That would make me a banana then – I ⁴ _____ (eat) loads of those recently.

Luke Ha ha, very funny ... ⁵ _____ (you/run) next Thursday as well?

8 ★★★ Complete the text with the correct perfect or continuous forms of the verbs from the box.

come   do   live   ~~notice~~   prioritise

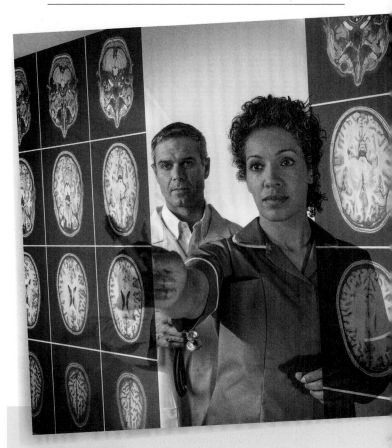

WHY THE BRAIN RESISTS CHANGE

One of the key reasons why people fail to change their bad habits is quite simply a lack of patience. They usually try to start a new habit, but give up when, after a few days or weeks, they ¹*haven't noticed* any dramatic changes.

Since the days when we ² _____ in caves, the brain ³ _____ survival. From a biological perspective, if we are still alive, what we ⁴ _____ must be working for us, so there is no need to change it.

For this reason, the brain naturally resists change. It rarely works to try and change everything overnight. Therefore, we should make incremental changes, until one day we look back and see how far we ⁵ _____.

9 ON A HIGH NOTE Write a paragraph about a habit you would like to give up.

1 What impact is it having on your life?

2 How will your life be different in six months' time if you succeed?

1E READING AND VOCABULARY

1 Read the article. Which of the following aspects of cultural difference does the author NOT mention?

  a speaking a different language
  b different kinds of foods
  c the way people dress
  d what is considered good manners

2 Read the article again and match questions 1–7 with paragraphs A–G. Each paragraph may be chosen more than once.

In which paragraph does the author …

  1 ☐ reflect on the long-term impact of her travels?
  2 ☐ indicate a possible explanation for reverse culture shock?
  3 ☐ highlight a disadvantage of limiting contact with the host culture?
  4 ☐ point out the potentially serious consequences of culture shock?
  5 ☐ emphasise that cultural acclimatisation is likely to be an ongoing process?
  6 ☐ mention a possible reason why culture shock may not be immediately apparent?
  7 ☐ list some social norms that resulted in her being initially confused?

3 What do the underlined words in the sentences from the article imply? Choose *A* for a judgement arrived at after some time or *B* for an immediate judgement.

  1 It requires strenuous effort to <u>deduce</u> all the unspoken rules.   A / B
  2 It's at this point that many people <u>conclude</u> that living in this new culture is not for them.   A / B

4 Complete the sentences with the highlighted words from the text.

  1 She's very *touchy-feely*, always hugging everyone.
  2 It's hard to _____ so much information so quickly.
  3 The accident looked bad at first, but in fact the damage was only _____.
  4 I used to live in the countryside, so found it difficult to _____ myself to big city life.
  5 She's physically quite small and slight, but rather _____ when she's angry.
  6 She screamed at the top of her voice, as a way of releasing all the _____ frustration.
  7 In the fog, I felt a strange sense of _____, with no idea which way was which.
  8 When you are exhausted, _____ in judgement are only to be expected.
  9 The trip to the Uffizi Art Gallery in Florence was a culturally _____ experience.
  10 Even after twenty years of marriage, he was still completely _____ with her.
  11 He is a better film actor than on stage, where the _____ of his facial expressions may be missed.
  12 Having forgotten his torch, he didn't _____ into the dark cellar.

ACTIVE VOCABULARY
Verbs with *-ize* or *-ise* endings

Many verbs in English can be spelt with either the suffix *-ise* or the suffix *-ize*. In most cases, both are acceptable, though you should be consistent in the spelling you choose.

Note that a few verbs are always spelt *-ise* (e.g. *advise, improvise, arise, compromise, despise, disguise*), and a very small number of verbs are always spelt *-ize*, (e.g. *seize, prize, capsize*).

5 Complete the sentences with the correct verbs formed from the words in the box. Be consistent in your spelling. Use a dictionary if necessary.

accessory advice agony ~~climate~~ custom fiction
ideal jeopardy priority

  1 The footballers arrived a few days before the match to *acclimatise/acclimatize* to the humidity.
  2 People often _____ their childhood, remembering it as always sunny and happy.
  3 She _____ her black dress with a simple silver necklace.
  4 She _____ him to work harder if he wanted to pass the exam.
  5 You need to _____ your work. There will be plenty of time for fun later.
  6 Rather than creating a documentary, they decided to _____ what had happened.
  7 Having _____ over what to do for several days, he finally decided that he would have to confess.
  8 The software can be _____ to meet your exact requirements.
  9 If she fails this exam, it could _____ her whole future.

6 **ON A HIGH NOTE** Write a paragraph giving advice to someone visiting your country. What aspects of your culture do you think people from other cultures might find hard to adapt to?

UNIT VOCABULARY PRACTICE > page 13

A I was well-brought-up, and frankly, I always assumed I had good table manners until I went to live in Brazil. Food is almost always eaten there with cutlery – and that includes chips, sandwiches and cake. If you absolutely have to use your hands, you hold the food in a napkin at all times. It's charming, and probably a lot more hygienic, but it's certainly very different, if not a little intimidating. It also took me a remarkably long time to fully comprehend that when a Brazilian invites you to their house for eight o'clock, it is considered impolite to turn up until at least thirty minutes later. These are just a couple of classic examples of the kinds of (often quite subtle) differences that can lead to a feeling of disorientation and culture shock when we travel abroad to work, live or study.

B At first, it can be hard to recognise what is going on, not least because the immediate impact of arriving in an alien culture may be overwhelmingly positive. Known as the 'honeymoon stage', everything is new and exciting. We may become infatuated with the food, the language, the people, the surroundings. On a short trip, we may never leave the honeymoon stage, and look back fondly on our time there.

C If we stay longer, however, small frustrations may start to creep in. Nothing is ever as easy as it was back home. You can't grasp the nuances of getting things done, and you are increasingly irritated by the way everyone pushes into the queue ahead of you. Everything seems to take longer and it requires strenuous effort to deduce all the unspoken rules. Excitement may give way to pent-up feelings of homesickness.

D This stage, often referred to as the 'negotiation stage', can kick in around the three-month mark within the host culture. You may find that your sleep is negatively impacted, and you may even develop physical symptoms such as headaches or stomach aches. Lapses in concentration are also common, which is particularly challenging if you are in the country to work or study. It's at this point that many people conclude that living in this new culture is not for them, and make plans to return home. Alternatively, they may decide to bury themselves as much as possible within the expat community, and venture out as rarely as they can. Tempting as this approach may seem, it is likely to leave you in a permanent state of culture shock as you never give yourself the opportunity to fully acclimatise or adapt to the new culture.

E For those who pass through the negotiation stage successfully, after six to twelve months they may expect to adjust to the new culture. It is likely that this will still be relatively superficial, and they may continue to come up against deeper cultural differences in the longer term. Gradually however, they will assimilate themselves into the culture, in some cases coming to see themselves as bicultural, particularly if they create family ties within the new culture.

F Strangely enough, it has been found that reverse culture shock, when the person returns to their home culture, can be even more challenging to deal with than the original culture shock. Perhaps even more surprisingly, it seems that those who found the most difficulty in assimilating are often those who suffer the most from reverse culture shock. It may be that they have created an idealised version of their home culture, in which none of the problems of the alien culture exist. Equally, if they have been away from home for some years, they may find that things have moved on at home, and that the culture there is no longer just as they remember it.

G I adjusted relatively quickly to life in Brazil, but did indeed struggle to a degree with reverse culture shock. Back home, people felt somewhat cold and unfriendly, and I found myself perceived as overly 'touchy-feely'. The experience of living in another culture profoundly changed me, and while I have probably reverted somewhat to my 'Britishness' since, I'm sure that much of that change was permanent. I have no regrets whatsoever, and believe that the experience was nothing if not enriching.

Give your blog post a catchy title.

Begin by introducing the memory.

Give some background information. How old were you? Where did this happen?

Use time linkers to show when things happened.

Describe the main events of the memory.

Comment on the memory from your present day perspective and explain why it is important to you.

A SWEET MEMORY

One of my fondest childhood memories is the day that, much to my delight, sugar rationing ended in Britain. It was February 1952, seven years after the end of the Second World War, and I was just six years old. I didn't even remember the war but, ¹___, sweets and chocolate had been things that were only available in very small quantities, as a special treat ²___.

Suddenly, sugar was freely available, and we were all determined to make the most of it. I clearly recall a van pulling up outside the school, and men coming in with armfuls of free lollipops. I didn't have a clue why this was happening, but I was very sure that I liked it a lot! That evening, my father came home from work with an enormous box of chocolates for my mother, and we were all allowed to eat as many as we wanted.

Of course, ³___ I realise that the nation was probably considerably healthier during those days of rationing. Rationing was introduced in 1940 and lasted fourteen years. ⁴___, life expectancy increased by six or seven years, far more than the average increase one might expect.

⁵___ I eat pretty healthily, and I don't have a particularly sweet tooth, but ⁶___ I see my grandchildren getting excited about sweets, it brings all the memories flooding back. I've never forgotten the wild joy of suddenly being able to have all the sugar I wanted.

1 Read the blog post and answer the questions.

  1 Why is the memory significant for the author?

  _____

  2 How did they feel at the time? _____

  3 How has their perspective changed? _____

2 Find any phrases that are used to introduce a memory or to explain why the memory is significant.

3 Match time phrases a–f with gaps 1–6 in the blog post.

  a ☐ for as long as I could remember
  b ☐ Nowadays
  c ☐ whenever
  d ☐ During these years
  e ☐ on rare occasions
  f ☐ with hindsight

4 USE OF ENGLISH Complete the second sentence using the word in bold so that it means the same as the first one. Use between two and five words, including the word in bold.

  1 I very rarely wore a tie. **OCCASIONS**

  I only wore a tie _on rare occasions_.

  2 Between 1990 and 1999 I lived in France. **DURING**

  _____ I lived in France.

  3 Looking back, I can see that I was often lonely. **HINDSIGHT**

  _____, I can see that I was often lonely.

  4 When I think of that time, it evokes so many memories. **FLOODING**

  When I think of that time, the memories _____.

  5 It affected me deeply. **PROFOUND**

  It had a _____.

5 WRITING TASK Write a blog post about a memory. Imagine yourself in old age looking back on a different time in your life.

ACTIVE WRITING | A blog post about the past

1 Plan your blog post.
  • Decide on the memory you will describe.
  • Say why the memory is significant for you.
  • Describe how you felt and what you thought at the time.
  • Describe how your perspective may have changed in old age.

2 Write the blog post.
  • Start by introducing the memory.
  • Describe what happened.
  • Say why it is significant.
  • Reflect on the memory from your perspective as an old person.

3 Check that ...
  • you have used time markers effectively.
  • it is clear why you have chosen to describe this memory.

UNIT VOCABULARY PRACTICE > page 13

UNIT VOCABULARY PRACTICE

1 1A VOCABULARY AND SPEAKING Complete the email with one word in each gap.

Dear Lucia,

How great that we're going to be penpals 😊! So, let me tell you a bit about myself. I'd say I'm quite **1** l**aid**-b**ack**, I don't easily get upset, and I'm definitely not **2** h_____ s_____. I'm not that **3** i_____ having loads of friends, I'd rather just spend time with a couple of good friends. Once I **4** c_____ with someone we tend to be friends for life. Perhaps that **5** s_____ a lot about me, I don't know!

I'm **6** n_____ a _____ the theatre. I really **7** g_____ a k_____ o_____ of being in a show. It doesn't have to be a big part or anything, I'm quite **8** h_____! Are you interested in acting or the theatre at all?

What else? Well, I value my family a lot. My mum is great, really **9** k_____-h_____, and always there for me. I also have a younger brother, Calum. He's very **10** h_____-s_____ and makes me laugh a lot.

Anyway, enough about me. What about you? Write back and tell me all about yourself and your family.

Best,
James

2 1B SPEAKING AND VOCABULARY Complete the sentences with appropriate idioms.

1 Don't expect him to give you a hug. He's such a *cold fish*.
2 The company is looking for investment and the _____ are all showing an interest.
3 You didn't say he could borrow the car yet again, did you? You're such a _____.
4 Don't be such a _____. You're too clever for your own good!
5 I had no idea you wrote poetry – you're a _____, aren't you?
6 Don't worry about the exams too much. You're a _____, you'll do fine.
7 We're looking to recruit a real _____ who is willing to work hard and be committed.

3 1C LISTENING AND VOCABULARY Replace the underlined words with their synonyms from the box.

destiny disposition hereditary imply moulded ~~offspring~~ proponents trait vulnerabilities

1 Her <u>children</u> obviously take after her. *offspring*
2 Did he <u>suggest</u> that you had been tactless? _____
3 Inevitably people are <u>shaped</u> by their experiences. _____
4 <u>Supporters</u> of this theory are usually quite forward-thinking. _____
5 His ability to laugh at himself is an endearing <u>characteristic</u>. _____
6 I want to be in charge of my own <u>future</u>. _____
7 She has a very good-natured <u>character</u>. _____
8 Is the shape of your ears <u>genetic</u>? _____
9 Genetics may lead to certain inherited <u>weaknesses</u>. _____

4 1E READING AND VOCABULARY Choose the correct words to complete the sentences.

1 It was so complicated I found it hard to *deduce / grasp* what she was saying.
2 I needed some time to *reflect / consider* on what to do next.
3 I can't *conceive / perceive* how someone could behave that badly.
4 From what I can *recognise / gather*, the project was a great success.
5 From the clues left behind the police are attempting to *gather / deduce* what happened.
6 I'm *contemplating / reflecting* changing my degree subject.
7 Female athletes are often *perceived / concluded* to be less robust.
8 I don't think she fully *comprehends / considers* the importance of this situation.
9 We shouldn't *assume / grasp* anything until we have all the facts.

5 1F WRITING AND VOCABULARY Complete the sentences with one word in each gap.

1 Much to my *delight*, my book was given the award.
2 It _____ as a bit of a shock to realise that he was twenty years older than I had imagined.
3 No _____ where I went, there he was.
4 Stupidly, I had _____ to realise that the clocks had changed to summer time.
5 He greeted me by name, but embarrassingly I didn't have a _____ who he was!
6 Can you just keep an _____ on the pasta and make sure it doesn't boil over?
7 I've eaten so much cake now I might as _____ finish it.

6 ON A HIGH NOTE Write a paragraph. What interests and hobbies do you consider to be part of your identity?

1 For each learning objective, write 1–5 to assess your ability.

1 = I don't feel confident. 5 = I feel confident.

	Learning objective	Course material	How confident I am (1–5)
1A	I can use compound adjectives to talk about personality.	Student's Book pp. 4–5	
1B	I can use paraphrases to check and summarise information.	Student's Book p. 6	
1C	I can understand the main points of a talk about genes and personality.	Student's Book p. 7	
1D	I can use continuous and perfect tenses.	Student's Book pp. 8–9	
1E	I can identify specific details in a text and use verbs connected with understanding.	Student's Book pp. 10–11	
1F	I can write a blog post about the past.	Student's Book pp. 12–13	

2 Which of the skills above would you like to improve in? How?

Skill I want to improve in	How I can improve

3 What can you remember from this unit?

New words I learned and most want to remember	Expressions and phrases I liked	English I heard or read outside class

GRAMMAR AND VOCABULARY

1 Replace the underlined words with the words from the box. There are three extra words.

frank   live wire   merciful   narrow-minded   smart cookie
soft touch   strong-willed   ~~tight-fisted~~   wet blanket

1 Have you noticed that Marta never buys anyone else a coffee – she's so <u>mean</u>! *tight-fisted*

2 If you ask him to tell you the truth, you can be sure he'll be <u>honest</u>. _____

3 She has been very <u>determined</u> ever since she was a baby! _____

4 He graduated with the highest grade in the year. What a <u>clever man</u>! _____

5 My brother was the <u>energetic one</u> and I was the quiet, shy one. _____

6 My dad is such a <u>kind person</u> – I can easily get what I want from him. _____

/ 5

2 Choose the correct words to complete the mini-conversations.

Amy Come on, hurry up and choose!

Sue I can't decide which flavour to **1***plump / pump* for.

Raj I'm just too tired to go out tonight.

Celia Don't be such a **2***damp / wet* blanket, it'll be fun.

Jim Be careful what you say to her, she's really **3***thin / fine* -skinned.

Kurt Oh, I know, she took offence last time I made a joke.

Norm I'm just looking for a pay rise that's in **4***line / lane* with inflation.

Aarav That's understandable, but the economic situation is very tricky at the moment.

Tina **5***Much / Such* to my delight, I've been awarded a prize.

Felicity That's amazing! Congratulations!

/ 5

3 Complete the sentences with the forms from the box.

had been walking   had walked   ~~have been walking~~
was walking   will be walking   will have walked

1 Recently, I *have been walking* upstairs instead of taking the lift.

2 By the time I finish walking the South Downs Way, I _____ 100 miles.

3 I _____ for about an hour before I gave up and rang for a taxi.

4 I _____ the route before, but last time I was on my own.

5 Pack some proper hiking shoes, we _____ a lot.

6 I _____ down the street when I bumped into an old friend of mine.

/ 5

4 Complete the diary entry with the correct perfect or continuous forms of the verbs in brackets.

Recently, I **1***'ve been trying* (try) to drink more water. I'm always so busy that I get to lunchtime and then realise that I **2**_____ (not have) a drink since I got up. I read somewhere that when you **3**_____ (feel) thirsty, that's a sign that you are already too dehydrated. Apparently, you should drink before you get to that stage. So, this morning I had a big glass of water as soon as I got up and felt very pleased with myself because I **4**_____ (already/make) a good start. And then I forgot all about it again and wondered why I **5**_____ (feel) thirsty. I'm a bit frustrated with myself – I **6**_____ (forever/make) the same mistake!

/ 5

USE OF ENGLISH

5 Complete the sentences with the correct words formed from the words in bold.

1 This is a complex situation and it's an *oversimplification* to just blame the government. **SIMPLE**

2 The film allows us to see the fears and _____ of the characters. **VULNERABLE**

3 He won't tell anyone, he has a great deal of _____. **DISCREET**

4 He has a complete lack of _____. **SPONTANEOUS**

5 I expressed doubts about the _____ of her offer. **SINCERE**

/ 4

6 Choose the correct words a–d to complete the text.

HOW MEMORY WORKS
Many people **1**___ to comprehend that memories are stored in many different ways.

The sensory memory **2**___ information for less than a second before transferring what it considers to be important to the short-term memory, where we can **3**___ on it for a while. Then a small percentage of that information may be transferred to the long-term memory.

It is not yet fully understood why some people are more **4**___ -minded than others, and it may be that a good memory is hereditary. However, even those of us who set great **5**___ by having a good memory probably don't remember as clearly as we think. We should never **6**___ that our memories must be accurate, as the brain easily changes old memories.

	a	**b**	**c**	**d**
1	lose	fail	suffer	weaken
2	gathers	deduces	concludes	assumes
3	perceive	recognise	reflect	comprehend
4	narrow	like	strong	absent
5	importance	store	value	priority
6	conclude	gather	recognise	contemplate

/ 6

/ 30

15

02 On the move

2A VOCABULARY AND SPEAKING

Verbs of movement, idioms related to movement, travel verbs

1 ★ Complete the definitions with the correct forms of the verbs from the box. Then match photos A–D with the correct sentences 1–8.

~~hobble~~ lurch shuffle stagger stride stumble surge wobble

1 Someone who has a bad leg _hobbles_.
2 Someone who is carrying something heavy _____.
3 Someone who is confident _____.
4 A crowd of people moving forward suddenly _____.
5 Someone who cannot balance _____.
6 Someone wearing shoes that are too big _____.
7 If a truck or train _____, it makes sudden movements forward or to the side.
8 Someone who _____, hit their foot against something and almost fell.

2 ★★ Choose the correct words to complete the sentences.

1 After asking my sister several times to turn down the music in her room, my father finally *wobbled / strode* into her room angrily and switched it off himself.
2 When the celebrity got out of the taxi, the fans suddenly *surged / shuffled* forward and nearly knocked over the barriers lining the red carpet.
3 It's a wonderful moment when a young child takes its first steps and *hobbles / wobbles* precariously across the room.
4 As the wind became stronger, the boat started to *lurch / stride* from side to side and we nearly capsized.
5 The train guard *stumbled / surged* over a bag in the aisle and nearly fell.
6 When the hockey ball hit her on the leg, she had to *shuffle / stagger* off the pitch to sit down for a while.
7 Since the operation on my knee, I find it much easier to drive my car to the shops rather than *lurch / hobble* down the road.
8 I remember my mother telling my brother, when he was very young, not to *stride / shuffle* but to pick his feet up properly when he was walking.

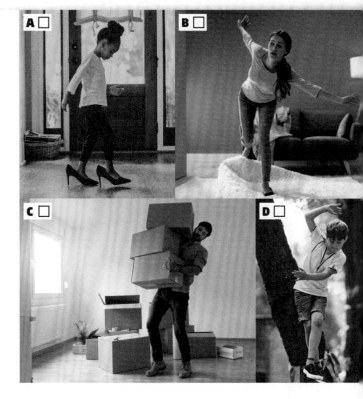

3 ★ Choose the correct words to complete the idioms in bold.

1 The business **has been going** ___ since the new company took it over.
   a downstairs   **b** downhill   **c** downward
2 Avoid the websites listed below if you do not want to **be taken for a** ___.
   a drive   **b** journey   **c** ride
3 The incessant noise of the roadworks outside his house **is driving my uncle up the** ___.
   a wall   **b** hill   **c** path
4 It's a good idea to **steer** ___ **of** making any financial commitment until you know more details.
   a clean   **b** neat   **c** clear
5 I've also got to retake my final exams next month – so we're **in the same** ___.
   a ship   **b** boat   **c** canoe
6 The MP for Hampshire has been **the driving** ___ **behind** the new regulations to control city pollution.
   a power   **b** fuel   **c** force
7 Once we get the bank to agree on the loan, setting up the business should be all _____ **sailing**.
   a clean   **b** plain   **c** open
8 I don't really understand why they chose to live right in the city centre, but – **whatever** ___ **your boat**!
   a sails   **b** rides   **c** floats

4 ★★★ Complete the mini-conversations with the correct forms of the idioms from Exercise 3.

Ann I'm planning to spend all evening finishing my assignment, so I won't be going to Tom's party.

Vicky I'm [1] *in the same boat* – I'm only half-way through mine.

Celia Can you recommend a vegan restaurant in town? My English friend, who's vegan, is coming for the week.

Tony Well, there's a good one in the High Street, but definitely [2]_____ the one opposite the bank. I didn't feel very well after eating there.

Nell I've got my driving test coming up on Friday and I'm a bag of nerves!

Kosmo Hey, don't worry. You're a great driver – it'll be [3]_____.

Mia It's great that students can now get reductions on all buses in the city. It's costing me much less to commute to college every day.

Yang I know! My uncle was [4]_____ behind the introduction of the scheme. He's on the town council.

David We're planning to book a holiday through the new travel website. It looks much cheaper than a lot of others.

Pierre Be careful you aren't [5]_____ – check out and compare prices before you book! It's had some bad reviews.

5 ★★ Complete the sentences with the correct forms of the verbs from the box. Then identify one sentence in which the verb is NOT used figuratively.

backpedal drive fly jump park ride ~~sail~~
stagger stumble

1 The student *sailed* through all the questions in the test and finished at least ten minutes before anyone else.

2 After the interview, Charlie was _____ when the manager asked him if he could start immediately.

3 When Professor Shaw had lost one page of his notes, he panicked and started _____ over his words.

4 I'm terrible when I'm reading – I often _____ to the end of a chapter to see what happens.

5 Some parents _____ their children too hard to do well at school and the kids end up with a lot of health issues.

6 Betty _____ down the stairs to open the door.

7 When Tim realised that his opinions were driving everyone up the wall, he tried to _____ very quickly.

8 The government's plans to reform the public sector have been _____ until after the general election.

9 He arrived _____ on a black horse.

6 ★★★ Complete the posts on a website with one word in each gap.

☐ **Aviator321**

I recently went on a trip to France by ferry and that was an interesting experience! The weather was really windy, and the ferry [1] *lurched* from side to side. Apart from feeling sick, I [2]s_____ over someone's bag which had slid across the floor and spent the rest of the trip [3]h_____ around with a bad ankle!

☐ **Digedd01**

My family went to London for the day last month and the train service is definitely going [4]d_____. To start with, we were completely [5]s_____ by the cost of the return tickets, and then the train was delayed by forty-five minutes. If you think you can get anywhere on time by train these days, I'd suggest you [6]p_____ that idea.

☐ **Katfish**

We really got taken for a [7]r_____ when we booked a flight to Paris last month. My dad bought the tickets online and they were really cheap. Also, it was so quick and easy to do – he [8]s_____ through the booking forms in minutes. But when we got to the airport, they'd imposed extra charges! In addition to this, the website didn't allow for priority boarding so everyone just [9]s_____ forward when the gate opened to allow people on the plane – my bag got dragged past me in the rush. Horrible experience.

7 ★★★ Read the conversation and tick the blog post in Exercise 6 that it refers to. Then complete the conversation with a word or a phrase in each gap.

Alia I hear your ferry journey wasn't much of a success. That's a real shame, because when I went on that boat a few years back the weather was great. The time just [1] *flew* by.

Bella You were lucky. It was a nightmare. So rough that everything on the tables was [2]_____ and nearly falling off! Apart from the weather and a sore ankle, the snack bar on board was terrible. If you go again, [3]_____ of the sandwiches – the bread was really stale. And I couldn't believe the queue for food. It was [4]_____! It took us twenty minutes!

Alia I have to admit, on our crossing, we [5]_____ the queue for the snack bar! People weren't very happy with us.

Bella I should have done the same! Also, we were sitting near the TV screen and the volume was so high it nearly [6]_____ the wall. The ferry was packed and we couldn't move anywhere else. Next time we'll fly!

8 ON A HIGH NOTE Write a short article about a travel experience (real or imagined) for your school website using ten of the new vocabulary items from this lesson.

2B READING AND VOCABULARY

1 Read the article quickly and choose the best summary.

   a What to wear in summer for an underground journey.

   b When it is best to travel on the underground in summer.

   c How to help people survive summer journeys on the underground.

2 Read the article again, ignoring the gaps. Tick the points that are mentioned in the text.

   1 ☐ You are not allowed to take animals on the underground.

   2 ☐ It would be physically difficult to provide cooling systems on some lines.

   3 ☐ Water is provided on all trains.

   4 ☐ Travellers must follow the rules about queueing displayed on every platform.

   5 ☐ People do not generally want to talk while travelling.

3 Match sentences A–G with gaps 1–7 in the article.

   A Now, you need to keep moving down the carriage aisle to maintain the flow of passengers.

   B Sometimes this can peak at over 34 degrees on the Central Line, one of the most frequently used lines of the whole system.

   C If you are lucky enough to get a seat, the rule is to give it up to anyone who looks in greater need of it than you.

   D This rule applies to all stages of your journey through the system.

   E Temperatures are reaching staggering highs on a daily basis, with no signs of abating.

   F And apologies to all those who unquestioningly already observe these points.

   G Some lines, such as the Central, are deep below some of the most densely populated areas of the city, and digging extra ones would be extremely difficult and expensive.

Vocabulary extension

4 Complete the sentences with the correct forms of the highlighted verbs from the text.

   1 You need to _ensure_ that your child receives a proper education.

   2 She had to _____ a few extremely painful operations on her leg.

   3 His racist comments have _____ civil rights activists.

   4 I believe that the function of television is both to entertain and _____.

   5 A good teacher should _____ confidence in students by showing that he/she knows the subject inside out.

   6 After the decision about reduced working hours was announced to the staff, a long silence _____.

ACTIVE VOCABULARY | Idioms with *go*

In addition to phrasal verbs, there are many idiomatic expressions that use the verb *go*.

Remember that apart from changing the form of the verb, other parts of the idiom should not be changed.

*It **goes** down well with ...*

*It **goes** without saying.*

5 Complete the idioms in bold with the words from the box. If necessary, use a dictionary.

~~down~~   flow   grain   motions   saying   tangent

   1 His proposal for a new timetable **went _down_ well with** the passengers and he was praised for his forethought.

   2 Sometimes it is important just to accept life as it is and **go with the _____**.

   3 Tanya was telling me all about some holiday friendships she'd formed and then suddenly she **went off on a _____** and started to talk about how expensive the car hire was!

   4 I organised a dinner for Rob's birthday, but I wasn't feeling very well and although I **went through the _____**, my heart wasn't in it.

   5 In the car race tomorrow, **it goes without _____** that John is going to win, but Jed stands a good chance of coming second, I think.

   6 It really **goes against the _____** to admit that my brother is ever right, but on this occasion, I think he made a very good decision.

6 **ON A HIGH NOTE** Write a paragraph about some of the unwritten rules at your school. Is it good to observe them?

UNIT VOCABULARY PRACTICE > page 25

Mid-July, London. The city is sweltering in a heat wave. [1]___ And you have no choice but to travel in stifling conditions even beyond the limit imposed by law for transporting animals. Welcome to the nightmare that is the London tube rush hour in summer.

Visitors to London may well wonder why travellers on the Underground have to endure such extreme heat in the carriages. [2]___ The problem is that when the tunnels were originally built, no space was left in the tunnels for installing extra equipment such as air conditioning units and there are few shafts through which hot air can escape. [3]___ There are hopes that measures might be taken by the year 2030, but in the meantime, it appears that the only advice from Transport for London is for passengers to carry water with them during hot spells.

There are, however, other things we can all do to make life a little easier on our daily commute, or while travelling between tourist sights. The heat engenders confrontations and outbursts that otherwise remain simmering just below the surface of tube users and often this is down to simple tube etiquette – that set of unwritten rules that we instinctively learn to follow.

So, let me enlighten you. [4]___ Firstly, the etiquette begins at the ticket barriers as you enter the system. When the stations are thronged with people, ensure that you have your ticket to hand and do not wait until the moment you are faced with the barrier to stop and search for it. [5]___ Never stop abruptly to check a map, answer your phone or read a message. Keep walking! On the escalators, if you want to stand, keep to the right. The left-hand side is for passengers who want to keep moving. Then once on the platform, be aware that there is a queueing protocol, although it may not be physically obvious. Wait your turn to board a train, do not jump the queue, and allow passengers to leave the train before attempting to board yourself. Otherwise panic ensues!

OK, so you have managed to board the tube and have not enraged fellow passengers so far. [6]___ A seat would be good, but unlikely during the rush hour, so hold on to the handrail and be sure to take any backpacks off and put them on the floor between your legs. Do not try to strike up a conversation with anyone, as most of us are simply trying to concentrate on surviving the journey. [7]___ Some might argue that people can be offended by someone assuming they are pregnant or aged and frail, but it truly is better to ask, than not. Also, remember that the arm rests between seats are not actually arm rests, but seat dividers and do not spread arms (or legs) beyond your allotted space. And another thing, loud music leaking from headphones or the strong tang of spicy food will not go down well with your fellow passengers!

It goes without saying that pushing and shoving is a big no-no on the underground, but breaking other forms of etiquette, as outlined above, will also earn you dark looks and anger from the sea of hot and tired passengers. One day, there will be air con on all trains. One day, there will be enough carriages to carry everyone who wants to travel, in comfort. Until then, visitors and commuters alike need to go with the flow and keep calm like a true Brit.

2C GRAMMAR

Inversion, cleft sentences and fronting

1 ★★ **What are these sentences example of? Choose *I* for inversion, *F* for fronting or *C* for cleft sentences.**

1 Faster and faster the car sped along the road.   I / F / C

2 Not only did we get more comfortable seats in First Class, but we also had excellent food.   I / F / C

3 Such was the anger that the company had to reinstate the employees.   I / F / C

4 Over the hilltop came the cyclists and everyone cheered.   I / F / C

5 Horrified, he read the email a second time.   I / F / C

6 What always surprises me is the speed he reaches.   I / F / C

2 ★★ **Complete the sentences with the words from the box.**

~~little~~   once   only   scarcely   so   such

1 *Little* did we know that he'd been driving in rallies for ten years.

2 _____ after we'd arrived did they tell us that the race had been cancelled.

3 _____ a steep hill was it that only one cyclist made it to the top.

4 Not _____ did the driver slow down all along the motorway.

5 _____ sharp were the bends that all the cars had to slow right down to take them safely.

6 _____ had the race started when it became clear who was going to win.

3 ★★★ **Rewrite the sentences using inversion.**

1 A passing driver waved at me to stop. Then I realised I had a flat tyre.
Only when *a passing driver waved at me to stop did I realise I had a flat tyre*.

2 The driving examiner was extremely strict. Very few students passed first time.
So strict _____
_____.

3 Katya was a very talented driver and won every race she entered for two years.
Such a _____
_____.

4 The experience was very traumatic and he never forgot it.
So traumatic _____
_____.

5 Jack didn't realise he'd won the race until he'd got out of the car.
Only after _____
_____.

6 It was the first time I had ever seen such an exciting event.
Never before _____
_____.

4 ★★★ **Put the words in order to make sentences that are examples of using fronting for emphasis.**

1 set off / her test / my friend / worried / to take
Worried, my friend set off to take her test.

2 an excited / in the day / got / I / phone call / later
_____

3 was / a blue car / our house / outside
_____

4 the driving seat / my friend / in / sat
_____

5 me / her driving licence / she / smiling / showed
_____

6 drove / jumped / she / and / off / in / I
_____

5 ★★★ **Rewrite the sentences using fronting and cleft sentences to emphasise information.**

1 I shall never know what he was intending to tell me.
What he was intending to tell me I shall never know.

2 Nobody knew where the road led, but we all turned off and followed it anyway.
_____

3 The members are discussing the new rules at this very minute.
_____

4 I later learned from the newspapers who came second in the race, but I didn't know at the time.
_____

5 It was a miracle how Lenny avoided the crash.
_____

6 The winner's name was highlighted in red on the results board.
_____

6 ★ **Choose the correct words to complete the sentences.**

1 *That / What* he enjoyed was the independence the car gave him.

2 The reason *because / why* I got a bike was to go to and from college.

3 *Only / All* I wanted was to be able to travel somewhere cheaply and quickly.

4 *The / A* thing I like most about beach holidays is sitting in the sun with a good book.

5 *It / There* was the choice on the menu that we all really appreciated.

6 The person *what / who* warned me about the high cost involved was a previous student.

7 ★Rewrite the sentences starting with the words given.

1 I wanted a mountain bike, not a road one.
It *was a mountain bike I wanted, not a road one*.
What _____ .

2 I only said that it was getting late.
The _____ .
All _____ .

3 I was thinking about driving over to visit my grandparents.
What _____ .
The thing _____ .

4 I first learned to ride a bike in a car park.
It _____ .
The place _____ .

5 Miss Saunders was my favourite teacher at primary school.
The person _____ .
It _____ .

6 I know everything about the course apart from the start date.
The only _____ .
What _____ .

8 ★★Complete the conversation with the words and phrases from the box.

how he managed   is how   is that   it was   it's not
little do   up to   ~~was he~~   what annoys   who he's

Filip Did you hear Shane bragging about his new car yesterday?

Ben Not only **1** *was he* bragging about his new car but also about the road trip he's going to take it on next month.

Filip **2**_____ the fact that he's got a new car that bugs me, it's the way he needs to let everyone know how fast it is and how much it cost.

Ben And **3**_____ me about it **4**_____ it was his dad who paid for it, not him.

Filip Yeah, **5**_____ the school gates he drove yesterday, stopping with a screech of brakes. **6**_____ not to drive into them is a mystery!

Ben **7**_____ going to get to risk their lives on a road trip with him is beyond me too!

Filip What I can't understand **8**_____ he actually passed his test.

Ben **9**_____ most people know that it took him three attempts to pass!

Filip Really?

Ben Yes. **10**_____ his sister who told me. It made my day!

9 ★★★USE OF ENGLISH Complete the text with one word in each gap.

HAPPY DAYS!

I did it! The day **1** *when* we take our driving test is usually an unforgettable one, and mine certainly was. Not only **2**_____ I pass, but I passed with flying colours! Well, **3**_____ my driving examiner actually said **4**_____ that I was his best driver of the day! OK, I was his FIRST driver of the day, but it felt good. Everything went really smoothly. The **5**_____ I'd been very worried about **6**_____ the reversing – but in fact **7**_____ was the reversing that I did really well on. **8**_____ I must admit is that I was petrified, and I hardly slept the night before. **9**_____ I managed to keep a clear head is beyond me. Afterwards **10**_____ I wanted to do was go home and sleep! **11**_____ when I woke up the next morning **12**_____ the full impact of what I'd achieved hit me. Now, I could drive completely alone! What an amazing feeling. I celebrated by driving my dad's car to the supermarket and back!

10 ON A HIGH NOTE Write a short paragraph about whether or not you think it is important for young people to learn to drive and give your reasons.

2D LISTENING AND VOCABULARY

1 🔊 **7** Listen to three conversations about space travel and match them with topics a–c.

Conversation 1 ☐   **a** an unusual object in space
Conversation 2 ☐   **b** a job in space
Conversation 3 ☐   **c** an experiment in space

2 🔊 **7** Listen again and choose the correct answers.

Conversation 1

1 The speakers disagree about
   a the need to be ambitious.
   b their childhood ambitions.
   c the requirements to become an astronaut.

2 The man gives the example of a British astronaut to point out how
   a long it can take to become one.
   b a dream can become a reality.
   c physically demanding the training can be.

Conversation 2

3 Regarding the experiment with twins, the man feels
   a critical of the way it was conducted.
   b concerned about one of the astronauts' health.
   c disappointed about the results.

4 The woman is unsure whether
   a the human body can endure long space journeys.
   b money should be invested in trying to reach Mars.
   c any astronaut would spend three years in space.

Conversation 3

5 The woman expresses
   a regret at not watching the launch.
   b concern about potential negative impacts.
   c scepticism about the motives for the project.

6 What the man likes about the project is that it
   a may make contact with other life forms in space.
   b will be in space forever.
   c showcases artistic achievement.

Vocabulary extension

3 Complete the sentences with the correct forms of the verbs from the box, which you heard in the recording in Exercise 1.

bring   hold   miss   push   ~~subject~~   whittle

1 The space station is such a confined space that astronauts are _subjected_ to all sorts of pressures.
2 I _____ out on a college trip to the space museum as I was down with flu that week.
3 The judges have _____ down the entries in the invention competition to five.
4 My dad watched the original moon landing and reading my project _____ it all back to him.
5 The college has decided not to _____ ahead with plans for new laboratories as funds are low.
6 If you want to work in the space industry, don't _____ back, even if it means moving to the USA.

Pronunciation

4 🔊 **8** Read some sentences from the recording in Exercise 1. Pay attention to how the voice tone rises or falls at the end of each clause. Listen and repeat.

   1 What's also important ↓↑ is being the right age and the right height. ↓
   2 I think it's something ↓↑ that we'll see in our lifetime. ↓
   3 It's the long-term effects that they can't really assess properly yet. ↓

ACTIVE PRONUNCIATION
Intonation in cleft sentences

Intonation in cleft sentences depends on what information we are focusing on.

- *What* clefts usually focus on information in the second clause.

  What I need to do tonight ↓↑ is to finish my assignment ↓.

  All it means ↓↑ is that I must switch off my phone. ↓

- In cleft sentences starting with *it*, the tone depends on the context. If the second part of the sentence is new information, the tone usually falls. If the second part is not new information, there is a fall-rising tone.

  They offered some funding ... and it was this money ↓ that allowed him to take on extra trainees ↓. (new news)

  He thought his application would fail because of his height ... but it was his age ↓ that stopped him joining ↓↑. (not news)

---

5 🔊 **9** Listen to the mini-conversations and repeat, paying attention to the fall-rise intonation pattern in the cleft sentences.

Lisa Would you like to holiday in space?
Will What I'd really like is to have a holiday in Egypt!

Eric What do you see as a priority for the space industry?
Lena What I'm wondering is whether we'll colonise other planets.

Ryu Are you going to get a long holiday this year?
Zac All I'm hoping for is a short break in Paris.

6 Decide which cleft sentences in each pair are adding news in the second part, and which are not.

   1 I'm worried about several exam papers, but
     a it's the History paper that really concerns me.
     b it's the History paper that I need to pass to get to uni.

   2 Long periods of space travel will affect astronauts in many ways, but
     a it's their physical health that has always worried scientists.
     b it's humanity's need for progress that will ensure that the projects continue.

7 🔊 **10** Mark the intonation patterns on the sentences in Exercise 6. Listen and check. Then practise saying them.

2E SPEAKING

1 🔊 *11* Listen and repeat the phrases. How do you say them in your language?

SPEAKING | Considering and comparing alternatives

CONSIDERING ALTERNATIVES

There's a lot to be said for a couple of days in the capital. **But on the other hand,** it might be expensive.

Alternatively, we could put forward the idea of going along the canal.

You have to consider the fact that it might be busy **and likewise with this option, there are some drawbacks too.**

There are a lot of points in favour of having a couple of days on the coast.

Well, you could argue that with everyone contributing it might be cheaper.

If you're thinking about cost, then that's got to be my favourite, **but if we're talking enjoyment, then it's a whole different ball game.**

GIVING PREFERENCES

I'd go for the countryside **anytime!**

A canal trip? **No question (about it)! Definitely!**

It's pretty clear cut to me that going by coach would be cheapest.

On balance, I'd say go for the train.

No two ways about it, my choice would be the city.

I'm split between the beach **and** the city.

I'm in two minds here. There are pros and cons for each.

If you really wanted to pin me down, I'd have to go for a trip to the beach.

---

2 Complete the blog posts with the correct phrases. Use the words in bold.

A ¹*There's a lot to be said for* (**SAID**) a staycation you know! If you're planning a trip abroad, ²_____ (**CONSIDER**) that it's likely to cost a fair amount. Also, ³_____ (**ARGUE**) that we shouldn't go off exploring other countries if we don't really know our own yet. ⁴_____ (**CLEAR**) to me that finding out about what's on your own doorstep can be really exciting.

B I get A's point. ⁵_____ (**THINKING**) cost, then a staycation has got to be the answer, but if we're talking excitement, then for me it's got to be an exotic location, ⁶_____ (**QUESTION**). And my country is definitely not exotic!

C It surely depends on what you want out of a holiday. This year ⁷_____ (**SPLIT**) going somewhere hot and staying in a nice hotel, and staying at home but spending days out travelling around. ⁸_____ (**BALANCE**), I would say that sitting on a beach would be more relaxing, but ⁹_____ (**WAYS**), it would be expensive. I need to save up a bit longer, I guess.

---

3 🔊 *12* USE OF ENGLISH Complete the conversation with one word in each gap. Listen and check.

Petra OK, so have you had any more thoughts on how we should go about this new tourist campaign for the area? Currently, most people coming to visit here know about it through family or friends, it's mainly word-of-mouth.

Jamie Yes. There's a lot to be ¹*said* for word-of-mouth, but if we want to reach a lot of potential visitors, we've got to advertise nationally, haven't we?

Petra No ²_____ about it! We need to put ³_____ the idea that a staycation in this area would be both cheap and fascinating. After all, we've got some wonderful natural attractions. The problem is national advertising costs money.

Jamie Not necessarily. There are lots of points in ⁴_____ of using social media to post pictures and information about coming here.

Petra You could ⁵_____ that there's not a lot of point in doing that unless we also have our own website where people can get more information.

Jamie Yes – it's ⁶_____ clear cut to me that we'll need a decent website. I'm in two ⁷_____ here about whether we develop it ourselves or get a professional in.

Petra OK, if we're ⁸_____ professional, then that will cost. But we ⁹_____ to consider the fact that local businesses will be willing to contribute, so that should allow us to bring someone in. And how about including podcasts from visitors to the area who have had a great experience? And opportunities for reviews and ratings?

Jamie I'm not convinced about that. There are some ¹⁰_____ to think about. You also get negative reviews sometimes which might put people off. And what about photos for the website – we really need professional ones, don't we?

Petra Well, ¹¹_____ with the website developer – it will cost. But on ¹²_____, I'd say it was worth it.

Jamie Great – I'll get onto local businesses and check out some …

---

4 ON A HIGH NOTE Write a short dialogue between Jamie and a professional photographer about possible locations to be photographed with alternatives and priorities.

Explain reason for writing.

Use correct register.

Use passive forms and clauses of concession where appropriate.

Use emphasis to show your dissatisfaction.

Use initial comment adverbs to indicate attitude.

Use a range of adverb–adjective collocations.

Explain how you expect the recipient to act on the information in your letter.

Dear Sir,

I recently attended an experience day at your race track, using a voucher given to me for my birthday. I am writing because I encountered several issues on the day. I feel that you should be made aware of these in order for you to improve the experiences of other people who wish to enjoy a session on your race track in the future.

I am a keen driver and had been looking forward to the supercar experience as detailed on my voucher. Whilst the instructor demonstration lap was excellent, other aspects of my day's experience were disappointing. The promise was that I would be able to drive three supercars, a BMW M2, a Ferrari F430 and the Aston Martin Vantage. I am sure you can imagine my disappointment when only two of the three cars were actually available for me to drive on the day.

In addition to this, I was completely taken aback when one of the cars I was driving developed a fault which resulted in me having to stop while an engineer checked out the car. I am fully aware that cars can be temperamental at times, particularly supercars of the calibre I was driving, but I would hope that all of your cars for this type of experience would be fully maintained at all times.

Not only did I lose time while the fault was being corrected, but I was also not given the full driving session as promised. Indeed, instead of the advertised three-hour session, mine was stopped after two hours, so I most certainly did not get the full value of the voucher.

I am afraid that in no way did the experience live up to what had been promised and I was deeply disappointed. At the very least, I would expect some financial compensation for the issues encountered or, preferably, an additional voucher for another day's experience at which I would hope that none of the aforementioned problems would reoccur.

Yours faithfully,

Marie Headly

1 Read the letter above and tick the issues the writer is complaining about.

1 ☐ increased cost
2 ☐ reduced driving time
3 ☐ badly maintained cars
4 ☐ delayed start
5 ☐ limited range of cars
6 ☐ incomplete prior information

2 Complete the sentences with the adverbs from the box.

blindingly deeply ~~drastically~~ vehemently wholly wildly

1 The service has _drastically_ improved since last year.
2 The hotel owners were _____ opposed to giving us any sort of refund.
3 The five-star reviews of the property were _____ unjustified.
4 It must be _____ obvious to any tourist that our area is unprepared for a significant influx of visitors during the summer months.
5 Predictions for financial investment in the space industry are _____ inaccurate.
6 My parents were _____ disappointed when the cruise was cancelled last month.

3 WRITING TASK Write a letter of complaint.

You have recently been on a weekend residential sailing course for beginners. There were certain problems over the weekend and you decide to write to the company that ran the course. Write your letter of complaint.

ACTIVE WRITING | A letter of complaint

1 Plan your letter.
- Consider what might go wrong – accommodation/ levels/number of people/catering.
- Make notes about the points you choose.
- Divide your notes into paragraphs.

2 Write the letter.
- Use an appropriate register.
- Say how you expect the recipient to respond.
- Use a range of vocabulary and grammatical structures including adverb-adjective collocations, passive forms and clauses of concession.

3 Check that ...
- you have used formal language and a range of complex structures.
- there are no spelling, grammar or punctuation mistakes.

UNIT VOCABULARY PRACTICE

1 2A VOCABULARY AND SPEAKING **Read the sentences and complete the words with one letter in each gap.**

1 I'd been ill in bed for two weeks and when I finally got up for the first time I was w_o_ _b_ _b_ _l_ _i_ _n_ _g_ all over the place.

2 On the journey home the train suddenly l_ _ _ _ _ _ _ as the track curved round a bend and our sandwiches ended up on a fellow passenger's lap.

3 My sister does a lot of exercise and when we go out for a walk together she always s_ _ _ _ _ _ ahead of me and I have trouble keeping up.

4 Danny got kicked in the shins while playing football on Saturday and had to h_ _ _ _ _ off the pitch.

5 I remember my mother getting really cross with my young sister when she found her s_ _ _ _ _ _ _ _ around in her best high-heeled shoes.

2 2A VOCABULARY AND SPEAKING **Complete the pairs of sentences with the correct forms of the same word.**

1 a It's nearly impossible to _park_ near the station these days because so many people commute from here to London every day.

b I think we'll have to _park_ that idea until there's enough money to consider funding the project.

2 a We were playing cards when suddenly our dog burst into the room. He jumped up at the table and all the cards _____ up in the air.

b It's often easier and sometimes even cheaper to _____ the couple of hundred miles from here to Edinburgh than to drive.

3 a It _____ me how quickly the concert tickets sold out online.

b Do you remember that ridiculous scene in the film where, although he's been shot several times, the hero _____ to the window to shout for help?

4 a Apparently Hannah _____ through the job interview and she's starting first thing on Monday morning.

b Whenever we go on holiday, it is never plain _____ and something always goes wrong on the flight or at the hotel.

5 a There's nothing better than going for an early morning _____ on my mountain bike when there's a low mist over the fields.

b Dad knew he'd been taken for a _____ when he saw the same offer advertised fifty percent cheaper on a different website.

6 a Most people never read all through the terms and conditions on a webpage – they just _____ to the end.

b My brother _____ at least a foot in the air when a spider ran between his legs.

3 2B READING AND VOCABULARY **Complete the sentences with the correct forms of the verbs from the box.**

adjust cease clutch heave relinquish ~~shove~~

1 As I was getting off the tube train someone _shoved_ me and I fell onto the platform.

2 I need to _____ the seat after my father's been driving as he's much taller than I am.

3 The deck of the boat was _____ in the rough sea and a lot of passengers felt very ill.

4 Adele _____ her bag tightly as she pushed through the crowds of people.

5 Our new dog is supposed to be a retriever, but he will never _____ his ball when he brings it back to me.

6 Finally, the whispering and rustling _____ and the play began.

4 2D LISTENING AND VOCABULARY **Complete the report with phrasal nouns formed from the verbs in the box.**

come cry cut lay set (x2)

There was a big turnout at the meeting yesterday evening – hundreds of people. However, from the [1]_outset_ it was clear that the council were not prepared to fund the initial [2]_____ required to set the new cycle lane scheme up and running any time soon. The representative made out that this was down to government [3]_____, but this will not please all those who have campaigned for so long for safer riding conditions in the town. Inevitably, the [4]_____ of the meeting was disappointment all round and the people's hopes of safe cycling suffered a [5]_____ as in no way had it addressed the public [6]_____ last summer over the number of accidents involving cyclists in the town.

5 2F WRITING AND VOCABULARY **Choose the correct adverbs to complete the sentences.**

1 The efficiency of the new train service has been _gravely / grossly / deeply_ overrated. Passengers have suffered delays nearly every day for a week now.

2 It is _fundamentally / infinitely / blindingly_ obvious to everyone that the bus service system needs investment.

3 The company are _wholly / grossly / vehemently_ unjustified in increasing fares for short flights while the on-board service is so poor.

4 For me, it's _gravely / wildly / infinitely_ preferable to travel outside the rush hour rather than have to stand up for an hour's journey.

5 The proposed new rail link will cost several billions of pounds and the majority of people are _grossly / blindingly / vehemently_ opposed to the project.

6 People are _infinitely / gravely / wildly_ mistaken if they think that the new speed limits will make much difference to drivers. Until there are speed cameras installed, nothing will change.

6 ON A HIGH NOTE **Write a short paragraph about how public transport could be improved in your local area to become more efficient and less damaging to the environment.**

25

1 For each learning objective, write 1–5 to assess your ability.

1 = I don't feel confident. 5 = I feel confident.

	Learning objective	Course material	How confident I am (1–5)
2A	I can use verbs and idioms related to movement to talk about travelling.	Student's Book pp. 18–19	
2B	I can understand reference devices and talk about public transport.	Student's Book pp. 20–21	
2C	I can use inversion, fronting and clefting to add emphasis.	Student's Book pp. 22–23	
2D	I can identify specific information in a conversation and talk about space.	Student's Book p. 24	
2E	I can consider and compare alternatives when talking about tourism.	Student's Book p. 25	
2F	I can write a letter of complaint.	Student's Book pp. 26–27	

2 Which of the skills above would you like to improve in? How?

Skill I want to improve in	How I can improve

3 What can you remember from this unit?

New words I learned and most want to remember	Expressions and phrases I liked	English I heard or read outside class

GRAMMAR AND VOCABULARY

1 Choose the correct words to complete the sentences.

1 The train guard *staggered* / *stumbled* over the name of the next station and some passengers got confused about where they were.

2 You are *infinitely* / *gravely* mistaken if you think we will ever use this travel website to book again.

3 The Formula 1 driver was driving at break- *back* / *neck* speed round the track.

4 We definitely got our fair *portion* / *share* of rain while we were on holiday in Barbados!

5 There are a lot of *fences* / *hurdles* to overcome if you want to reach the very top of your profession.

/ 5

2 Replace the underlined parts of the sentences with the words and phrases from the box.

a breakthrough ~~a knock-on effect on~~ brag
drives me up the wall fidget outlook

1 A train delay in the morning has <u>consequences for the whole network during the day</u>. *a knock-on effect on*

2 My classmate always used to <u>move in her seat or play with her pens</u> if she was bored. _____

3 He's made <u>an important discovery</u> in keeping the human body healthy in space. _____

4 When my brother is driving, he whistles some weird tune and it <u>really irritates me</u>. _____

5 Really successful people don't feel the need to <u>talk about their achievements</u> all the time. _____

6 The <u>forecast</u> is for clouds and showers today.
_____

/ 5

3 Use the prompts to write sentences.

1 Last year / not only / we / go to Spain / but we went to Portugal too
Last year not only did we go to Spain, but we went to Portugal too.

2 So / difficult / be / the test that she could not even get past the first three questions
_____

3 Only after / I / pass / my driving test next year / I / be able / drive without a passenger
_____

4 Under no circumstances / be / people / allowed / to open the train door while the train is moving
_____

5 Little / we / know / that an airport strike would delay our flight for four hours
_____

6 Such a / big / discount / be / it / on my dream car / that I immediately booked a test ride online
_____

/ 5

USE OF ENGLISH

4 Complete the text with one word in each gap.

CABMEN'S SHELTERS

At various points in London you can see strange little green huts actually on, or near the road. **¹***What* you might not know **²**_____ that these are historic little buildings that are fully operational cafés. Back in the nineteenth century, **³**_____ that the drivers of horse drawn carriages wanted during their breaks **⁴**_____ some hot food and a place to shelter from the bad weather. If they went to an inn, not **⁵**_____ might they lose customers, but **⁶**_____ they had to pay someone to protect their cab. So, in 1875 a charity built sixty-one shelters throughout London. **⁷**_____ was also the charity **⁸**_____ provided cooking facilities and often paid an attendant to make tea and hot food for the drivers. Today, thirteen of these shelters are still working cafés and **⁹**_____ you'll find interesting is their distinctive ornamental design. The public can buy from them, but it **¹⁰**_____ only cab drivers **¹¹**_____ can sit inside them.

/ 10

5 Complete the second sentence using the word in bold so that it means the same as the first one. Use between three and six words, including the word in bold.

1 In addition to becoming Formula 3 champion, he was named Young Driver of the Year. **BECOME**
Not only *did he become Formula 3 champion*, but he was also named Young Driver of the Year.

2 We were delayed for hours and hours and the airline company gave us a complete refund. **DELAY**
So _____ that the airline gave us a complete refund.

3 We had no idea that all the planes had been grounded for the day. **KNOW**
Little _____ all the planes had been grounded for the day.

4 I'd been hoping to buy a Mercedes, but I couldn't really afford it. **WAS**
What I _____ a Mercedes, but I couldn't really afford it.

5 We couldn't board the ferry until the staff had cleared up after the previous passengers. **ONLY**
The staff cleared up after the previous passengers and _____ to board the ferry.

6 The future is unknown. **HOLDS**
What _____ is unknown.

/ 5

/ 30

27

03 Hard sell

3A VOCABULARY AND SPEAKING

Business-related vocabulary, compound nouns, phrasal verbs

1 ★ Read the definitions and complete the words with one letter in each gap.

1 A feature of a product or service which makes it different from the rest. U _S_ _P_

2 A new business project that involves taking risks.
v _ _ _ _ _ _

3 A piece of paper with a price attached to a product.
p _ _ _ _ _   t _ _ _

4 (Of a price) Extremely cheap. b _ _ _ _ _ _ _
b _ _ _ _ _ _ _

5 A product made specially for a particular customer.
b _ _ _ _ _ _ _

6 When you bring a product onto the market for the first time. l _ _ _ _ _

7 The price a company says they will charge for a service. q _ _ _ _

8 The amount of business a company does over a period of time. t _ _ _ _ _ _ _ _

9 Brings the best possible profits for the lowest possible price. c _ _ _ - _ _ _ _ _ _ _ _ _

10 When you start to do something different from what you usually do. b _ _ _ _ _   o _ _

2 ★ Match the two parts of the sentences.

1 ☐ I asked several companies to give me

2 ☐ It isn't cost-effective to heat the whole house

3 ☐ He has unusually large feet

4 ☐ After working for the company for a few years,

5 ☐ The venture may be lucrative,

6 ☐ Once we've worked out what our USP is,

7 ☐ I was staggered by

8 ☐ You can't expect to get good quality

9 ☐ Everything is online now,

a how high his turnover was.

b so he needs bespoke shoes.

c a quote for remodelling the kitchen.

d if you're only working in one room.

e but it's also risky.

f she decided to launch her own business.

g the rest will be plain sailing.

h at bargain-basement prices.

i so I think the days of bricks and mortar are over.

3 ★ Choose the correct words to complete the sentences.

1 The *price tag / quote* is missing. How much is it?

2 Shops sometimes put sweets by the cash desk to encourage *luxury goods / impulse buys*.

3 If you have positive *upfront investment / word-of-mouth*, you may not need to advertise.

4 It was a *start-up / venture*, so there wasn't much money to pay good salaries.

5 They're offering free cinema tickets as a *word-of-mouth / sales gimmick*.

6 Do some research before choosing your *quote / tradename*.

7 Expensive cars are *bespoke / luxury* goods. When the market drops, people buy standard cars instead.

8 If the *USP / profit margin* is only five percent, you need to sell a lot of units.

9 There is a *niche / cost-effective* market in shoes for vegan women that is growing quickly.

4 ★★ Complete the sentences with the correct forms of the compound nouns from Exercise 3.

1 They spend far too much on __luxury goods__ such as perfume and jewellery.

2 I try to avoid _____ by taking a shopping list to the supermarket.

3 Inevitably, most _____ will fail in their first year.

4 It's really important what your business is called. You must have a memorable _____.

5 Pet owners who want personalised products for their pets are quite a profitable _____.

6 There are little plastic toys in the cereal, given away as a _____.

7 There will be a significant _____, but it will be well worth the money in the long run.

8 We get most of our work through _____ referrals and recommendations.

9 When I looked at the _____, I almost passed out. It was so expensive!

5 ★ **Complete the sentences with the correct forms of the phrasal verbs from the box.**

~~build up~~ knock off pass up set up sign up
spring up win over

1 She *built up* the business very gradually, over a number of years.

2 He _____ a few pounds as the packaging was damaged.

3 While bricks and mortar retail is doing badly, coffee shops and barbers are _____ all over the place.

4 I _____ to her mailing list because I was interested in what she had to say.

5 Initially, I wasn't sure I wanted such a big car, but the salesman _____ me _____.

6 There are a lot of upfront costs in _____ a business, such as premises and insurance.

7 Never _____ the chance to tell someone about your business. They might become your customer.

6 ★★ **Complete the conversation with the correct verbs.**

Aaron Have you tried that new cake shop on Regent Street?

Lenny No, I can't say that I have.

Aaron It's not like you to ¹*pass* up the opportunity for cake ...

Lenny I didn't know there was one! When did that ² _____ up?

Aaron Oh, I found out about the place a week ago. The owner was standing outside offering free cake.

Lenny That's a good way to ³ _____ people over. It would work for me, anyway!

Aaron Yes. She was also getting people to ⁴ _____ up for her newsletter. If you gave her your email, she ⁵ _____ twenty percent off the price of a cake.

Lenny She's obviously working hard at ⁶ _____ up the business.

7 ★ **USE OF ENGLISH Complete all three sentences with the same word.**

1 _____
a There's an excellent ___ margin on these goods.
b Damaged goods mean lost ___.
c A ___-making business can surely also be ethical.

2 _____
a A satisfied ___ will create good word-of-mouth.
b We need to create ___ loyalty, so they will come back time and time again.
c Our ___ service representatives are highly trained.

3 _____
a The United States can be a difficult market to ___ into.
b It is still a mystery how they managed to ___ out of prison.
c The train rushed along the tracks at ___-neck speed.

8 ★★ **Complete the online article with one word in each gap.**

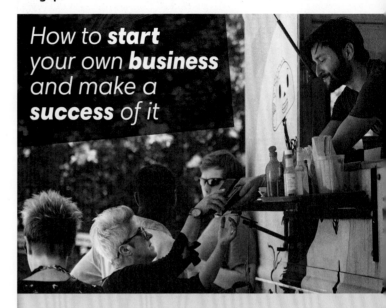

*How to **start** your own **business** and make a **success** of it*

Got an idea for a new business ¹v*enture*? Here's how to get started ...

If you are entrepreneurial, you are probably juggling lots of ideas. But which business ²c_____ is the best? Think about which one you have the most passion for as a new ³s_____ will require a great deal of time and energy.

Then think about your customers. If it's too much of a ⁴n_____ m_____, perhaps you won't be able to find enough people interested in buying what you're selling. On the other hand, if you want to ⁵b_____ into an already crowded market, you'll need a ⁶U_____.

However great you think your idea is, research it thoroughly. If no one else is doing it, does that mean you're a genius, or that everyone else knows that there's no ⁷p_____ m_____ in what you're considering?

Finally, are you thinking of an online business, or a ⁸b_____ and m_____ one? If the latter, remember that hiring premises will involve a significant ⁹u_____ i_____.

Once you've decided on your idea, you need to think about how you're going to ¹⁰l_____ the business. It probably isn't that ¹¹c_____-e_____ to start by paying a lot for advertising. If you can provide really excellent customer service, and ¹²w_____ o_____ some loyal fans, you'll get more business through ¹³w_____-of-m_____, and can build your business up that way. You might not get rich quick, but the freedom of being your own boss is hard to beat.

9 ON A HIGH NOTE Write a paragraph about one of your favourite businesses. Why do you like their products or services? What is their USP?

3B LISTENING AND VOCABULARY

1 🔊 *13* **Listen to a radio interview. What is the main topic? Choose the correct answer.**

  a the history of sales and marketing

  b a case study of sales techniques

  c making ethical business decisions

2 🔊 *13* **Listen again and choose the correct answers.**

  1 Sarah says that William Wrigley's early experiences

    a were relatively unique to him.

    b caused him great suffering.

    c may have motivated him.

    d were inappropriate for his age.

  2 Joe implies that Wrigley offered freebies because he

    a felt it provided better value to the customer.

    b understood their psychological impact.

    c learned this from his father's company.

    d liked the idea of getting something for nothing.

  3 Joe feels that Wrigley's decisions were

    a largely calculated risks.

    b unnecessarily hazardous.

    c an example to follow.

    d impossible to reproduce nowadays.

  4 Wrigley learned from the depression in 1907 that

    a people made small purchases to lift their mood.

    b chewing gum could have significant health benefits.

    c he could manipulate people into impulse purchases.

    d people needed a reason to buy his product regularly.

  5 How do you think Sarah feels about William Wrigley?

    a She admires him as a go-getter who achieved success.

    b She wonders if his spontaneity was always good.

    c She is somewhat taken aback by his determination.

    d She thinks he must have been very strong-willed.

Vocabulary extension

3 🔊 *14* **Complete the sentences from the interview in Exercise 1 with the words from the box. Listen and check.**

> acumen   brainwave   flair   freebie   knack   lightbulb   ~~stroke~~

  1 While risky, what he did was a *stroke* of genius, probably never replicated to this day.

  2 It's clear that he had a _____ for selling even then.

  3 He had a _____ – he would start giving away baking powder as a _____ when people bought soap.

  4 Using his _____ for marketing, he prevailed upon people to buy gum to chew after a meal.

  5 And his business _____ didn't stop there. A few years later he had another _____ moment.

Pronunciation

4 🔊 *15* **Read some words from the interview in Exercise 1. Count the number of syllables in each word. Listen and check. What do you notice?**

  1 different   **5** happening

  2 interesting   **6** especially

  3 family   **7** complimentary

  4 necessary   **8** suppose

ACTIVE PRONUNCIATION
Words that drop a syllable

In British English, vowels tend to be left out in natural speech and the word loses an unstressed syllable. This usually happens before:

- /r/ (e.g. *different, interesting, necessary, complimentary*).
- /l/ (e.g. *especially, dreadfully, family, marvellous*).
- /n/ (e.g. *happening, educational, definite, prisoner*).

In a few words, the dropped syllable comes before a consonant (e.g. *vegetable, medicine, suppose*).

---

5 🔊 *16* **Listen and find the vowels which are left out in natural speech. Then practise saying the words.**

  1 correct   **4** secondary   **7** perhaps

  2 frightening **5** memory   **8** mystery

  3 national   **6** thankfully

6 🔊 *17* **Look at the texts and find four words in each text where vowels may be left out. Listen and check. Then practise reading the texts aloud.**

> The (government) plans to introduce a series of national measures to improve performance in secondary schools. The proposals were announced by the Education Secretary.

> The centre offers a specialist complementary therapy service, offering a range of different treatments which can be safely used alongside traditional medicine.

UNIT VOCABULARY PRACTICE > page 37

3C SPEAKING

1 🔊 *18* **Listen and repeat the phrases. How do you say them in your language?**

SPEAKING | Negotiating

ASKING FOR WHAT YOU WANT

This is a bit awkward, but I was bought this top as a birthday present, and it just doesn't suit me.

Would you be prepared to give me a store gift card so I can buy something else from the store?

I'm wondering if there's any flexibility in moving this deadline.

How about if we were to say 11.30? Would that be OK?

REFUSING AN OFFER

I'd like to say yes, but I'm afraid it isn't company policy.

I'm afraid that's a bit out of my price range/budget/a bit less than I'd be willing to accept.

The bottom line is – this is a good flat and I won't have any difficulty finding a tenant.

At the end of the day, the children really won't be any bother, they're quite self-sufficient.

It has to be a 'no'.

ACCEPTING AN OFFER

Great, you've got yourself a deal.

Let's shake on that, then.

OK, I can live with that.

TRYING TO GET TO A WIN-WIN SITUATION

I can see what you're saying, but it's clearly from this shop.

Is there any room for compromise?

Provided you knock £10 off the price, **I see no reason why I couldn't** pay cash on the spot.

Can we try and meet halfway on this?

How does that sound?

2 **Choose the correct words to complete the sentences.**

1 The *bottom / important* line is that it has to be worth my while.

2 I'd like to say *agreed / yes*, but the price is still too high.

3 This is a bit *awkward / sorry*, but would you be willing to accept less?

4 I'm sorry, but it has to be a *'yes' / 'no'*. That just isn't enough.

5 How does that *sound / hear*?

6 At the *end / beginning* of the day, it's got to be worth more than that.

7 I can *see / know* what you're saying, but from my perspective it just isn't worth it.

8 How about if we *where / were* to try and meet in the middle?

9 OK, I can *leave / live* with that.

10 Would you be *in agreement / prepared* to accept an offer?

3 **USE OF ENGLISH Complete the second sentence using the word in bold so that it means the same as the first one. Use between three and six words, including the word in bold.**

1 I can't manage that. Could we try and reach an agreement we're both happy with? **ROOM**
   I can't manage that. Is there any *room for compromise*?

2 Great, we're agreed then? **DEAL**
   Great, you've _____.

3 I'm wondering if we can negotiate? **FLEXIBILITY**
   I'm wondering _____.

4 I'm afraid that's a bit too expensive for me. **RANGE**
   I'm afraid that's a bit _____.

5 Let's agree to that deal then. **SHAKE**
   Let's _____ then.

4 🔊 *19* **USE OF ENGLISH Complete the conversation with one word in each gap. Listen and check.**

Scarlett Hi, you must be Sam? I've come about the bike you advertised online. So how much were you looking for?

Sam £150.00.

Scarlett Oh, that's a bit out of my price ¹*range*. Would you be ²_____ to accept a bit less?

Sam Well, ³_____ you could pay cash, I see no reason why I couldn't knock a bit off. Say, £130?

Scarlett This is a bit ⁴_____ , but I was thinking more like £70.00.

Sam Oh. That's really less than I'd be ⁵_____ to accept.

Scarlett Is there any ⁶_____ for compromise here? At the end of the ⁷_____ , it is second hand.

Sam Well, yes, but it's in perfect condition. How about if we ⁸_____ to say £120?

Scarlett I could probably do £100.

Sam I'd ⁹_____ to say yes, but I just can't take any less than £120.

Scarlett OK, I can live ¹⁰_____ that. £120 it is.

Sam Great, you've got yourself a ¹¹_____ then.

Scarlett Let's ¹²_____ on that.

5 **ON A HIGH NOTE Jake is hoping to buy a second hand computer from a friend of his sister's. Write a short dialogue where they negotiate the price.**

31

3D READING AND VOCABULARY

1 Read the article. Does either of the sayings below represent the author's attitude towards money?

Money doesn't grow on trees.

You can't take it with you when you die.

2 Read the article again and choose the correct answers.

1 What does the writer say about 'comparison-itis'?

  a It's too easy to imagine you have the facts when you don't.

  b It is likely to make you feel dissatisfied with your situation.

  c It is unwise to make negative judgements about other people.

  d It is unlikely to be a problem unless you feel insecure in the first place.

2 What does the writer recommend in Paragraph 3?

  a Ensuring that you avoid any financial problems.

  b Putting in the effort required to earn a higher income.

  c Understanding that earning more isn't necessarily the solution.

  d Never spending more than you have in the bank at that time.

3 What is the writer's purpose in Paragraph 5?

  a To make a counterargument.

  b To introduce a new concept.

  c To summarise an idea.

  d To expand on a point.

4 The writer believes that having a negative attitude towards money

  a is better than ignoring it altogether.

  b can affect your earning potential.

  c is something you shouldn't talk about.

  d may make you envious of others.

5 What would be a suitable subtitle for this article?

  a Unhealthy attitudes to avoid.

  b How to get rich and stay rich.

  c Why understanding your money mindset is vital to success.

  d Becoming financially independent.

3 What are the highlighted phrases from the text about? Choose *SA* for saving or *SP* for spending.

1	squirrel money away	SA / SP
2	have disposable income	SA / SP
3	be stingy	SA / SP
4	be frugal	SA / SP
5	be a cheapskate	SA / SP
6	squander money	SA / SP
7	throw money down the drain	SA / SP

4 Complete the sentences with the correct forms of the words and phrases from Exercise 3.

1 She <u>squanders</u> her money on magazines, coffees and sweets.

2 If you pay for a monthly gym membership and never go, you're _____.

3 He never takes his turn to buy coffee. He's such a _____!

4 We live pretty _____ and very rarely go out to eat.

5 He has a job, but his parents don't charge him rent, so he has a lot of _____.

6 You only spent £5 on his birthday?! That's a bit _____.

7 As soon as I get paid, I _____ a chunk of money towards my holiday.

ACTIVE VOCABULARY | The prefix *dis-*

The prefix *dis-* combines with verbs to mean an action which reverses the effect of the original word (e.g. *appear – **dis**appear, entangle – **dis**entangle*).

It is also used with nouns and adjectives to mean something which is the opposite of the original word (e.g. *passionate – **dis**passionate*).

However, there are many words where it is not possible to clearly identify the original word (e.g. **dis**posable, **dis**gruntled, **dis**miss, **dis**play).

5 Match the definitions with the correct words formed from the words in the box. Use the prefix *dis-*.

content ~~courteous~~ incentive infect inherit integrate obedient quiet

1 Rude and careless of other people's feelings. *discourteous*

2 Something which makes people not want to do something. _____

3 Not doing what you are told to do. _____

4 Prevent someone from receiving your money after you die. _____

5 Be destroyed by breaking into small pieces. _____

6 Not happy with a situation. _____

7 Worry or anxiety. _____

8 Clean using chemicals to kill bacteria. _____

6 **ON A HIGH NOTE** Write a paragraph describing some of your beliefs or attitudes about money.

UNIT VOCABULARY PRACTICE > page 37

money mindset

1 Have you ever taken the time to consider your money mindset? What beliefs about money do you have? Perhaps you always heard people in your family saying things like, 'money doesn't grow on trees' or 'you need to save for a rainy day'. These kinds of notions and beliefs can be helpful of course. If you were brought up this way, you've probably got some savings squirreled away already.

Being aware of what money you have to spend is never a bad thing. If you have never delved deep into what you're spending, saved up for something, or drawn up a budget – why not start? They are all useful life skills, especially once you begin to become more financially independent from your parents. If this all sounds a bit of a yawn, remember that people who actually have money almost always spend time taking care of it. Research shows that millionaires spend on average 8.4 hours a month on money management.

2 A common pitfall in developing a healthy approach towards money is 'comparison-itis', or comparing yourself (often unfavourably) with others. It may seem that all your friends have more disposable income than you do, but you don't know the intimate details of their family's finances, and it's really none of your business if they have a propensity to spend money like water. And before you start to feel disgruntled or jealous, consider that your parents may well feel that they are actually preparing you better for the real world by not giving you constant handouts.

3 Bear in mind that managing money doesn't mean you have to be stingy with it. You don't want to go too far, and become known for being a bit too frugal, or even a cheapskate, rather than simply economical. It's all about balance. People often fall into the snare of thinking that they will be able to disentangle themselves from any financial problems once they have more money, and then find that their spending simply accelerates to keep pace with their new income. They find themselves in a spiral of working harder and harder and still never feeling that they have enough.

4 If you find yourself squandering money like it's burning a hole in your pocket, that may also be down to your unconscious beliefs about money. It could be that you keep throwing money down the drain, because you simply don't feel comfortable having it. Just think for a minute about the language we often use to describe those who are loaded. They're 'filthy' or 'stinking' rich. That doesn't exactly sound inviting. Maybe if you had money, people would judge you as spoilt or greedy. There are lots of well-known sayings around this too. 'Money is the root of all evil' for example, leaving us with the uneasy idea that having or wanting money will inevitably lead to wickedness.

5 Having negative feelings about money can also be detrimental to your chances of actually getting enough of it. Once you're working, perhaps you'll subconsciously opt for a less well-paid job, or avoid setting your sights on a promotion?

6 So, if you want to manage your money well, be able to put some aside for a rainy day, but also know when something is money well spent, it is vital to understand your money mindset. Perhaps you believe that people 'like you' don't ever have money? Perhaps you even believe that you don't deserve it? Visualise yourself having money. Does it feel uncomfortable? What are some of your earliest memories around money? What do they tell you about the role of money in your family?

7 Money is something that many people prefer not to talk, or sometimes not even think about. But burying your head in the sand and hoping for the best is rarely a good strategy. Only when you really understand your money mindset and have taken steps to change any aspects that are not really serving you well, can you start to make truly dispassionate financial decisions.

3E GRAMMAR

The Passive

1 ★ Find and correct one mistake in each sentence.

1 Leeds Corn Exchange built in 1863. *was built*

2 It is a grade 1 listed building which means it cannot altered without permission. _____

3 In Victorian times corn traded there. _____

4 Recently, it been refurbished and is now home to many independent shops and designers. _____

5 The interior of the building considered to be one of the finest of its kind in the country. _____

6 In a few years, the Corn Exchange have been serving the people of Leeds for 150 years. _____

2 ★ Rewrite the sentences using the Passive.

1 We will prosecute all shoplifters.
All *shoplifters will be prosecuted*.

2 Reading a review has convinced eighty-two percent of consumers to make a purchase.
Eighty-two percent _____.

3 The manager sacked the shop assistant.
The shop assistant _____.

4 Genuine individual online reviews of products influence over ninety-three percent of consumers.
Over _____.

5 People think that shopping will always be a social experience.
It _____.

6 People are integrating social media into more and more commercial sites.
Social _____.

3 ★★ Match reasons for using the Passive a–f with sentences 1–6 from Exercise 2.

a ☐ We want to sound more objective or talk about general opinions.

b ☐ There is a tendency to put the new or most interesting information at the end of the sentence.

c ☐ It is obvious who carried out the action.

d ☐ We want to avoid personal responsibility or blame.

e ☐ We are more interested in the action (e.g. a process) than who does it.

f ☐ There is a tendency not to start a sentence with a long complex subject.

4 ★ Choose the best continuation for each sentence.

1 My sister makes customised jeans.
  a They are sold by her online.
  b She sells them online.

2 Leeds is a popular shopping destination.
  a It was visited by over three million people last year.
  b Over three million people visited it last year.

3 This jumper has shrunk.
  a Did you read the washing instructions?
  b Were the washing instructions read by you?

4 Alison is an excellent salesperson.
  a More is sold by her than anyone else on the team.
  b She sells more than anyone else on the team.

5 Oxford Street is a famous shopping street in London.
  a The street was originally built by the Romans.
  b The Romans originally built the street.

6 Oxford Street is heavily polluted by traffic.
  a They are therefore considering pedestrianisation.
  b Pedestrianisation is therefore being considered.

5 ★★ Complete the sentences with the correct forms of the verbs in brackets.

1 It is often difficult *to see* (see) the outside world when you're in a shopping mall.

2 This is because they _____ (design) to make people lose track of time.

3 For the same reason, it is unusual _____ (come across) a clock.

4 This deliberate confusion _____ (know) as the Gruen Transfer.

5 The transfer _____ (occur) when you stop looking for a specific item and start shopping in general.

6 This effect _____ (name) after Victor Gruen, an Austrian architect who designed shopping malls.

7 Unfortunately, it _____ (say) that Gruen did not intend to create this effect at all.

8 He simply wanted shopping to _____ (experience) as a social event.

6 ★★ Complete the text with the most appropriate phrases from the box. There are six extra phrases.

certain companies launched it	to be stopped in
has been ordered	to stop
has ordered	will be delivered
have been being used	will be ironed out
have been using	will deliver
~~it was first launched~~	will iron out

Why voice shopping may not be the next big thing after all

When ¹*it was first launched*, it seemed as if voice shopping might be the next big thing. Let's say you notice that your printer is getting low on ink. There's no longer any need ²_____ what you were doing and go online to buy it. Just say, 'buy printer ink', and it ³_____ the very next day.

And yet, only a tiny percentage of consumers ⁴_____ voice shopping. One reason may be the high percentage of miscommunications. Unless the transaction is extremely simple, or it's an item which ⁵_____ before, there's a very real risk that a completely wrong item will turn up on your doorstep. It may be that as the technology develops, these glitches ⁶_____, but for now, it's simply not taking off as a trend.

7 ★★ Rewrite the Passive sentences using a different subject.

1 A lot of gift vouchers were given to me for my birthday.
I was given a lot of gift vouchers for my birthday.

2 All employees will be offered a discount.
_____

3 I am owed a refund.
_____

4 I have been shown the plans for the new shopping mall.
_____

5 She had been given a shopping basket.
_____

6 All the customers were given a freebie.
_____

8 ★★★ USE OF ENGLISH Complete the online blog with one word in each gap.

A magical bookstore

The Livraria Lello bookstore in Porto, Northern Portugal, is probably my most favourite shop in the world. They ¹*pride* themselves on their customer service, and their selection of books is second to none. However, most of their customers tend to ²_____ enticed inside by the sheer gorgeousness of the building.

Opened in 1906, it ³_____ designed in the Gothic style by architect Xavier Esteves. The building is celebrated for its staggeringly beautiful staircases and stained-glass windows. Every detail has ⁴_____ considered carefully, such as the pillars, which are ⁵_____ with carved figures from Portuguese literature.

⁶_____ is thought that JK Rowling, ⁷_____ was employed as an English teacher in Porto in the 1990s, may have based her descriptions of Hogwarts on the Livraria Lello, especially as she ⁸_____ known to frequent the café there.

Up until fairly recently, it was possible to visit the bookstore free of charge, but with up to 4,000 visitors a day, most of whom bought nothing, it was decided to introduce a small charge to enter. This charge is fully refundable against any book ⁹_____ in the store.

9 ON A HIGH NOTE Write a paragraph about your favourite shop. Use a mixture of the Active and the Passive.

Summarise the topic of the essay using your own words.

Outline both points of view. You may also give your point of view, or thesis, here.

Give arguments either for or against which are not your overall opinion.

Then use the remaining space to make your arguments.

Summarise your argument and offer your opinion again.

SHOPPING AS A LEISURE PURSUIT: A POSITIVE OR NEGATIVE TREND?

Many people nowadays seem to prefer to spend their leisure time in shopping malls, rather than playing sports, going for walks or even taking up creative hobbies. While I can see some ªpositive sides, in my opinion, the negative aspects ᵇoutweigh these for the reasons I ᶜoutline below.

ᵈIt should be said that shopping malls do offer people a relatively safe and comfortable environment in which to meet and socialise. Friends can ¹mooch round the shops together, take the opportunity to ² _____ up on a few essentials, or have a coffee.

ᵉNotwithstanding this, by encouraging people to see shopping centres as places to socialise, we are also encouraging them to go on a shopping ³ _____, and potentially spend money just to keep up with their peers who may have more ⁴ _____ income.

ᶠThen there is the question of what other pursuits they are potentially sacrificing in order to spend time in the mall. Wouldn't that time be spent more fruitfully playing a game, where they could be developing physical prowess as well as team working skills?

Finally, we should consider the detrimental impact of shopping as a leisure pursuit on the environment. Take fashion ᵍfor example. Many shops change the products they ⁵ _____ every few weeks, and huge quantities of unsold clothes end up in landfill. Even what has recently been purchased may often be quite quickly disposed of as fashions change. Such cheap items are also often the result of ⁶ _____ slavery, where workers are poorly paid and suffer terrible conditions.

In conclusion, ʰgiven all of these factors, it is almost impossible to see this trend as anything but negative, and something we should strive to change.

1 Read the essay and put the arguments against shopping as a leisure pursuit in the order they are mentioned.

a ☐ A fast turnover in products, and a lot of waste.

b ☐ People squandering money they don't really have.

c ☐ Exploitation in order to create low cost products.

d ☐ A replacement for more productive hobbies.

2 Complete collocations 1–6 in the essay with the words from the box.

carry   disposable   modern   ~~mooch~~   spree   stock

3 Match phrases 1–8 with underlined parts a–h from the essay with a similar meaning.

1 ☐ as a case in point
2 ☐ beneficial
3 ☐ having said
4 ☐ it is inarguable
5 ☐ lay out
6 ☐ override
7 ☐ taking all of this into account
8 ☐ we should also consider

4 WRITING TASK Read the topic and choose the best thesis statement. Then write your essay.

More and more shopping is being done online. What are the benefits of this, and what possible drawbacks might there be? Discuss and give your opinion.

A Over the last couple of decades, the popularity of online shopping has increased year on year. While there are clear advantages, we should also consider the potential downsides.

B Now that almost anything can be bought from the comfort of our own home, why would we feel the need to venture into bricks and mortar stores? Surely, online shopping is both cheaper and more convenient.

ACTIVE WRITING | A for-and-against essay

1 Plan your essay.
- Make a note of arguments in favour of and against the topic.
- Decide what your conclusion will be.

2 Write the essay.
- Start with a thesis statement.
- Paraphrase to use your own words and to avoid repetition.

3 Check that ...
- you have considered both sides of the argument.
- there are no spelling, grammar or punctuation mistakes.

UNIT VOCABULARY PRACTICE

1 **3A VOCABULARY AND SPEAKING Replace the underlined parts of the sentences with the correct forms of the phrasal verbs from the box.**

branch out   break into   break out   build up
~~knock sth off~~   pass up   sign up for   spring up

1 It was slightly damaged so they <u>reduced the price by £5</u>. *knocked £5 off the price*

2 They <u>escaped from</u> prison and fled the country.
_____

3 I'm not going to <u>reject</u> a free meal! _____

4 Have you <u>joined</u> the cinema club this year?
_____

5 There are new shops and cafés <u>appearing</u> every day.
_____

6 We're trying to expand and <u>get started in</u> the Chinese market. _____

7 It took a while to <u>grow</u> the business, but it's doing well now. _____

8 They started with womenswear, but now they're <u>expanding</u> into girlswear. _____

2 **3A VOCABULARY AND SPEAKING Complete the text with one word in each gap.**

The Something Store

Here's an unusual business ¹concept. Instead of spending ages choosing what to buy, why not just buy 'something' from The Something Store? Literally something, because the ²U_____ is that until it arrives, you don't know what it is. Have they ³l_____ their marbles? Well, it may be a sales ⁴g_____ , but the ⁵v_____ has already been able to ⁶w_____ over thousands of customers who just love the surprise element, and ⁷w_____-of-mouth has seen the company grow very rapidly. The upfront ⁸i_____ is $10, which isn't going to break the bank, and the company guarantee that the item will be worth at least that amount.

3 **3B LISTENING AND VOCABULARY Complete each sentence with the correct forms of TWO words from the box with a similar meaning.**

clever   ~~coerce~~   crafty   devious   entice   gullible
ingenious   naive   open   ~~pressure~~   seduce   trusting

1 He was innocent, but had been *coerced/pressured* into making a confession.

2 Putting sweets near the checkout _____/_____ people into buying things they don't really want.

3 If you are _____/_____ enough to believe that, you'd believe anything!

4 The child gave me a warm _____/_____ smile.

5 That's _____/_____! How do you come up with such great ideas?

6 Don't trust him, he's really _____/_____.

4 **3B LISTENING AND VOCABULARY Complete the sentences with the correct words formed from the words in bold.**

1 When you watch her paint it looks so easy and *effortless*. **EFFORT**

2 His opinion changed so dramatically, the _____ was that someone had told him what to say. **INFER**

3 Try a little gentle _____ – I'm sure he'll change his mind. **PERSUADE**

4 This approach is too _____ to deal with such a complex situation. **SIMPLE**

5 I wasn't able to bake because there was a _____ of flour. **SCARCE**

6 He was so charming that his _____ victims trusted him completely. **SUSPECT**

5 **3D READING AND VOCABULARY Complete the text with the correct forms of the words and phrases from the box.**

adverse effects   ~~bear in mind~~   fall prey to   notion
outweigh   palatable   pitfall   plough on   propensity

THE CURSE OF KNOWLEDGE

One cognitive bias that all of us should ¹*bear in mind* is something often referred to as 'the curse of knowledge'. It's a ²_____ we fall into when we don't realise that just because we understand a particular ³_____, that doesn't mean that everyone else does. Some of the ⁴_____ can include a ⁵_____ to use jargon other people don't understand, skip vital steps in our explanations, and, instead of checking understanding, simply ⁶_____ regardless.

To avoid ⁷_____ this bias, make sure that you ask for feedback when preparing a speech or piece of writing. Negative feedback may not always be ⁸_____ , but the benefits far ⁹_____ any temporary embarrassment.

6 **3F WRITING AND VOCABULARY Choose the correct words to complete the sentences.**

1 I'm just popping out to *make / run* a few errands. Do you need anything?

2 I really can't be bothered to shop *around / out* for the best deals.

3 I do a big shop every month to stock *in / up* on essentials.

4 The major downside *for / to* online shopping is all the packaging.

5 It's usually cheaper to buy food *on / in* bulk.

6 I've got some birthday money so I'm going *to / on* a shopping spree!

7 **ON A HIGH NOTE Write a paragraph about your spending habits. Are you a saver or a spender? What do you spend most of your money on?**

37

1 **For each learning objective, write 1–5 to assess your ability.**

1 = I don't feel confident. 5 = I feel confident.

	Learning objective	Course material	How confident I am (1–5)
3A	I can use compound nouns and phrasal verbs to talk about business ideas.	Student's Book pp. 34–35	
3B	I can infer meaning, opinion and attitude from an interview and talk about persuasion.	Student's Book p. 36	
3C	I can accept or refuse an offer in a negotiation.	Student's Book p. 37	
3D	I can identify specific details in an article and talk about behavioural economics.	Student's Book pp. 38–39	
3E	I can use the Passive to focus on the action and be more objective.	Student's Book pp. 40–41	
3F	I can use paraphrases when writing a for-and-against essay.	Student's Book pp. 42–43	

2 **Which of the skills above would you like to improve in? How?**

Skill I want to improve in	How I can improve

3 **What can you remember from this unit?**

New words I learned and most want to remember	Expressions and phrases I liked	English I heard or read outside class

GRAMMAR AND VOCABULARY

1 Complete the sentences with one adjective in each gap.

1 A b*espoke* product is something tailored specifically to your requirements.

2 If you e_____ someone, you persuade them by offering something they want.

3 If something has a d_____ effect, the impact is negative.

4 Someone who is i_____ is not biased in any way.

5 If you are s_____, you are able to judge a situation accurately and make it work for you.

6 If you always believe what you are told, and are therefore easily deceived, you are c_____.

/ 5

2 Find and correct one mistake in each sentence.

1 With bargain-cellar prices like these, you can snap up a bargain! *bargain-basement*

2 I would always prefer to visit a bricks and walls store than go online. _____

3 At the beginning of the day, you have to provide good value. _____

4 The top line is that I simply can't afford it. _____

5 I love spending hours just mooning around the shops. _____

6 I think we shouldn't plough through this plan - it won't work. _____

/ 5

3 Rewrite each sentence in two different ways, both using the Passive.

1 They will offer him a refund.
He will be offered a refund.
A refund will be offered to him.

2 They sent the purchases to the customer.
_____
_____

3 Someone has promised this customer a refund.
_____
_____

4 The chef is creating a dish from unusual ingredients.
_____
_____

/ 6

4 Choose the best options in each case.

1 **a** You must dry clean this garment.
   b This garment must be dry cleaned.

2 **a** He was attracted by the idea of setting up a website.
   b The idea of setting up a website attracted him.

3 **a** The company will make a payment within a week.
   b Payment will be made within a week.

4 **a** The CEO has been interviewed by a journalist.
   b A journalist has interviewed the CEO.

/ 4

USE OF ENGLISH

5 Complete the second sentence using the word in bold so that it means the same as the first one. Use between two and six words, including the word in bold.

1 After seven years working for the company, she started her own business. **BRANCH**
After seven years working for the company, she *branched out on her* own.

2 Could you offer me a discount on this price? **KNOCK**
Could you _____ this price?

3 He persuaded me to take the job. **SWEET**
He _____ the job.

4 Can we come to a compromise on this? **HALFWAY**
Can we _____ on this?

5 They eventually convinced her to accept the agreement. **PREVAILED**
She _____ to accept the agreement.

/ 4

6 Choose the correct words a–d to complete the text.

Trust The Rabbit

Imagine you have a job which needs [1]___, but that you don't have the time or expertise to do yourself. If this is a specialist job, such as decorating or building, you would probably know where to go. But what about if you just needed someone to run some [2]___?
Task Rabbit is an app which [3]___ to match freelance labour to local demand. 'Taskers' offer low-skill but important help with basic DIY, cleaning and shopping. The business [4]___ is based on the fact that many people nowadays are 'time poor' and therefore [5]___ to pay well for even very simple services. This isn't just a gimmick – the company now has a [6]___ of millions of dollars.

1 **a** being done **b** done **c** to do **d** to be done
2 **a** shopping **b** errands **c** purchases **d** tasks
3 **a** is setting up **b** setting up **c** was set up **d** set up
4 **a** concept **b** fallacy **c** propensity **d** snare
5 **a** set up **b** coerced **c** inclined **d** seduced
6 **a** quote **b** turnover **c** credit note **d** USP

/ 6

/ 30

4A VOCABULARY AND SPEAKING

Adjectives to describe food, partitives

1 ★ Label the pictures with the words from the box.

clove dab handful heel scoop ~~segment~~ slab
slice sprig sprinkle

1 segment

2 _____

3 _____

4 _____

5 _____

6 _____

7 _____

8 _____

9 _____

10 _____

2 ★ Choose the correct words to complete the phrases. Sometimes more than one answer is possible.

1 a slice of *salad / cake / bread*
2 a clove of *onion / garlic / tomato*
3 a scoop of *mashed potato / milk / butter*
4 a sprig of *parsley / cucumber / peas*
5 a segment of *cheese / grapefruit / orange*
6 a handful of *sauce / nuts / ketchup*
7 a sprinkle of *breadcrumbs / grated cheese / cream*
8 a dusting of *baked beans / cheese / icing sugar*

3 ★ Choose the correct words to complete the sentences.

1 My mother always puts a *handful / piece* of fruit in my sister's lunch box.
2 At the local market, you can buy big *segments / slabs* of meat for really low prices.
3 You shouldn't have more than a *drop / pinch* of salt with your meal, otherwise it's unhealthy.
4 In winter, we make crumbs from a *slab / heel* of bread to put out for the birds.
5 My favourite Italian restaurant serves very large *portions / items* of pasta, which I adore!
6 You only need to add a couple of *dabs / drops* of vanilla essence to a cake mix to give it a great flavour.

4 ★★ Complete the conversation with the singular or plural forms of the words from Exercises 1 and 2.

Erden You know everyone is supposed to eat five or more **1** *portions* of fruit and vegetables a day?

Caria Yes. But I don't think I always do!

Erden Last night I made a meal for my flatmates and I got five in!

Caria You – cooking? Go on then. Astound me …

Erden OK. First off, I made a quick starter. I used **2**_____ of avocado, spread prettily over the plate, and a **3**_____ of paprika pepper over the top, with a couple of **4**_____ of mayonnaise. Ben's got a huge appetite, so I served it with a **5**_____ of crusty bread.

Caria I love the 'prettily spread' – you artist you!

Erden Remember we start eating with our eyes! Then I cooked a **6**_____ of beef very slowly in the oven with several **7**_____ of garlic and just a **8**_____ of curry powder. I cut it into bite-sized chunks and served it with a **9**_____ of rice and a **10**_____ of peas and green beans. Oh yes, and I put some **11**_____ of parsley and rosemary on the meat.

Caria Very pretty!

Erden Absolutely. For dessert, I arranged some **12**_____ of orange around the dish, with a couple of **13**_____ of ice cream in the centre and a **14**_____ of chocolate powder over the lot. Clean plates all round.

Caria Sounds very healthy, apart from the mayo, chocolate and ice cream!

5 ★★ Choose the correct meanings for the underlined words.

1 The meat is <u>gristly</u>.
  a hard and chewy   **b** tasty and well-seasoned

2 The cake is <u>gooey</u>.
  a bit dry and crumbly   **b** sticky and soft

3 The sauce is <u>velvety</u>.
  a thick and lumpy   **b** smooth and soft

4 The pudding is <u>stodgy</u>.
  a heavy and solid   **b** delicious-looking

5 The fish is <u>tender</u>.
  a tough and chewy   **b** easy to cut and eat

6 The meat is <u>succulent</u>.
  a undercooked   **b** moist and tasty

7 Here's a cup of <u>scalding</u> tea.
  a extremely hot   **b** really strong

8 The sandwich is all <u>soggy</u>.
  a wet and soft   **b** fluffy and chewy

9 The bread is <u>mouldy</u>.
  a spongy   **b** old and inedible

6 ★★ Complete the mini-conversations with the words from the box.

chewy	greasy	~~mouldy~~	scalding	tempting	tender

Sue Can we have some cheese?
Mia Sorry, I had to throw it away – it was ¹*mouldy*.

Jasper Would you like some more chips?
Jim No, thanks. They're a bit too ² _____.

Kurt This meat is so ³ _____. How did you cook it?
Mina Oh, I just bought good quality, that's all.

Martin I think I'll have the cheesecake.
Tina It looks really ⁴ _____, but I haven't got room!

Felicity Oh, have you burned your lip?
Will Yes, I had some soup earlier and it was ⁵ _____.

Fidel My steak was OK. But you didn't eat yours.
Ryu No, it was really tough and ⁶ _____.

7 ★★★ Complete the words in reviews A–D with one letter in each gap.

A Five-star rating for this new restaurant! The menu had a range of ¹te *m p t i n g* options and it was difficult to make a choice, but the waiter made some recommendations and I followed his advice. I started with a ²v __ __ __ __ __ __ __ parsnip soup which was just the right temperature – neither ³s __ __ __ __ __ __ __ __ nor too cold, with some crusty bread. I followed this with a ⁴f __ __ __ __ __ cheese omelette and afterwards I treated myself to a piece of ⁵g __ __ __ __ __ chocolate gateau with a couple of ⁶s __ __ __ __ __ __ __ __ __ of cream. A quality meal at affordable prices. Highly recommended.

B Avoid this restaurant, unless you want to waste money and maybe end up with a stomach upset! A starter consisting of a couple of ¹s __ __ __ __ __ __ __ __ of grapefruit with a ²s __ __ __ __ __ __ __ __ of sugar and a ³s __ __ __ __ of brown toast doesn't really float my boat. I had chicken which, for some reason, had a ⁴s __ __ __ __ __ __ __ of cheese on it and a salad with what must have been a single ⁵d __ __ __ __ of French dressing. The cheese and biscuits that followed were equally disappointing. The cheese was old and ⁶m __ __ __ __ __, and the biscuits were dry and tasteless. Needless to say, I refused to pay!

C My meal at the restaurant left me slightly ambivalent. On the one hand, the meat in my main course was tough and ¹c __ __ __ __ __ and the boiled cabbage was ²s __ __ __ __ __. But on the other hand, when I sent it back, I was then given another serving with extremely ³s __ __ __ __ __ __ __ __ lamb and clearly fresh vegetables. Later, I was treated to dessert on the house – a generous ⁴s __ __ __ __ __ of delicious homemade chocolate ice cream decorated with delightful ⁵s __ __ __ __ __ of mint. Because of this, I shall definitely return. Customer service like this is excellent.

D The marketing for this restaurant makes much of the fact that the kitchen is run by a top chef. I regret to say that on my visit he must have been having an off day. I had a heavy ¹s __ __ __ of ²g __ __ __ __ __ __ meat with so many ³c __ __ __ __ __ __ of garlic in it that it was almost inedible, with a couple of chips . A ⁴h __ __ __ __ __ __ __ of chopped carrots and peas added colour, but little else to the dish. To finish, I was served a chocolate pudding that was sugary and ⁵s __ __ __ __ __ __. The bill was extortionate! In no way would I ever recommend this eatery to anybody.

8 ON A HIGH NOTE Describe a meal that was particularly memorable. Give reasons and say what could have improved it, if anything.

1 Read the introduction to the article. Tick the points which might be raised in the article. Then read the article quickly and check your ideas.

1 ☐ the history of food waste
2 ☐ the effect of food waste on the environment
3 ☐ ways of dumping food waste
4 ☐ ways of reducing food waste

2 Read the article again and match questions 1–10 with writers A–D. Each writer may be chosen more than once.

Which writer ...

1 ☐ mentions an environmental bonus to purchasing a particular product?
2 ☐ cites the appearance of certain foods as a contributory factor to a problem?
3 ☐ believes that information can have an effect beyond its target audience?
4 ☐ emphasises that buyers share responsibility for food waste?
5 ☐ is keen to encourage early awareness of the impact of food waste?
6 ☐ feels that changes should be implemented by the big corporations?
7 ☐ is encouraged to find that creative uses of unwanted produce are well represented in shops?
8 ☐ clarifies different terminology related to food excess?
9 ☐ has recently realised the extent of a particular issue?
10 ☐ appears determined to change a habit?

3 Complete the sentences with the correct forms of the highlighted words and phrases from the text.

1 She's very *choosy about* what airline she travels with.
2 I believe it's the powerful advertising agencies that should be _____ the rise in sales of unhealthy food products.
3 Grapes and olives grow _____ in Greece.
4 The show will continue for another month _____.
5 Don't _____ perfectly edible food because you have bought too much of it – share it with others.
6 The factory is struggling to _____ environmental _____.

ACTIVE VOCABULARY
Verbs and nouns with the prefix *mis-*

You can add the prefix *mis-* to verbs and nouns to indicate something has been done wrongly or badly.

- Sometimes the word form remains the same, e.g. *calculation* (n) – **mis***calculation* (n).
- Sometimes adding the prefix creates a new word form, e.g. *fit* (v) – **mis***fit* (n).
- Sometimes the base word needs another change, e.g. *shape* (n, v) – **mis***shapen* (adj).

4 USE OF ENGLISH Complete the sentences with the correct words formed from the words in bold.

1 We all have to be aware of the spread of *misinformation* online. **INFORM**
2 Students are sometimes sent home for continued _____ in class. **BEHAVE**
3 I'm afraid there has been a _____ about who will be conducting the report. **UNDERSTAND**
4 My grammar was fine, but I lost marks for _____ some common words. **SPELL**
5 It's easy to _____ instructions – you need to check things carefully before you start. **INTERPRET**
6 A lot of food loss is down to a _____ between supply and demand. **MATCH**
7 I _____ my arrival and got to the party just as it was finishing! **TIME**
8 I have some _____ about the way the project is being organised. We need to look at this again. **GIVE**

5 ON A HIGH NOTE Write a short paragraph adding a contribution to the posts based on your own recent experiences with food waste.

Hungry for some answers?

We asked for your thoughts on food waste and you haven't disappointed us! Read contributions from four readers.

top-quality, wonky veg

A Miss Fit

Before starting to research a college project on food waste, I had not realised how much of a problem this really is. I knew, as we all do, that we buy more food than we consume and that we need to reduce how much we throw away, but I was astounded to discover statistics that indicate food waste produces 6.7 percent of all greenhouse gases. What really surprised me was the amount discarded before it gets to the stores, or even into the food processing systems at all! Although food waste isn't only down to us as individuals, some of it is our fault. Apparently, we as customers are too choosy about the shape and size of the pieces of fruit or individual vegetables we want to buy. We don't like our carrots to be wonky or our cucumbers to be curly. Spare a thought for the poor speckled banana – due to popular demand, they need to be a nice bright yellow with no spots whatsoever. And what happens to all these misfits? They get thrown away, rot and contribute to pollution.

B Al Green

I was looking in a store recently for some ketchup and I came across something that really cheered me up. It was a bottle of sauce made from produce that would normally have ended up as waste. Extremely reassuring was the fact that this was only one of a whole series of products made by different companies targeting food that did not meet quality standards. Simply because an onion is too small to fit into a peeling machine or a carrot is not straight enough to fit into a pack for sale on a supermarket shelf, there is no reason why it should be discarded. By turning these into sauces or pickling them in jars, they can still be used and enjoyed. Small enterprises can make a good living and help reduce food waste with this type of creativity, and I really admire them for it. I shall definitely buy more of these products going forward.

C Miss Happen

Farms produce crops in abundance to supply supermarkets and food stores all year round, but often they produce an *overabundance*, far more than needed. This can be due to miscalculations on the part of the food producers or to overestimations of what the buyers will actually need. Whatever the reason, the result is inevitably tonnes of additional mouldy waste – although, to be precise, this should be referred to as food *loss*, rather than food *waste* – which is what consumers or retailers throw away. But all in all, the amount is about 1.3 billion tonnes globally according to some sources. This can, and must, be reduced. Supermarkets should be held to account for overforecasting demand. In addition to this, they should be encouraged to invest in retailing products that are created from initially unacceptable produce. One that immediately springs to mind is a range of different flavoured waters that uses misshapen and overripe fruits. A bonus is that these are sold in recycled and recyclable cans and glass bottles. Perhaps large companies should consider following this example and invest more in developing products like these.

D Ned Less

In my opinion, education about food waste and its effect on climate change should start at a very early age, so I was encouraged to see a documentary last week about how primary school children are being taught about this. The children featured in the programme were clearly very proud of how they were helping the environment, even on a very small scale. They had charts that they had completed about how their parents used leftovers to rustle up meals, and they also brought examples of wonky fruit into class to compare. What struck me was that although, on the surface, this was about educating the children, indirectly it was also about educating, or re-educating, their parents. I am convinced that more parents were experimenting with using leftover chicken, for example, as a result of the child in the family needing to complete their chart. And I particularly liked the posters children had made with drawings of knobbly carrots and bent parsnips!

4C GRAMMAR

Advanced conditional structures, inversion in conditional forms

1 ★ **Match each pair of sentences with their meanings.**

1 ☐ If I'd spent more on the steak, it wouldn't have been so chewy.

2 ☐ If I'd spent more on the steak, it wouldn't be so chewy.

    a They are eating.
    b They have eaten.

3 ☐ If I were a more experienced cook, I'd have given you a hand with the meal.

4 ☐ If I were a more experienced cook, I'd help you with the meal.

    a The meal has been cooked.
    b The meal has not been cooked.

5 ☐ If I don't put the chicken in to roast now, it won't be ready on time.

6 ☐ If I put the chicken in to roast now, it would be ready too early.

    a The speaker doesn't want to start cooking.
    b The speaker wants to start cooking.

7 ☐ If he'd invited me, I would have come.

8 ☐ If he invited me, I would come.

    a The party has happened.
    b The party hasn't happened.

9 ☐ If the chef hadn't been so liberal with his cloves of garlic, the lamb would be much tastier.

10 ☐ If the chef weren't so liberal with his cloves of garlic, I would have chosen the lamb.

    a I didn't choose the lamb.
    b The garlic spoiled the taste of the lamb.

2 ★★ **Choose the correct forms to complete the sentences.**

1 If we *thought / think* more about the consequences of our actions, we *'d have stopped / stopped* these practices long ago.

2 If cattle *graze / grazed* on ecological grass, we *'ll have got / 'll get* healthier meat and milk.

3 If they *had opened / opened* an organic café near us, I *'d / will* go there regularly.

4 If those young city children *didn't go / hadn't been* on a farm visit last year, they *'d still be thinking / will still think* that milk was produced in factories!

5 If companies *didn't / don't* use so much packaging on produce, it *is / would be* better for the environment.

3 ★★ **Choose the correct words to complete the sentences. Sometimes both words are correct.**

1 The restaurant wouldn't be doing so well *but / if it weren't* for your help.

2 If he *should / were to* ask you what the recipe is, you mustn't tell him.

3 If *it hadn't been for / there should have been* you, the improvements would have taken much longer.

4 *If / As long as* the store sold more products for vegans, it would do more trade.

5 If *it hadn't been for you rustling / you were to rustle* up omelettes, I'm sure we'd all devour them in no time!

4 ★★★ **Complete the sentences with one word or a contraction in each gap.**

1 If you ___should___ ever ask Dan over for a meal, remember that now he's a vegan, so there's a fair amount of products he won't eat.

2 If it _____ been for governments banning those really dangerous pesticides years ago, the situation would be significantly worse than it is.

3 As _____ as you cook it slowly in the oven for a few hours, it will be wonderfully tender.

4 _____ for the sprigs of parsley, there would be no greenery on the plate at all.

5 If it hadn't _____ for the need to share the buffet with the group, I would have eaten everything in sight.

6 If we _____ to leave parts of our gardens untended, it would encourage biodiversity and the insects would flourish.

5 ★★ **Complete the sentences with the words from the box.**

assuming   condition   should   ~~supposing~~   unless without

1 ___Supposing___ I brought some eggs? Would that help at all?

2 _____ knowing about different cultures' eating habits, you're bound to put your foot in it at some point.

3 _____ we start buying wonky fruit, the practice of throwing away good food is not going to change.

4 _____ everyone likes avocados, we'll be fine for a starter.

5 I'll eat again at that restaurant on _____ that they bring down some of their prices.

6 _____ I only get one piece of bread again, like last time, I'll complain.

6 ★★ Rewrite the sentences starting with the words given.

1 We'd have finished by now if we'd started eating when I suggested.

Had *we started eating when I suggested, we'd have finished by now*.

2 If farmers adopted new techniques, insecticides would have no place in agriculture.

Were _____.

3 Without Maria's experience, we wouldn't be eating this amazing meal.

Had_____.

4 If it turns out that the restaurant breached hygiene standards, they will have to close.

Should _____.

5 I'm going to die of hunger if we don't start eating soon.

Unless _____.

6 If it hadn't been for the creative ideas of one small company, this trend would not have developed.

But _____.

7 ★★★ 🔊 20 Complete the conversation with the correct forms of the words in brackets. Use inversion wherever possible. Listen and check.

Danny Hi! I'm Danny, the new waiter. I guess you're Trevor?

Mr Bell I am. But **1**_should you need_ (you/need) to address me in future, please call me Mr Bell.

Danny OK, Trev ... Mr Bell. Sorry if I'm a bit late.

Mr Bell **2**_____ (you/be) another minute late, management **3**_____ (have to) terminate your employment.

Danny But it's my first day!

Mr Bell If you wish to work at a five-star restaurant, you have to provide five-star service. That includes punctuality. To be honest, **4**_____ (not be) for your excellent references, I doubt that the boss **5**_____ (take) you on. Apparently, your interview was not a complete success.

Danny Well, if I'd done that badly, I **6**_____ (know) it. I thought it went pretty well. Anyway, do you have any advice for my first evening?

Mr Bell Remember that our dishes are designed and cooked by world-class chefs. **7**_____ (customers/enquire) why there are no condiments on the tables, inform them politely that the seasoning has been carefully balanced by the chef.

Danny OK. And what happens if **8**_____ (someone/have) specific requirements – like they're vegan or diabetic or something?

Mr Bell Provided that the guest **9**_____ (give/us) prior warning of the situation, there will be a record of this, and you need only to take the name.

Danny And if anyone **10**_____ (complain) about any description, who do I take it to?

Mr Bell We do not receive complaints here. But **11**_____ (you/fail) to provide good service, for example, **12**_____ (you/spill) food on a guest, you **13**_____ (replace) immediately.

Danny No – I'm usually careful. That's important when it comes to tipping!

Mr Bell Tips are forbidden here at Cloud 9. **14**_____ (customer/offer) you money, you should refuse politely. If you **15**_____ (want) to supplement your salary through tips, you **16**_____ (never/apply) here.

Danny That's OK. I'll manage, Mr Bell. And finally, when do you reckon I can get away?

Mr Bell On condition that the **17**_____ (tables/all/lay) for tomorrow, it's likely that you will be able to leave at 12.30.

Danny And supposing I **18**_____ (be) under the weather one day and can't come in, who do I contact?

Mr Bell We do not get ill here at Cloud 9. However, **19**_____ (you/involve) in an accident, the hospital will contact us. Now, **20**_____ (you/have) no more questions, please get to work.

8 ON A HIGH NOTE Write a short post for a website describing how you would survive on a desert island.

4D SPEAKING

1 🔊 *21* Listen and repeat the phrases. How do you say them in your language?

SPEAKING
Proposing solutions, giving reasons and justifications

PROPOSING OPTIONS

Another way forward could be organising courses.

In my opinion, we should also be looking at giving online advice.

We need to address this problem by getting people into saving water.

Given the difficulty/urgency of the problem, we need to move quickly.

GIVING REASONS (JUSTIFICATIONS)

My reason for saying that is because the solution doesn't get to the root of the problem.

The reasoning behind that is that it'd be more of a long-term solution.

The logic underpinning such an approach is that we are in control of our world.

What I'm trying to say is that some people would prioritise other things over food.

ACKNOWLEDGING ANOTHER PERSON'S SUGGESTIONS

Yes, I see where you're going with that.

Actually, that's a really feasible option.

Good thinking. You're spot on!

2 Match the two parts of the sentences.

1. ☐ As far as I'm concerned, we should also be
2. ☐ The logic underpinning such an approach is
3. ☐ That's interesting and I can
4. ☐ We need to address the issue of food shortages
5. ☐ Given the urgency of the current problems,
6. ☐ Another way forward could

a. ☐ looking at alternative sources of food for future needs.
b. ☐ see where you're going with that.
c. ☐ be to ban all movement of livestock during the crisis.
d. ☐ we need to pool ideas worldwide.
e. ☐ by investing in creative ways of using supplies.
f. ☐ that the global population is increasing rapidly.

3 USE OF ENGLISH Complete the second sentence using the word in bold so that it means the same as the first one. Use between three and six words, including the word in bold.

1. You're exactly right with your explanation of the situation. **SPOT**

   You *are spot on* with your explanation of the situation.

2. I simply cannot understand why this approach has been taken. **LOGIC**

   _____ such an approach is inexplicable.

3. We need quick action to be taken because the problem is so urgent. **URGENCY**

   _____ the problem, we need quick action to be taken.

4. Consulting scientists is an alternative approach. **WAY**

   _____ could be to consult scientists.

5. We need to deal with the problem of malnutrition. **ADDRESS**

   We need _____ problem of malnutrition.

6. I'm saying that because such an approach would benefit the majority of the population. **BEHIND**

   The _____ such an approach would benefit the majority of the population.

4 🔊 *22* USE OF ENGLISH Complete the conversation with one word in each gap. Listen and check.

James The situation of rough sleepers is becoming a real concern in this area.

Maddie I know, not only are they having to deal with the weather, but also they desperately need to eat more nutritious food. When they do get ill, they get very ill.

James Absolutely. Action on this is well overdue. We need to ¹*address* this problem immediately by ensuring that they can get a regular supply of healthy meals at least once a day.

Maddie You're ²_____ on. In my opinion, we should also be ³_____ at getting them to understand what they should be eating.

James I see where you're ⁴_____ with that, but for most of these people, it's not about having a choice, is it? ⁵_____ the urgency of the problem, we really need to get food on the streets. We could set up more outdoor food stalls at various points in the area. The ⁶_____ behind that is that many of these people feel safer in their own environment.

Maddie Good ⁷_____. Another way ⁸_____ might be to follow the example set in other cities – where in some cafés, paying customers can donate a meal to a homeless person.

James Actually, that's a really feasible ⁹_____. It gets local businesses involved too.

Maddie The ¹⁰_____ underpinning such an approach in other places is also that it encourages these people to come inside and make social contact.

James I really like that idea! It could dramatically improve life for some of these people.

4E LISTENING AND VOCABULARY

1 🔊 **23** Look at the painting and listen to a lecture on table manners. Why does the lecturer refer to the painting? Choose the correct answer.

a To talk about paintings that show table manners through the years.

b As an example of how we know about table manners through the years.

c To emphasise how bad our table manners are nowadays compared with the time of the painting.

2 🔊 **23** Listen to the lecture again and complete the sentences with a word or a short phrase in each gap.

1 The lecturer uses the word _outrageous_ to describe some people's table manners today.

2 The lecturer mentions an early example of table manners in literature in the _____ century .

3 The lecturer refers to an image of _____ to show that people were becoming less clumsy at the table.

4 The practice of taking _____ was mainly to mix with other people.

5 The lecturer uses the word _____ to describe the connection between Mrs Beeton's cooking tips and today's cooks.

6 Mrs Beeton's book lay down rules about requesting a _____ at dinner time.

7 According to the lecturer, Oxbridge colleges _____ outdated table manners.

8 The lecturer wonders about table manners in a _____ time.

Vocabulary extension

3 Complete the sentences with the words from the box, which you heard in the recording in Exercise 1.

| dreamed face ~~hazard~~ odds ostracised wind |

1 I wouldn't like to _hazard_ a guess as to how many people will turn up at the celebration.

2 You realise that you'll be flying in the _____ of family tradition if you don't have a dinner on your birthday.

3 The chef's manner can change like the _____. One minute he's really happy and kind and the next he's angry and shouting at everyone.

4 It's _____ on that no one else will pay the bill, so it will be me again.

5 This recipe was _____ up by my grandmother and I think it's delicious.

6 A colleague at work has been _____ because he told the boss that several of us had left early last week.

4 **ON A HIGH NOTE** Write a short paragraph about phone etiquette at meal times, in restaurants or cafés, etc.

Pronunciation

5 🔊 **24** Read some sentences from the lecture in Exercise 1. Listen and compare your pronunciation.

1 What is amazing is how rapidly trends come and go.

2 However, it serves to show us that manners were important and at that time extremely strict.

3 Pictures of beautifully fragile Venetian drinking glasses indicate how impossible it would have been to handle these roughly.

ACTIVE PRONUNCIATION
Emphatic syllable stress

When we use emphatic adverbs, we usually stress these words. Additionally, we tend to emphasise the stress of one syllable over the others to focus attention. The voice rises slightly on this syllable.

The situation could **ra·pidly** *deteriorate.*

Crops will **ine·vitably** *fail, won't they?*

It's **rema·rkably** *difficult to plan these things.*

Adverbs of emphasis include: *absolutely, certainly, clearly, completely, definitely, desperately, inevitably, naturally, obviously, positively, rapidly, really, remarkably, significantly, simply, undoubtedly.*

---

6 🔊 **25** Listen and choose the correct sentence, a or b, that contains a stressed syllable.

1 This move would significantly benefit large numbers of people.   a / b

2 We desperately need to research alternatives.   a / b

3 This could completely change how our food is sourced.   a / b

4 It's clearly one of the most difficult problems mankind has ever faced.   a / b

5 It is blindingly obvious that everyone needs to do their part in controlling food waste. a / b

7 🔊 **26** Find the stressed syllables in the words in bold. Listen and check.

1 This option would cost **considerably** less than what has been suggested.

2 To say that nothing can be done is **completely** ridiculous.

3 This would **dramatically** reduce our reliance on government funding.

4 Providing shelters in some areas is **rapidly** becoming unsustainable.

VARIETY IS THE SPICE OF DINING

Engage the reader from the start.	Not another cookery programme! In recent years, our TV screens seem to have been dominated by programmes related to cooking in some shape or form. You can't look at a TV guide without being confronted by different chefs wanting to talk us through complex recipes, or competition after competition where both professionals and amateurs vie to take home awards, win the chance to cook for special people, or simply tour different countries, consuming enviable amounts of mouth-watering specialities. By way of contrast, the series *Come Dine With Me*, sought to do something refreshingly different, and I still find it quite addictive.
Use phrases of similarity and contrast.	
Give brief information about the programme.	What attracts me to the programme is the unpretentiousness of it, the sincerity. Take a group of ordinary people, from a range of backgrounds and get them to take turns to cook for each other. It's a simple premise. The viewers follow the preparations and learn a little about the host's home and hobbies, and then we witness the actual meal and listen in on the conversations and reactions to the food.
Use nominalisation.	The variety of food served is endless. It ranges from haute cuisine with tiny portions of exquisitely flavoured food, to hearty family suppers that would stave off any hunger pangs for days! Monday's meal might include delicate morsels of tender beef, or expensive fish served with a spoonful of light, velvety sauce, whereas Tuesday's might be a thick farmhouse stew with a heel of bread and a stodgy chocolate pudding!
Use synonyms to avoid repetition.	However, the thing that has made me watch each episode without fail, is the difference between the initial reactions of the guests to a meal, and the final official assessment they give when the host is not present. I thoroughly enjoy attempting to guess the final verdict as they rate each meal. So, if you haven't yet been tempted to *Come Dine With Me* – you have been missing out. I cannot praise it highly enough.
Offer a recommendation.	

1 Read the review. Why does the writer like the series? Choose the correct answer.

  a It features food that he enjoys.

  b It shows us how other people live.

  c It shows people cooking who are not specialists.

2 Choose the correct words to complete the sentences.

  1 In *similarity* / *common* with many other programmes of this nature, its interest value is low.

  2 Other writers have done *likewise* / *equally*.

  3 *As* / *So* many other chefs have done, Katy Wild opened her own restaurant within a five-star hotel.

  4 If you're *wanting* / *looking* for something quite out of the ordinary, then this could prove interesting.

  5 This hotel *needs to* / *should* be a first choice for a wedding reception in this area.

  6 I *could* / *would* have to say that this store doesn't score *top* / *highly* on the value for money scale.

  7 *Should* / *Unless* the overcrowding issue be solved quickly, then I wouldn't hesitate to recommend this restaurant.

3 **WRITING TASK** Write a review of a new café (real or invented) that has recently opened in your area.

ACTIVE WRITING | A review

1 **Plan your review.**

  • Give a brief background description.

  • Note down points you could include, either positive, negative, or both.

  • Engage the reader.

2 **Write the review.**

  • Use synonyms to avoid repetition.

  • Make comparisons where possible.

  • Give your opinion and clear recommendation.

3 **Check that ...**

  • you have used a range of vocabulary and grammatical structures, including nominalisation where appropriate.

  • there are no spelling, grammar or punctuation mistakes.

UNIT VOCABULARY PRACTICE

04

1 4A VOCABULARY AND SPEAKING Complete the words in the sentences with one letter in each gap.

1 The meat is so te**nder** that it almost falls apart.

2 If I eat s_ _ _ _ _ cake or pudding just before bed, I don't sleep very well.

3 I'm afraid we can't have macaroni cheese tonight because the cheese in the fridge has gone m_ _ _ _ _.

4 Have you got a cloth I can wipe my hands with because my fingers are all g_ _ _ _ _.

5 Be careful – the water from the hot tap is s_ _ _ _ _ _ _.

6 The meat in the stew was very g_ _ _ _ _ _ _. I think it must have been a really cheap cut.

2 4A VOCABULARY AND SPEAKING Choose the correct words to complete the sentences.

1 Use a *scoop / heel* of bread to make breadcrumbs to put out for the birds. Don't waste it!

2 I usually take a *pinch / spoonful* of sugar in coffee, but none in tea.

3 After mixing in the flour, add a *handful / clove* of raisins to the mix.

4 It's a good idea to roast lamb with a few *sprigs / dustings* of rosemary as it brings out the flavour.

5 Take a couple of *cloves / segments* of garlic, peel and then crush before frying with some onion.

6 There was a light *drop / dusting* of snow across the lawn this morning and it looked just like icing sugar!

3 4B READING AND VOCABULARY Match the two parts of the sentences.

1 ☐ Adverts for healthy eating options bombard you

2 ☐ Did you ever sneak into the kitchen at night to

3 ☐ I'm on a health kick at the moment and trying hard not to waver

4 ☐ While I was out of the kitchen, our dog sniffed out the slab of meat on the worktop

5 ☐ While I was at college, Mum baked some bread and the smell

6 ☐ There's not much in the fridge, but I can rustle up

a and devoured the lot.

b whenever you go online.

c wafted down the path to greet me as I came home.

d raid the fridge if you got hungry?

e some scrambled eggs on toast if you like.

f from my plan not to eat cakes and biscuits.

4 4B READING AND VOCABULARY Complete the sentences with one word in each gap.

1 After a tennis match I'm usually so hungry that I'll eat everything in *sight*.

2 It's a _____ indulgence I know, but a tempting gooey dessert after a good meal just finishes everything off beautifully.

3 Whenever I pass the fish and chip shop, my stomach gives a _____ and I remember how hungry I am.

4 It's always a good idea to let your dinner _____ down before doing any strenuous sport or exercise.

5 My brother is an absolute _____ for any two-for-one deals at the supermarket.

6 If you come round later, I'm sure I can _____ up something for a quick snack.

5 4E LISTENING AND VOCABULARY Complete the sentences with the words and phrases from the box.

by the board   home to me   over the coals
sinking feeling   ~~slurped~~   thing of

1 Dad was exhausted: he bent his face over the steaming bowl of soup and *slurped* loudly.

2 Our teacher used to haul us _____ if we didn't wear our full uniform to school.

3 It's common to get a _____ that moment before you turn over an exam paper.

4 Sharing a family meal every day at the table has, unfortunately, become a _____ the past.

5 Watching the costume drama on Channel 3 last night really brought it _____ how far mealtime etiquette has changed since Victorian times.

6 Manners can often go _____ when you're really hungry!

6 4F WRITING AND VOCABULARY Complete the blog with one word in each gap.

There was a great deal of **1***hype* surrounding the opening of the new clothes shopping complex in what used to be known as the Docklands area. The marketing **2**_____ out that it provided a range of stores that catered to all tastes and pockets. It certainly catered to all tastes, I'll **3**_____ it that. From today's fashion to vintage, you can find practically any items of clothing you might be looking for, but as far as 'all pockets' goes, I would have to disagree. The stores are all high end, and unaffordable to most. After searching for a good couple of hours, I found nothing that I would call **4**_____ for money. So, in that respect it was a definite **5**_____ – total disappointment. If you're feeling rich – then fine, it's a good place to shop, but otherwise I would give the whole place a very wide **6**_____!

7 ON A HIGH NOTE Write a short paragraph about how you think meals, manners and mealtimes might change in the future, giving your reasons.

49

04 Self-assessment

1 For each learning objective, write 1–5 to assess your ability.

1 = I don't feel confident. 5 = I feel confident.

	Learning objective	Course material	How confident I am (1–5)
4A	I can use adjectives and partitive expressions to talk about food.	Student's Book pp. 48–49	
4B	I can identify paraphrases in an article and talk about appetite triggers.	Student's Book pp. 50–51	
4C	I can use conditional forms to make hypotheses about the past, present and future.	Student's Book pp. 52–53	
4D	I can propose solutions, and give reasons and justifications when talking about food.	Student's Book p. 54	
4E	I can understand the development of ideas in a vlog and talk about table manners.	Student's Book p. 55	
4F	I can write a restaurant review.	Student's Book pp. 56–57	

2 Which of the skills above would you like to improve in? How?

Skill I want to improve in	How I can improve

3 What can you remember from this unit?

New words I learned and most want to remember	Expressions and phrases I liked	English I heard or read outside class

GRAMMAR AND VOCABULARY

1 Choose the correct words to complete the sentences.

1 My sister used to like to put milk in her bowl, then put the cake in it until the bottom went *tempting / soggy*! Strange tastes some people have.

2 Add several *drops / dabs* of vanilla essence to the cake mixture before stirring well.

3 All my good intentions went by the *board / coals* as soon as I smelled the pizzas cooking.

4 We were starving after the ten-mile walk and *devoured / slurped* all our sandwiches in a couple of minutes.

5 While I was living in the USA for a year, I *trawled / yearned* for a good strong cup of English tea.

/ 5

2 Read the sentences and complete the words with one letter in each gap.

1 My father is an absolute s u c k e r for foreign sports cars.

2 My stomach gives a l_ _ _ _ when I smell burgers and fried onions. I just have to eat one!

3 No one's been shopping today so I shall just r_ _ _ _ _ up a snack from the leftovers in the fridge.

4 I love this old picture of me and my friends s_ _ _ _ _ _ _ milkshakes in our garden when we were about ten years old.

5 My sister and her friends shared a flat above a fish and chip shop and the smell of vinegar and greasy chips w_ _ _ _ _ through their windows all evening.

6 The bread's gone m_ _ _ _ _ – it's all green and disgusting!

/ 5

3 Complete the sentences with the correct forms of the words in brackets.

1 If it *weren't* (not be) for getting the grant, you _____ (not study) here right now.

2 I _____ (never/enter) the competition if it _____ (not be) for your suggestion last week. Thanks!

3 _____ (you/not study) English at college, you _____ (not get) this job in London.

4 _____ (you/need) any help with sourcing a recipe, just give me a call.

5 If _____ (I/like) spicy food, I _____ (go for) the chicken curry, but I don't, and this sweet and sour is lovely.

6 If my mum _____ (not buy) me several cooking classes when I was twelve, I _____ (not be) a successful restaurateur now.

/ 5

4 Complete the message with the words from the box. There are two extra words.

but for   condition   long as   provided   ~~supposing~~
unless   without   would

It would be great to meet up for a snack tomorrow after college. [1]*Supposing* I message you when I'm finished? That should be around 4.30 [2]_____ the lesson overruns. Perhaps we can go to the new pop up café? It's really good, [3]_____ that you like cheese! Otherwise, we could go to Albie's. [4]_____ knowing what the weather's going to be like, it's hard to say whether we'll be able to sit outside, but it [5]_____ be good if we could as [6]_____ you're not allergic to the sun, of course. Speak tomorrow!

/ 5

USE OF ENGLISH

5 Complete the text with one word in each gap.

AN UNEXPECTED HERO

The huge salaries of professional sports people have given them a bad reputation, but if it hadn't [1]*been* for one celebrity footballer, the food crisis in this local community [2]_____ be a lot worse than it is. The footballer started a campaign which has resulted in government funding to help provide meals for children from families that [3]_____ would be surviving on food banks. [4]_____ for his presence on the campaign, the funding would [5]_____ stopped last week. And to be honest, he is not the only celebrity contributing. If it [6]_____ not for the generosity of many people like him, who are also donating secretly, more children would be going hungry today.

/ 5

6 Complete the second sentence using the word in bold so that it means the same as the first one. Use between three and six words, including the word in bold.

1 My teacher encouraged me to become a chef. **HAD**
Had it not been for my teacher, I wouldn't have become a chef.

2 Don't rush off for a run until you've allowed your dinner to digest. **GO**
You should _____ rushing off for a run.

3 If you do the washing up, I'll cook the meal. **CONDITION**
I'll cook _____ you do the washing up.

4 Watching programmes like these makes you realise that famine can be really devastating. **HOME**
Watching programmes like these _____ how devastating famine can be.

5 The restaurant didn't observe safety regulations and had to close. **NOT**
If the restaurant had observed safety regulations, _____ today.

6 I'll quickly make a couple of steaks for lunch. **UP**
I'll _____ a couple of steaks for lunch.

/ 5

/ 30

51

05 | *Do your best*

5A VOCABULARY AND SPEAKING

Idioms (studying), collocations with *attempt* and *effort*, verbs + dependent prepositions

1 ★ **Choose the correct words to complete the idioms in bold.**

1 When you start a new job, you **are** always **on a steep learning** *track / curve*.

2 We were all struggling with the grammar, but he *blew / breezed* **through it** all.

3 Don't talk to me! I need to **get my** *brain / head* **down** and get this work finished.

4 As soon as the exam started, **my mind went** *empty / blank* and I couldn't remember anything.

5 The importance of being polite **was** *drummed / dragged* **into us** from an early age.

6 As long as you can **keep** *up / on* **track**, you should do well this year.

7 I really need a holiday! **I've been** *running / breezing* **on empty** for months now.

8 I just can't *get / grasp* **the hang of** hula-hooping – the hoop always crashes down.

9 I don't know if I'll succeed, but **I'll give it my** *best / biggest* **shot**.

2 ★ **Match the idioms from Exercise 1 with their meanings a–i.**

a ☐ have no energy left

b ☐ try your hardest

c ☐ focus on something

d ☐ learn a lot very quickly

e ☐ teach something by repeating it many times

f ☐ learn how to do something

g ☐ do something successfully and easily

h ☐ have no knowledge or understanding

i ☐ continue to do what you are doing now

3 ★ **Match the two parts of the sentences.**

1 ☐ The rescuers made a last-ditch effort to

2 ☐ He made a misguided attempt to

3 ☐ We made a detour in a futile attempt to

4 ☐ They didn't really have much time so they only

5 ☐ If we want to get this finished today,

6 ☐ He sped up towards the end of the race

a avoid the bad weather, but still got soaked.

b made a half-hearted effort to find the missing luggage.

c reach the people before the building collapsed.

d we will have to make a sustained effort.

e untangle the fishing rod and fell into the river.

f in a valiant attempt to overtake me.

4 ★ **Choose the correct words to complete the sentences.**

1 Knowing that he was almost out of time, he made a *frantic / misguided* attempt to finish the essay.

2 She made a *strenuous / futile* effort to get there on time and, luckily, succeeded.

3 He made a *half-hearted / valiant* effort to keep up, and soon gave up.

4 It isn't just about trying hard today, but about making a *sustained / frantic* effort over the next few weeks.

5 At least you tried. It was a *misguided / valiant* effort, well done.

5 ★ **Complete the sentences with the correct prepositions.**

1 I don't think you can cram another scoop of ice cream *into* that bowl!

2 We all stood gaping _____ the porcupine in the back garden. Where could it have come from?

3 A sticking plaster solution can easily backfire _____ you and make things worse.

4 Never let anything deflect you _____ pursuing your dreams.

5 Why are you munching _____ that heel of bread? Isn't it stale?

6 The problem with cramming _____ exams, is that you will forget everything afterwards.

7 You won't pass unless you start applying yourself _____ your work.

8 Snacking between meals is associated _____ unhealthy eating.

9 Start by sorting the names _____ alphabetical order.

10 'Don't talk to strangers' was a message my mum drummed _____ me when I was young.

6 ★★ Complete the conversation with the correct verbs and prepositions from Exercise 5.

Luke My mum asked me to help my little brother revise for his Spanish test, but he's driving me crazy. He just sits there **1** _munching on_ crisps and every time I ask him a question, he **2** _____ me blankly.

Eloise That would drive me insane. Maybe you could make the revision more of a game? You know, maybe get him to **3** _____ vocabulary words _____ different piles, that kind of thing? This way he may start **4** _____ studying _____ fun? I've heard that learning through play makes children more self-confident and more willing to engage in new experiences.

Luke Yes, I've tried everything. He just won't get his head down and **5** _____ himself _____ his work! Literally everything can **6** _____ his attention _____ his set tasks!

Eloise Well, to be honest, I don't really think it's your job to try and **7** _____ knowledge _____ his head. He's not a baby, he has to take some responsibility himself, doesn't he? That kind of attitude is really going to **8** _____ him as he gets older.

Luke You're right. I need to talk to my parents about it. Now I'm going to check up on him and see if he's **9** _____ the test, little monkey!

7 ★★★ USE OF ENGLISH Complete the second sentence using the word in bold so that it means the same as the first one. Use between three and five words, including the word in bold.

1 He didn't really try to win the prize. **HALF-HEARTED**
He _made a half-hearted attempt_ to win the prize.

2 The car was really full with six of us. **CRAMMED**
There were _____ the car.

3 He shouldn't have attempted to swim across the river. **MISGUIDED**
He _____ to swim across the river.

4 All that matters is that you do your best. **SHOT**
All that matters is that you _____.

5 I had to learn a lot of new skills very quickly. **CURVE**
I was _____.

6 I completely forgot everything. **BLANK**
My _____.

7 I passed my practical driving test with no trouble at all! **BREEZED**
I _____ my practical driving test!

8 It's time you started working and did some revision. **HEAD**
It's time you _____ and did some revision.

9 I've been so exhausted lately but I just need to study for the final exams. **EMPTY**
I _____ but I just need to study for the final exams.

8 ★★★ Complete the online article with one or two words in each gap.

"WHERE DID I PUT THAT PIECE OF INFORMATION?"

VISITING THE MEMORY PALACE

The Memory Palace sounds like it might be the name of a band, but it's actually a technique invented by the ancient Greeks for memorising anything that you need to **1** _cram_ into your head. You might not see the point of learning how to memorise facts and figures when everything can be found at the touch of a button, but there are still a surprising number of occasions when developing a super memory will be useful. Not least if you're **2** _____ for an exam. If you master this technique, your mind may never **3** _____ again!

The idea behind the Memory Palace is to **4** _____ the information you want to remember with a place that you know very well, such as your own home. Close your eyes and imagine walking through this location. As you go, visually put each piece of information in a specific place. The more visual and memorable you can make the image, the better. For example, let's say you want to remember the expression 'make a **5** _____ effort'. You might imagine a knight in armour making an effort to open your front door, which is badly stuck.

When you later want to recall the items, just imagine yourself walking the same mental route, and the items should come back to you without even really having to **6** _____ yourself to it. With practice, you'll soon get the **7** _____ of it, and be able to **8** _____ through any exams with ease.

9 ON A HIGH NOTE Write a paragraph about a challenge which put you on a steep learning curve.

5B GRAMMAR

Modal and related verbs

1 ★ Complete the sentences with the modal verbs from the box.

can't (x2) may ~~must~~ mustn't oughtn't

1 Jane left the exam room after just ten minutes. She _must_ have failed.

2 I don't know what to do! I have broken my right arm and I _____ write with my left hand!

3 That result is disappointing. You _____ to have taken so much time off.

4 Jimmy _____ have failed, he's the strongest student in the class.

5 You _____ start writing on the exam paper only when I say so.

6 You _____ make any noise in the exam room or you'll be thrown out.

didn't need to   have to   might have   must needn't have   should have

7 I did so badly in my mock exams, I _____ work harder if I want to pass.

8 I wish I had known the lecture didn't start until ten. I _____ got up so early.

9 It was a mistake to tell her about it. I _____ kept quiet.

10 I _____ get up early that day so I had a lie-in until midday.

11 I was sick today, so I _____ take the exam tomorrow instead.

12 Don't worry. You _____ done better than you think – you can't know until the results come out.

2 ★ Match the sentences from Exercise 1 with their functions a–l.

a ☐ not have the ability to do something

b ☐ not be allowed to do something

c ☐ be almost certain that

d ☐ be possible that

e ☐ have permission to do something

f ☐ it wasn't necessary so I didn't do it

g ☐ be almost impossible that

h ☐ be a good idea to have done something

i ☐ it wasn't necessary to do something but I did it

j ☐ have no choice but to do something (someone else makes you do it)

k ☐ not be a good idea to have done something

l ☐ have no choice but to do something (you feel this way)

3 ★★ Rewrite the sentences from Exercise 1 using the paraphrases from Exercise 2.

1 _Jane left the exam room after just ten minutes. It is almost certain that she failed._

2 _____

3 _____

4 _____

5 _____

6 _____

7 _____

8 _____

9 _____

10 _____

11 _____

12 _____

4 ★ 🔊 **27** Listen to the pairs of sentences. What do they express? Choose *C* for a complaint or *P* for a possibility.

1 a He might have helped me. C / P

   b He might have helped me. C / P

2 a You could pick that up. C / P

   b You could pick that up. C / P

3 a They could have tried it. C / P

   b They could have tried it. C / P

5 ★ Choose the correct forms to complete the sentences.

1 Beatrice *must / can't* have been here earlier, that's her umbrella on the table.

2 You *don't have to / mustn't* leave your email address, it's entirely optional.

3 You *could / may* have given me a lift! I saw you drive past in your fancy car!

4 I don't know where my wallet is. I *should / could* have left it at home, I guess.

5 I *didn't need to rush / needn't have rushed* because he was going to be late.

6 *Could / May* you introduce us, please?

6 ★★ Complete the sentences with the correct modal verbs. Sometimes more than one answer is possible.

1 Mr Jones thinks there _might_ be a question on Ophelia in the exam because the topic hasn't come up for a while.

2 You _____ have told me you were going to be out. It was a wasted journey for me.

3 He _____ have been a big star, but he decided against acting as a career.

4 You _____ use a green pen on the exam paper – blue or black only.

5 Who _____ be calling at this time of night? It's nearly midnight!

6 Could you help me, please? I _____ reach the top shelf because I'm too short!

7 ★★ Complete the conversation with the verbs from the box.

<del>banned</del> been able to couldn't had to managed
must must have oughtn't to

Claire	Have you ever had anything funny happen to you in an exam?
Valentina	Not to me, no, but my cousin was almost ¹<u>banned</u> from an exam once!
Claire	He ² _____ done something really bad!
Valentina	Not really, or at least he didn't mean to. You see, he'd been very busy revising so he hadn't ³ _____ do any washing. So, on the day of the exam, he ⁴ _____ find any clean …
Claire	Perhaps you ⁵ _____ tell me this story. Isn't it a bit personal?
Valentina	No, not at all. You ⁶ _____ be the only person I haven't already told! It's such a good story … Anyway, he finally ⁷ _____ to find some clean socks which someone had bought him as a joke.
Claire	So, what happened?
Valentina	Nothing, at first. And then his socks started playing a tune, in the middle of the exam. He didn't even realise it was him at first, so the music went on and on before they finally identified the culprit! He ⁸ _____ do the rest of the exam in bare feet.
Claire	Hilarious!

8 ★★★ USE OF ENGLISH Complete the second sentence using the word in bold so that it means the same as the first one. Use between three and five words, including the word in bold.

1 Students should bring a ruler to the exam. **SUPPOSED**
   Students *are supposed to bring* a ruler to the exam.
2 My parents told me I had to study harder. **FORCED**
   I _____ by my parents.
3 We didn't buy a train ticket at the station, but were able to buy one on the train. **NEED**
   We _____ a train ticket at the station because we were able to buy one on the train.
4 The school says that students have to wear a uniform. **REQUIRED**
   Students _____ wear a uniform.
5 The school said that pupils were not allowed to wear earrings. **BANNED**
   The pupils _____ earrings.
6 You shouldn't have told him the answers. **MEANT**
   You _____ the answers.

9 ★★★ USE OF ENGLISH Choose the correct words a–d to complete the text.

MANAGING EXAM-RELATED ANXIETY

A certain amount of anxiety ¹__ be useful when taking an exam. Adrenaline signals to the body, and the brain, that we ²__ to focus and pay attention, and it ³__ even improve our performance.

However, after a certain point, anxiety could lead to negative thoughts about our performance, 'I just ⁴__ do this!', which is clearly not helpful.

In the run-up to an exam, you ⁵__ pay particular attention to eating and sleeping well. You ⁶__ give up junk food altogether, but be careful to ensure that your diet is balanced and includes plenty of protein, fruit and vegetables. There's no benefit in staying up late studying, especially if you are ⁷__ to get up early on the day of the exam.

You ⁸__ also benefit from learning some relaxation techniques, such as deep breathing or mindfulness, which you ⁹__ use when you feel the anxiety levels starting to rise.

	a	**b**	**c**	**d**
1	should	can	must	has to
2	need	didn't need	needn't have	needn't
3	ought to	can't	may	needs to
4	mustn't	couldn't	didn't have to	can't
5	ought	shouldn't	can	ought to
6	might	needn't	mustn't	can't
7	banned	not allowed	required	able
8	might	could have	can	must
9	may	can	need	ought

10 ON A HIGH NOTE Write a paragraph about your worst/best exam experience.

5C READING AND VOCABULARY

1 Do you listen to music while you study? What do you think might be the benefits and drawbacks?

2 Read the article. Match paragraphs A–E with gaps 1–4 in the text. There is one extra paragraph.

Vocabulary extension

3 Match the highlighted words from the text with the definitions.

 1 Carried out. _undertaken_
 2 Possible results (often negative). _____
 3 Support a claim with facts. _____
 4 Anything which blocks something from happening. _____
 5 Accept or recognise something. _____
 6 Clear and easy to understand. _____

4 Complete the sentences with the correct forms of the words from Exercise 3.

 1 She is generally _acknowledged_ as a leader in her field.
 2 Meeting the other people face to face helped to break down _____ between them.
 3 The government's plan needs to be _____ and easy to follow.
 4 Candidates will be required to _____ a personality test.
 5 Before you make a decision, you should consider all the possible _____.
 6 The initial reports have not yet been _____ with any proof.

ACTIVE VOCABULARY
Synonyms for things getting better or worse

When writing about the outcomes of research, we will often want to describe how something has improved or got worse. For example:

... the students' performance was **enhanced** _after listening to Mozart._

... whether music helped or **hindered** _performance._

Using a variety of synonyms will make your writing less repetitive and more engaging to read.

5 Write the words from the box in the correct column.

~~boost~~ deteriorate diminish enhance enrich hinder impair rectify undermine

Improve	Get/Make worse
boost	

6 Choose the correct words to complete the sentences.

 1 Various sales gimmicks were tried in order to _boost / enrich_ sales.
 2 Knowing you has greatly _enriched / rectified_ my life.
 3 Any errors should be _enhanced / rectified_ before handing in the essay.
 4 Despite the doctors' best efforts, his health continued to _deteriorate / erode_.
 5 You should support me, not _undermine / impair_ me!
 6 The heavy rain _diminished / hindered_ our progress up the mountain.
 7 The company's shares have significantly _diminished / hindered_ in value since the scandal.
 8 Winning an Oscar considerably _rectified / enhanced_ her career.

7 **ON A HIGH NOTE** Write a paragraph describing what impact, if any, reading the article may have on your studying habits. Explain why.

Is silence golden?

Do you listen to music while you study? According to a recent survey carried out at an American high school, ninety-four percent of students had background music on while they did their homework or crammed for an exam. But is this actually beneficial, or could it perhaps even be a destructive habit?

1 ___ Another justification people often give for listening to music while studying, relies on what has become known as the 'Mozart effect'. Put simply, this refers to a finding from research where students were asked to listen to a piano sonata by Mozart, or relaxation music, or sit in silence before performing a reasoning test. The study found that the students' performance was enhanced after listening to Mozart. However, before you leap at this as the answer to all your prayers, note that the effect was not sustained for very long (around fifteen minutes), it only seemed to apply to this specific kind of task, and, crucially, no one has ever successfully reproduced the effect.

2 ___ Researchers from Cardiff Metropolitan University divided students into four groups: the first revised in silence, the second revised while listening to music with lyrics they felt positively about, the third listened to music with lyrics they didn't like and the fourth listened to purely instrumental music.

3 ___ Students who listened to music without any lyrics at all did better than those who had been processing words as well as sounds, but were not as successful as those who worked in silence. So, it would seem that silence is definitely golden.

4 ___ Which brings us to the next factor: personality. Another study investigated the impact on students depending on whether they had self-identified as extrovert or introvert, and on the type of cognition required for the task. These researchers found that introverted people found background music distracting while carrying out abstract reasoning tasks, while more extroverted individuals were unaffected. Neither personality type was adversely affected by music while working on verbal reasoning tasks, however. We can perhaps conclude from this that task complexity may be a key factor, especially if you are more on the introverted spectrum.

So, if you listen to music while studying, could it backfire on you? As is so often the case with research into memory and the brain, the answer in a nutshell is 'it depends'. Considerations may include the kind of music, the type of task, and even the type of person you are. It does seem clear however, that for more complex processing tasks, any kind of music is probably best avoided.

A So, it seems that this research is not, after all, perhaps all that pertinent to our question. Let's look at some other research which aimed to focus not only on whether music helped or hindered performance in comparison with silence, but on what impact the kind of music, and the students' attitudes to the music might have.

B Another study compared 'unpleasant or aggressive' music with 'pleasant, calm' music, and found, probably unsurprisingly, that performance was worse with the 'unpleasant' background music. The question though would have to be in whose opinion the music was unpleasant, and whether enjoyment of more loud and raucous music might make all the difference to students' performance. In general, when looking at this kind of research, it is important to consider all the possible variables.

C Intuitively, many people feel that music relaxes and calms them, making it easier to focus on the job in hand. There is some evidence to substantiate this. Research carried out in 2005 found that music could improve mood, and thus motivation to study. However, this was a relatively small impact, and other factors need to be taken into account, as we shall see.

D That said, there are, as I mentioned earlier, a number of other factors which we should perhaps take into consideration. Firstly, we probably need to consider the nature of the task being undertaken. Another study showed that listening to classical music (without lyrics) had a positive impact on studying vocabulary, leading to better test results overall. This supports other research showing that music may help with verbal reasoning, but proves a barrier for more abstract reasoning tasks. However, the author of this study did also acknowledge that not all participants benefited to the same degree.

E The results were surprisingly coherent. Those students who had revised in a quiet environment did over sixty percent better in a subsequent test than those who had been listening to music with lyrics. So, it appears that lyrics definitely did get in the way. And, interestingly enough, it made no difference at all whether the students liked the lyrics or hated them, the ramifications were the same.

5D LISTENING AND VOCABULARY

1 🔊 *28* Listen to four short extracts from a radio phone-in. What is the main topic? Choose the correct answer.
  a trying something new
  b performing in public
  c rising to a challenge

2 🔊 *28* Listen to the extracts again. For Task One, match each speaker with the trigger for their anxiety. For Task Two, match each speaker with the strategy they used to overcome their anxiety. There are two extra options for each task.
  Task One – Speaker: 1 ☐ 2 ☐ 3 ☐ 4 ☐
  a being judged by others
  b low blood sugar
  c conflict
  d feeling overwhelmed
  e making a mistake
  f money worries
  Task Two – Speaker: 1 ☐ 2 ☐ 3 ☐ 4 ☐
  a slow breathing
  b talking to someone about your feelings
  c relaxing your muscles
  d eating balanced meals
  e going for a walk
  f challenging your self-talk

Vocabulary extension

3 Match the expressions from the box, which you heard in the recording in Exercise 1, with their definitions.

egg someone on	go without a hitch
get over yourself	not hear a peep
give someone a dirty look	put a sock in it
go through the roof	~~run into difficulties~~

  1 Encounter problems. *run into difficulties*
  2 Experience silence. _____
  3 Stop thinking of yourself first. _____
  4 Tell someone to stop making a noise. _____
  5 Urge someone to do something bad. _____
  6 Increase to a very high level. _____
  7 Show disapproval. _____
  8 Go smoothly. _____

4 Complete the sentences with the correct expressions formed from the words in bold.
  1 He stopped laughing when Sally *gave him a dirty look*. **DIRTY**
  2 It started off well, but they soon _____. **DIFFICULTIES**
  3 I'm trying to sleep, can you please _____? **SOCK**
  4 It isn't always about you, you need to _____. **OVER**
  5 He would never have done it if she _____. **EGGED**
  6 Overnight the company's share price _____. **ROOF**
  7 They must be asleep, I can't _____. **PEEP**

5 ON A HIGH NOTE Write a paragraph about a time when you were pushed out of your comfort zone, but ended up being glad that it happened.

Pronunciation

6 🔊 *29* Listen to some sentences from the recording in Exercise 1. What do you notice about the pronunciation of the underlined words?
  1 I've never really thought of myself as a <u>singer</u>.
  2 I think I'm a <u>stronger</u> person for the experience.
  3 So, I had three <u>passengers</u> ...
  4 I didn't want to put us in any <u>danger</u>.
  5 The queues at lunchtime were much <u>longer</u> ...
  6 Lots of people suffering from <u>hunger</u> ...

ACTIVE PRONUNCIATION
Words that end in -nger

The cluster *nger* can be pronounced in three different ways:
  • /ŋə/ (e.g. ha**nger**)
  • /ŋgə/ (e.g. a**nger**)
  • /ndʒə/ (e.g. gi**nger**)

---

7 🔊 *30* Write the underlined words from Exercise 6 in the correct column. Listen, check and repeat.

/ŋə/	/ŋgə/	/ndʒə/
	stronger	

8 🔊 *31* Read some less common words. How is the cluster *nger* pronounced? Choose 1 for /ŋə/, 2 for /ŋgə/ or 3 for /ndʒə/. Listen and check.

1 scavenger	1 / 2 / 3		**6** ranger	1 / 2 / 3
2 linger	1 / 2 / 3		**7** zinger	1 / 2 / 3
3 plunger	1 / 2 / 3		**8** whinger	1 / 2 / 3
4 banger	1 / 2 / 3		**9** malinger	1 / 2 / 3
5 sponger	1 / 2 / 3		**10** warmonger	1 / 2 / 3

5E SPEAKING

1 🔊 *32* **Listen and repeat the phrases. How do you say them in your language?**

SPEAKING | Buying time

I'm sorry, I'm really nervous and my mind has gone blank. Let me think about it for a minute.

I'm not certain I follow you. Could you explain a bit more about what you mean?

Well, I'm glad you asked that question.

So, let me see ... I suppose she portrays Sir William Elliot.

That's quite a tough question. Let me have a minute to think about it.

Well, to be honest, that requires a bit of thought.

Actually, I don't really have strong feelings one way or the other, but if I had to choose, I'd say working in the kitchen.

Could you just explain what you mean by that?

Wow, that really needs a moment's thought.

I suppose it depends on what you mean by that.

2 **Choose the correct words to complete the sentences.**

1 I'm not certain I *go with* / *follow* you.
2 That's quite a *chewy* / *tough* question.
3 I'm sorry, my mind has *become* / *gone* blank.
4 It depends *on* / *in* what you mean by ...
5 Well, I'm *sad* / *glad* you asked that question.
6 If I *had* / *have* to choose, I would say ...
7 So, let me *see* / *look* ... I suppose ...

3 **Replace the underlined parts of the sentences with the phrases from the Speaking box. Use the words in bold.**

1 I'm quite neutral about that. **STRONG**
   I don't really have strong feelings one way or the other.

2 That's quite a tricky thing to ask. **TOUGH**
   _____

3 Wow, I really need to take some time to think about that. **MOMENT**
   _____

4 I'm sorry, I'm really nervous and I can't think what to say. **BLANK**
   _____

5 That's a great question! **GLAD**
   _____

6 Well, let me see, I probably need to think about that for a minute. **REQUIRES**
   _____

7 I'm not sure I completely understand what you're saying. **FOLLOW**
   _____

4 🔊 *33* **What function does the underlined word have in each sentence? Listen and repeat.**

1 <u>Well</u>, let me see, that's a bit tricky ...
2 <u>Actually</u>, to be honest, I might need a moment to think.
3 <u>So,</u> I suppose it depends on what you mean by that.

5 🔊 *34* **Complete the mini-conversations with no more than three words in each gap. Listen and check.**

Interviewer	So, what's your biggest achievement so far?
Interviewee	Well, I'm ¹<u>glad</u> you asked that question. Er, I think it probably has to be when I worked together with a team to raise over £1,000 for charity.
Interviewer	That sounds great. Tell me more about it.
Interviewer	Where do you see yourself in five years' time?
Interviewee	Well, to ²_____, that requires a ³_____. I guess I'd like to be doing something positive in the world, and really using my qualifications.
Interviewer	What are your weaknesses?
Interviewee	That's ⁴_____ question. Let me have a minute to think about it. Er, I guess I have sometimes struggled with lack of confidence, but this is something I'm working on.
Interviewer	Can you give a specific example of how you've overcome this?
Interviewee	I suppose ⁵_____ what you mean by 'overcome'. OK, let me tell you about something which happened last year ...
Interviewer	Do you prefer to work alone, or with other people?
Interviewee	Actually, I don't really have ⁶_____ one way or the ⁷_____. Both can work really well, it depends on the task.

6 **ON A HIGH NOTE Write three mini-conversations. Use the interview questions below.**

1 Tell me about a time you made a mistake.
2 How would you deal with someone who got annoyed with you?
3 Why do you want to study here?

5F WRITING AND VOCABULARY | An essay

Summarise the topic of the essay and state your position on the matter.

Choose the first point of two (from the three options given). Explain the reasons for your choice. Use the opinions given if you wish, but remember to paraphrase them in your own words.

Choose the second point of two. Use your own ideas to back up the point, and give reasons and examples.

Summarise the main points and restate your opinion on the topic.

Without doubt, a developed society is an educated society. It is clear that while education has a financial cost to any society, the benefits far outweigh any costs.

It is not debatable that lack of education is the root cause of poverty. If all children left school with basic reading skills, 171 million people worldwide would not have to contend with extreme poverty in their daily lives. We also know that taken as an average, each extra year of education can result in an extra ten percent in terms of earnings. These benefits are felt not just by the individuals concerned, but by society as a whole, as there is a positive correlation between literacy rates and the economic health of the entire country. For these reasons, the potential for education to reduce levels of poverty should be seen as the key benefit.

[1]**Following closely behind**, however, is the impact of education on equality, particularly gender equality. It is almost impossible to achieve equal opportunities for both men and women, when so many women receive only a very rudimentary education. In fact, on a global level, [2]around two thirds of those who are unable to read and write are female, **leaving them significantly disadvantaged**, and reliant on male family members to manage many essential tasks on their behalf. This can have many serious knock-on effects, as mothers may be unable to read advice on looking after their children, for example. [3]**Having had a primary education** also significantly cuts maternal death rates, so there is a lot at stake.

In conclusion, I believe that education, particularly literacy, is essential in creating a fairer and more equal society. That is why we should all focus on ensuring that all children round the world, have access to at least the basics. In this way, we have the potential to make a real difference to so many people's lives.

1
Read the task below and the essay. Which of the benefits did the author choose to write about and which opinions did they refer to?

Your class has listened to a radio discussion on the benefits of education for society. Here are your notes:

Benefits of education for society:
1 reducing levels of poverty
2 promoting equality
3 discouraging crime

Some opinions expressed in the discussion:
a 'Education gives people more opportunities so they don't need to turn to crime.'
b 'Almost two thirds of the world's illiterate adults are women.'
c 'On average, people earn ten percent more with each extra year of education.'

Write an essay discussing two of the most important benefits listed above.

2
Rewrite the underlined sentences from the essay without using the participle clauses in bold.

1 The impact _____
_____ .

2 Around two thirds of those who are unable to read and write are female, _____
_____ .

3 Maternal _____
_____ .

3
WRITING TASK Read the task and write your essay.

Your class has discussed the best ways to prepare young people for work. Here are your notes:
• teaching career skills such as leadership in class
• providing opportunities for work experience
• inviting speakers to tell students about their careers

Some opinions expressed in the discussion:
'Young people need practical experience of work.'
'It is difficult to know what you want to do if you're unaware of all the options.'
'Career skills should be given more priority in schools.'

Write an essay discussing two of the ways in which schools can prepare young people for work. Explain which way is more important and give reasons.

ACTIVE WRITING | An essay

1 **Plan your essay.**
   • Choose two ways you think are most important.
   • Make notes and decide on your reasons.
   • Choose the opinions given or think of your own.
2 **Write the essay.**
   • Use a formal/semi-formal writing style.
   • Give reasons for your opinions.
   • Paraphrase any vocabulary from the question.
3 **Check that ...**
   • you have followed the instructions.
   • there are no spelling, grammar or punctuation mistakes.

UNIT VOCABULARY PRACTICE > page 61

1 5A VOCABULARY AND SPEAKING Complete the sentences with the prepositions from the box.

| at   on (x4)   through   with |

1 Having a study buddy can help to keep you _on_ track.
2 I am proud to be associated _____ this project.
3 He appeared to breeze _____ his exams effortlessly.
4 When I told him he'd got an 'A', he gaped blankly _____ me, unable to believe it.
5 When I first joined the company, I was _____ a steep learning curve.
6 I've been working for twelve hours straight and I'm really running _____ empty now.
7 Can't you find something healthier than crisps to munch _____ while you study?

2 5A VOCABULARY AND SPEAKING Complete the online article with one word in each gap.

You may believe that you work much better under pressure, and so you only ever get your ¹h_ead_ down a few days before the exam. However, this attitude can really ²b_____ on you, as, while making a ³l_____ -d_____ attempt to ⁴c_____ something into your head is probably better than nothing, you will do much better if you ⁵a_____ yourself to studying steadily throughout the year.

If you really want to ⁶d_____ something into your head, it works best to study it several times, leaving time between each occasion that you try to learn it.

3 5C READING AND VOCABULARY Match the words and phrases 1–8 with situations a–h.

1 ☐ natural aptitude
2 ☐ boundless energy
3 ☐ stubborn streak
4 ☐ rivalry
5 ☐ exuberance
6 ☐ tenacity
7 ☐ willingness to make sacrifices
8 ☐ self-conviction

a If his brother gets something, he has to get it too.
b He's like a machine! Never gets tired.
c He never gives up.
d She's always been really musical.
e She's full of high spirits and has a zest for life.
f He always puts his family first.
g She isn't easily persuaded.
h She has a lot of faith in herself.

4 5C READING AND VOCABULARY Replace the underlined words with the words or phrases from the box. Make any other necessary changes.

| adroit   barrage   laughable   mediocrity   perseverance   ~~pertinent~~   raw talent |

1 I don't think that question is relevant to the discussion. _pertinent_
2 The plot was so unbelievable it was ridiculous. _____
3 She needs training, but her natural ability is undeniable. _____
4 She will probably get her pay rise, she is a skilful negotiator. _____
5 It may be difficult at first, but with determination you will succeed. _____
6 He faced a stream of difficult questions from the interviewer. _____
7 I would rather fail spectacularly than risk being average. _____

5 5D LISTENING AND VOCABULARY Rewrite the sentences using the words in bold.

1 He started the race in the lead, but then started to get tired. **STEAM**
 He started the race in the lead, but then started to run out of steam.
2 I have to pass this exam – it's really important. **STAKE**
3 Lucy is easily the best player on the team. **FAR**
4 Don't give up hope, it will happen. **FAITH**
5 He's been ill, so I call him every day to see he's OK. **UP**
6 You deserve congratulations for that performance. **PAT**
7 The park again? Let's go to the seaside instead. **CHANGE**

6 5F WRITING AND VOCABULARY Choose the correct words to complete the sentences.

1 It is _debatable / debated_ whether this approach is the right one.
2 Thank you for the offer, but I can do this _aided / unaided_.
3 After six weeks in bed, her muscles had _misguided / atrophied_.
4 Critics _content / contend_ that the policy is flawed.
5 Anyone who _discards / deflects_ litter in the street should have to pay a fine.
6 That attitude is _basic / outmoded_ and even offensive.
7 I only have very _rudimentary / boundless_ German.
8 It was _incredibly / utterly_ incomprehensible.

7 ON A HIGH NOTE What makes a good student? Write a paragraph with your answer.

1 **For each learning objective, write 1–5 to assess your ability.**

1 = I don't feel confident. 5 = I feel confident.

	Learning objective	Course material	How confident I am (1–5)
5A	I can use verbs and dependent prepositions, collocations and idioms to talk about studying.	Student's Book pp. 64–65	
5B	I can use modal and related verbs to complain or express possibility.	Student's Book pp. 66–67	
5C	I can identify specific details in an article and talk about success.	Student's Book pp. 68–69	
5D	I can recognise word clusters in fast speech and talk about motivation.	Student's Book p. 70	
5E	I can use phrases to buy myself time to think.	Student's Book p. 71	
5F	I can write an essay considering other people's points of view.	Student's Book pp. 72–73	

2 **Which of the skills above would you like to improve in? How?**

Skill I want to improve in	How I can improve

3 **What can you remember from this unit?**

New words I learned and most want to remember	Expressions and phrases I liked	English I heard or read outside class

GRAMMAR AND VOCABULARY

1 Complete the sentences with one word in each gap.

1 It is d*ebatable* whether this research was really worthwhile.
2 He made a v_____ attempt to win, but ended up coming second.
3 If you don't use muscles, they will a_____.
4 He tried hard, but all his efforts were f_____.
5 He l_____ up from the sofa when I came in.
6 Nothing can d_____ me from reaching my goal.

/ 5

2 Find and correct one mistake in each sentence.

1 The way she danced was poetry in (movement) *motion*
2 We need to focus, there's a lot in stake here. _____
3 Cramming into your exams is not a good strategy. _____
4 It was dark but the faces slowly went into focus. _____
5 You deserve a pat to the back for those results! _____
6 She was making a determined effort to give up chocolate! _____

/ 5

3 Choose the correct words to complete the sentences.

1 Why did you tell him? The party *was supposed / had* to be a surprise!
2 You're so selfish! You *must / could* have given me a lift.
3 I don't think you *ought to / must* have said that. Wasn't it a secret?
4 He was banned *from coming / to come* into the building.
5 I *could sleep / managed to sleep* eight hours last night.

/ 5

4 Complete the conversation with the phrases from the box. There are two extra phrases.

can't have   didn't need to   forced to   managed to
might have   must have   needn't have   supposed to

Josie Did I ever tell you about the time I was an hour late for an exam?
Lily Seriously? You ¹*can't have* done it on purpose, that's not like you, so what happened?
Josie I'd been working really hard and not going out or seeing anyone, and it really backfired on me because I ²_____ totally miss the fact that the clocks had gone forward an hour for summer time.
Lily Oh goodness. It ³_____ been such a shock when you realised!
Josie It was. Luckily, we were ⁴_____ get there thirty minutes early so I only missed half an hour.
Lily Imagine if you'd decided that you ⁵_____ get there early?!
Josie It ⁶_____ been the biggest mistake of my life!

/ 5

USE OF ENGLISH

5 Complete all three sentences with the same word.

1 _____
a You must eat something and have a rest. It isn't good for you to __ on empty like this.
b Stop trying to __ the show! I'm in charge here.
c I often start a new project with great excitement and then quickly __ out of steam.

2 _____
a This is a feel-good book which provides __ and warmth to readers.
b _____ eating doesn't provide a solution to your problems and may make them worse.
c He chose to do nothing and stay in his __ zone.

3 _____
a Stop messing about and get your __down and study.
b I can't cram any more information into my __.
c __ for the big hill. The park will be on your left.

4 _____
a You might think it's weird to always carry a compass, but it __ in handy when we got lost.
b It was dark, but as my eyes got used to it, the room __ into focus.
c The accident __ about because he hadn't checked the tyres properly.

/ 4

6 Complete the text with the correct words formed from the words in bold.

The Power of Passion

Is it possible to do well at something, even if you don't have a natural ¹*aptitude* (**APT**) for it? Angela Duckworth would definitely say yes. Author of the book *Grit: The Power of Passion and* ²_____, (**PERSEVERE**) she claims that if we believe that anything other than hard work and determination is the answer to success, then we're ³_____ (**GUIDE**).

Nothing is as ⁴_____ (**DESTROY**) to success as believing that because you have raw talent, you don't need to try.

Instead, Duckworth tells us that we need to be willing to commit to a goal, have ⁵_____ (**TENACIOUS**) in the face of setbacks, and be willing to step out of our comfort zone again and again.

The ⁶_____ (**SIMPLE**) of this approach is appealing, but can it really be true that grit is all you need to rise above ⁷_____ (**MEDIOCRE**)? Perhaps not, but it certainly has to be a key ingredient.

/ 6
/ 30

63

6A VOCABULARY AND SPEAKING

Body language, body-related collocations and idioms

1 ★ **Match the two parts of the sentences.**

1 ☐ When Mark argued with the teacher, she **folded her**
2 ☐ My dad always **furrows his**
3 ☐ Harry gets impatient and often **drums his**
4 ☐ My grandfather used to **purse his**
5 ☐ I really like that TV presenter who always **rubs his**
6 ☐ They say people **cross their**
7 ☐ In the photograph, you can see five-year-old Elsa **tilting her**
8 ☐ I remember how our mother used to **steeple her**

a **hands** to try to look serious when she told us off.
b **head** while she's listening closely to the story.
c **ankles** when they're nervous, but I'm not too sure about that.
d **hands together** when he's talking about good news.
e **lips** a lot when he was younger, and now he's got loads of wrinkles.
f **fingers** on the kitchen table. It's infuriating.
g **brow** when he's doing the crossword.
h **arms** and told him that he had no idea what he was talking about.

2 ★ **Complete the sentences with the correct forms of the collocations in bold from Exercise 1.**

1 I know you've been waiting for a long time, but could you please stop *drumming your fingers* on the desk?
2 It's a dead giveaway when you are discussing something with Dad and he feels a bit threatened because he always _____.
3 You don't need to _____ and look so happy because it's my turn to clean the kitchen this week!
4 Check out that cute clip online where the dog keeps _____ to one side when his owner talks to him.
5 At an interview, try to relax and don't _____ as that can show you're a bit worried.
6 My mother doesn't like my sister's friend Damien and she _____ in irritation whenever she's told he's coming round.

3 ★ **Choose the correct words to complete the sentences.**

1 My friend is an amateur actor and she always *checks / clears* her throat just before going on stage. The audience can hear her doing this, and the director always tells her off about it.
2 Something that really irritates me is when people *shrug / wrinkle* their shoulders when they don't know something. Why they can't simply say, 'I don't know!' is beyond me.
3 I've got an interview for the job I was telling you about this afternoon. *Twirl / Cross* your fingers for me!
4 Luke has got to have a lot of dental work done soon because he used to *bite / grind* his teeth during his sleep. He's not very happy.
5 If you had a different hairstyle, you wouldn't keep *rubbing / twirling* your hair in your fingers – you know, it can be very off-putting when you're having a conversation!
6 The bank has given us the *thumbs / fingers* up to start work on the new project. Everyone is very excited.
7 If you watch a young child when he's concentrating hard, you'll often find that he *purses / bites* his lip completely unconsciously.
8 Jacky is a real poser. You often see her *flicking / stroking* her hair back from her face like she's seen film stars do.

06

4 ★★ Complete the conversation with the correct words.

Annie Have you seen the video Tom took of us at Rita's party? I'd forgotten how much fun it was!

Billy Yes. He showed it to me this morning. It was a great evening – but I always come across as looking so grumpy in videos. I mean – I'm sitting at the table with my **¹**_arms_ folded as though someone's having a go at me. And when I lean across to talk to Beth, I actually **²**_____ my hands! I look like our teacher!

Annie Oh – body language is weird. I didn't realise I **³**_____ my shoulders so much, and I always seem to be **⁴**_____ my chin, as if I'm thinking deeply about something. I got a bit bored at one point, but I notice that I've got my head **⁵**_____ as though I'm listening!

Billy I have to admit it was funny watching Rita give her birthday speech! She clears her **⁶**_____ every ten or so words, and she's twirling her **⁷**_____ all the way through. Poor Rita. She hates speeches.

5 ★ Complete the body-related idioms in bold with the words from the box.

back   chin   feet   head   ~~lips~~   nose   shoulder

1 We've arranged a date for the wedding, but I can't tell you anything yet as **my _lips_ are sealed**!

2 It's easy to **get in over your** _____ if you take on extra work without checking out what you've already got planned.

3 I offered Jonas a cheese sandwich and he **turned his _____ up** at it because he'd been expecting something better.

4 Petra overheard me talking about her behind her back and she**'s been giving me the cold** _____ ever since.

5 I know I agreed to give a speech at the party, but I'm not good at public speaking and I've **got cold _____**.

6 Everyone fails at things at some points in their lives – it's just a matter of **keeping your _____ up** and trying again.

7 Why don't you **get off my _____**. I'm doing my best.

6 ★★ Complete the sentences with the correct forms of the idioms from Exercise 5.

1 Dan and I had an argument. He _gave me the cold shoulder_ for days afterwards.

2 You know I can't tell you about that! My _____.

3 I just knew that Kurt wouldn't go for the interview. He's _____.

4 I'm sorry! I followed the recipe exactly. Don't _____ at it!

5 I wish the teacher would _____ – I'll get the project finished by tomorrow.

6 Everything will be fine, I promise. _____.

7 After a week on the new course I realised that I'd _____ – I couldn't understand anything.

7 ★★★ Complete the text with the correct idioms using the words in bold.

TRY REFLECTING

Recently, I read an interesting article about mirroring body language – I can't say where I saw it **¹**_off the top of my head_ (**TOP**) – but it was on some website, while I was doing research for a project. It was a fascinating insight into how we can make good impressions on people, often something we do completely subconsciously. So, if you're the sort of person who tends to **²**_____ (**COLD**) before interviews or when you're trying to make up with someone who's been **³**_____ (**SHOULDER**), apparently, all you need to do is copy the other person's body language! If the interviewer **⁴**_____ (**TILT**) a little, tilt yours. If he **⁵**_____ (**ANKLES**), try doing the same. If he **⁶**_____ (**FLICK**), do likewise. But don't overdo it. Just a subtle gesture (or two) can do the trick. It makes the other person feel at ease with you and builds trust. However, it's a big no-no to copy negative body language – like **⁷**_____ (**FOLD**) when they do, or **⁸**_____ (**SHOULDERS**) in imitation. And definitely don't **⁹**_____ (**DRUM**) on the table or **¹⁰**_____ (**LIPS**)! Also remember that if you mirror somebody too obviously, the other person might notice it and think you're mocking them.

8 ON A HIGH NOTE Write a short paragraph about people's body language that you've observed today and your interpretation of it.

UNIT VOCABULARY PRACTICE > page 73

6B READING AND VOCABULARY

1 Look at the photos and read the article quickly. What do you think the people are doing?

a playing a game

b learning about and teaching body language

c using communication signs

2 Read the article again and choose the correct answers.

1 In Paragraph 1, the writer cites the example of learning a second or third language to

a illustrate how the brain helps in second language learning.

b compare the problems encountered when learning different languages.

c draw attention to the role the brain plays in language acquisition.

d point out the importance of speaking more than one language.

2 What does the writer say about sign language?

a It is not yet widely recognised in society.

b It is an international language.

c It may soon be possible for everyone to learn it.

d It is a skill actors are expected to have.

3 One advantage Makaton has over sign languages is

a it can be understood in more than one country.

b it encourages people to learn to vocalise.

c it has more word resources and concepts.

d it is a better communication tool.

4 In Paragraph 5, the writer expresses

a surprise at the range of people using Makaton.

b concern that Makaton may be used with non-impaired children.

c wonder at some of the ways Makaton is used.

d admiration for the way it links signing and speech.

5 According to the writer, Braille

a was originally designed for a specific deaf person.

b is unlikely to be replaced by other systems.

c is still used in military campaigns.

d was an extension of a previous idea.

6 The purpose of the article is to

a promote the use of artificial language systems.

b give an overview of available artificial language systems.

c explain the different types of brain impairments.

d discuss some people's communication problems.

Vocabulary extension

3 Match the highlighted adjectives and adverbs from the text with the definitions.

1 Extremely, deeply. _profoundly_

2 Difficult to handle, awkward to use. _____

3 When a decoration or design is raised on a surface. _____

4 When a surface is identifiable, pleasant or attractive to touch. _____

5 Weakened, damaged or disabled. _____

6 In a way that is clear and can be understood. _____

ACTIVE VOCABULARY | Prefixes *en-*/*em-*

We can add the prefixes *en-* and *em-* to words in order to form verbs that mean:

• 'to cause to be something' (e.g. *enable, enrich, empower*).

• 'to put into or onto something' (e.g. *enclose, encircle, enslave, embed*).

The prefix *em-* is used with words that begin with the letters *m*, *b*, and *p* and the prefix *en-* with other letters.

4 Complete the sentences with the correct forms of the verbs from the box and the prefix *em-* or *en-*.

able   bitter   body   close   ~~dear~~   force   rich   trust

1 The actor has _endeared_ himself to the nation with the wonderful roles he had played over four decades.

2 English vocabulary has been _____ over the years by the addition of words from French, German and many other languages.

3 I have _____ a hard copy of the receipt you requested.

4 The current basketball team _____ the fighting, competitive spirit of our school.

5 Increased funding would _____ us to add signing to more films and programmes.

6 Years of unemployment and poverty have _____ the old man.

7 It's all very well having the regulations in place, but who is going to _____ them?

8 Many families _____ our vets with the care of their animals.

5 ON A HIGH NOTE Write a short paragraph about your first experience of learning English. Was it enjoyable? What was interesting about it?

A sign of the times

1 We take language for granted. For the vast majority of people, expressing ourselves through speech, and the ability to understand what we read or hear is something that is automatic and unquestioned. When a child is born, we assume that he or she will move through the various stages of language acquisition until they are fully able to communicate with those around them and use their language to access all the sources of education and entertainment that will enrich their lives in so many ways. What we are not all fully aware of is the complexity of the language learning process and how the brain deals with it. Endeavouring to study a second or third language later in life can show us how difficult it can be once the natural brain process involved in first language acquisition has faded. However, the brain continues to enable us to instantaneously decipher and produce our native language without our ever giving it a second thought. What happens then if, for some reason, the brain stops cooperating in this process, when the ability to hear or speak coherently is damaged? Without some artificial form of help, people would be imprisoned in silence and unable to enter the worlds of others, or bring them into their own.

2 When we think of an inability to communicate, perhaps our thoughts immediately turn to the deaf community who use sign language – a developed series of signs and gestures which enable the hearing impaired to interact with others. Each country has its own language, and we are now used to seeing 'signed' performances in theatres or news broadcasts. It is even on the cards that learning sign language could be an option for all children at school, an example of how important inclusivity has become in society today.

3 People who use sign languages such as BSL (British Sign Language), although often profoundly deaf, are by and large not usually limited in other ways. However, there are a significant number of people who have impairments that go beyond the physical loss of hearing. Victims of strokes, for example, may lose the ability to speak – that is either the ability to vocalise sounds, or the ability to produce coherent continuous speech. This is down to disruption of certain neural pathways in the brain. Other examples would be people with learning difficulties and those whose own linguistic development has been delayed for some reason.

4 In order to address the needs of people such as these, the Makaton language programme was invented by three speech therapists in the 1970s, and has been adapted for use in more than forty countries. It focuses on using gestures, signs and symbols in combination with speech to express words and concepts. That way it empowers people to communicate on an international level. The notion of using speech at the same time as signing means that as the user gradually gains (or regains) their ability to speak, the signs ascribed to words and concepts can be dropped naturally. Amazingly, the system has a resource vocabulary of over 7,000 concepts and there are more than 100,000 people, including adults and children, using it today.

5 Interestingly, the fact that Makaton uses speech at the same time as signs has made it attractive and useful for adults to use with healthy babies for whom the ability to understand precedes the ability to speak. They can be taught to use Makaton to express their basic needs and feelings, and in this way relieve the frustration they feel when they cannot say what they need. The sight of a baby who cannot even walk making the sign for 'eat' or 'drink' is quite remarkable and highly useful.

6 We should not forget that communication through the written word is also a vital element in accessing information. For the visually impaired, reading and writing used to be an impossibility. Over the centuries this barrier has been broken down. Braille, a type of alphabetical code which involves a series of embossed dots identifiable by touch, was developed in 1824 by a deaf French teenager, Louis Braille. He turned something already in existence into a fully working form of communication. In Napoleon's time, the military had created a system called 'night writing' which was designed for use by soldiers at night. It was unsuccessful, being very unwieldy, involving combinations of twelve raised dots for each letter. Louis Braille reduced the number to six dots, and a version of his tactile system with sixty-four possible combinations is still used today. Using Braille has radically changed the lives of huge numbers of people since its inception, but technology is causing a decline in use. With screen readers, voice recognition and other amazing advances, the visually impaired are no longer dependent on a touch system.

Summing up, the ingenuity of humans to develop systems and technologies which support or bypass damaged brain function to enable communication is quite awe-inspiring. And the opening up of silent worlds is an absolute life-changer for the people who use them.

6C GRAMMAR

Reporting verbs and verb patterns, impersonal reporting structures

1 ★ Choose the correct words to complete the sentences.

1 He explained to the assistant that *he had / having* bought the computer only two weeks previously.

2 I complimented Paul *that he gave / on giving* such an excellent acceptance speech at the ceremony.

3 The manager offered *to give / giving* Mason a full-time job in the sales department.

4 We wondered whether you *like / might like* to come with us to laughter yoga later this afternoon.

5 I immediately regretted *to send / sending* the email because I hadn't checked it for errors.

6 My college lecturer convinced me *to download / downloading* a copy of the book on body language.

7 Doctors claim *laughter being / that laughter is* extremely good for reducing blood pressure.

8 The article generally discourages people *from constantly suppressing / to constantly suppress* their emotions.

2 ★ Match the two parts of the sentences.

1 ☐ The teacher advised me
2 ☐ The teacher convinced me
3 ☐ The teacher criticised me
4 ☐ The teacher maintained
5 ☐ The teacher predicted
6 ☐ The teacher notified me
7 ☐ The teacher asked me
8 ☐ The teacher suggested

a that I needed to take more breaks between studying.

b to try to smile all through the interview.

c how long I had spent revising.

d rewriting the assignment and addressing all her comments.

e that the Earth was flat! Would you believe that?

f for handing in my essay without checking it thoroughly first.

g that my oral test was going to be held in Room 15.

h that the whole class would pass with flying colours.

3 ★★ Complete the sentences with the correct forms of the words in brackets.

1 My parents blamed *me for starting* (me/start) the argument with my brother, but I didn't.

2 I really regret _____ (not work) harder when I was first studying English.

3 Psychologists urge _____ (everyone/do) breathing exercises to reduce any apprehension we may have before doing a difficult task.

4 Chris maintained _____ (do) the exercises only exacerbated his injury.

5 I wondered _____ (who/be next/give) their presentation in English class.

6 Have you suggested _____ (Katie/try/stop/grind) her teeth?

4 ★★ Rewrite the underlined parts of the conversation in reported speech.

Adam Did Sara tell you what happened when she and Andy went to the theatre last night?

Ben I asked her, [1]'<u>How did the evening go?</u>' but then it was time for class. What happened?

Adam Well, apparently, during the play Sara got the giggles. She started laughing and just couldn't stop. The people in front of them complained, [2]'<u>We can't concentrate on the play. You should leave.</u>'

Ben Oh wow! I've seen Sara get the giggles before and it's very funny. Laughter is so contagious. I remember [3]<u>I got the giggles</u> with her once in class. The teacher criticised us, [4]'<u>You should both be able to control yourselves.</u>' He recommended, [5]'<u>You should try to think of something serious whenever you feel the urge</u> to giggle like that again.' It doesn't work, I'm afraid! So, did they both leave the theatre?

Adam Oh, yes. The people in front threatened, [6]'<u>We'll call the management if you don't leave.</u>' Sara blames Andy for making her laugh. She claims, [7]'<u>He told me a joke</u> about something on the stage.'

Ben Oh, that's a shame. I would ask, [8]'<u>Can I get a refund on the tickets?</u>' It was a comedy they were watching after all, wasn't it?

Adam I'm afraid not. It was the death scene in *Romeo and Juliet*!

Ben Seriously? But that's not so bad. I went to the cinema with Pete the other day and he's got a problem with anyone eating crisps or slurping. Unfortunately, we were surrounded by people with arms full of snacks. Pete warned me, [9]'<u>I'm going to make a scene!</u>' And then he stood up and angrily asked [10]'<u>Any chance you could choose another cinema to eat your crisps in, please?</u>' Well, at least he tried to be nice, didn't he?

1 *how the evening had gone*

2 _____

3 _____

4 _____

5 _____

6 _____

7 _____

8 _____

9 _____

10 _____

5 ★★ Complete the sentences with the correct passive forms of the reporting verbs in brackets.

1 It *is believed that* (believe) laughter can lower high blood pressure.

2 It _____ (show) getting the giggles is more widespread than used to be thought.

3 It _____ (demonstrate) at the exhibition last month that photographs of clowns can lift our spirits.

4 It _____ (assume) smiling all the time could make us feel better, but a report last year found this theory to be false.

5 It _____ (announce) the circus dates are to be put back for several months.

6 It _____ (expect) there will be a high turnout at the lecture.

6 ★★★ Rewrite the sentences using impersonal reporting structures.

1 Scientists suspect that new antibiotics will be discovered relatively soon.

It *is suspected that new antibiotics will be discovered relatively soon*.

2 They have estimated that tuition costs at universities have risen by more than ten percent in the last decade.

It _____.

3 Doctors used to recommend that people eat five portions of fruit and vegetables a day, but now they say getting ten portions is important.

It _____.

4 People now think that supressing emotions is bad for our health.

It _____.

5 They have agreed to introduce laughter therapy sessions at the clinic.

It _____.

7 ★★★ Rewrite the sentences using the passive forms of the reporting verbs. Start with the underlined phrases.

1 It is believed that body language habits are formed during childhood.

Body language habits are believed to be formed during childhood.

2 It is thought that the first modern circus was staged in 1777.

_____

3 It is understood that Shakespeare was living in Stratford when he died in 1616.

_____

4 It was intended that the change in rules was for a temporary period.

_____

5 It is rumoured that the criminal is hiding somewhere in this locality.

_____

6 It was claimed that an English man developed the invention, but it was in fact an American.

_____

8 ★★★ USE OF ENGLISH Complete the email with one word in each gap.

Hi Paul,

If you're still working on that project about comedy, I really advise you **1** *to* read up about World Laughter Day!

2 _____ is said that the first World Laughter Day took place in India in 1998, where 12,000 people are claimed to **3** _____ come together for a day of laughter sessions. We know that laughing is supposed **4** _____ have all sorts of benefits for our health, but this gathering really tops everything! These enormous groups of people **5** _____ believed to spend hours marching, laughing and then marching again. Sounds great fun to me!

My brother Luke suggested **6** _____ to the next gathering, which will be on the first Sunday in May. He's always complaining about **7** _____ getting the giggles, so perhaps if it's an official 'giggle' day, he won't moan and will join in! He asked me **8** _____ you'd like to come too. So, how about it?

Good luck with the project. Miss Dean is rumoured to **9** _____ chasing everyone about our handing in projects late. Jake admitted **10** _____ behind with his, but mine should be ready on time.

Speak soon,

Grace

9 ON A HIGH NOTE Write a short email to a friend about an interesting interview you have seen recently, reporting what was said and by whom.

6D LISTENING AND VOCABULARY

1 🔊 *35* **Look at the photo used to advertise an animal documentary series. What do you think the documentary series might be about? Listen and check.**

   a how humans communicate with animals

   b the hearing abilities of animals

   c the effect of music on animals

2 🔊 *35* **Listen again and choose the correct answers.**

   1 Dave mentions cats to

      a explain how his interest in animal hearing began.

      b compare the abilities of domestic animals.

      c illustrate how a pet knows about an owner's return.

      d exemplify a relationship between hunter and prey.

   2 Dave refers to 'a rumble of thunder' because he wants to

      a describe clearly what an elephant might hear.

      b point out that elephants need to follow rainclouds to access water.

      c explain that elephants do not only depend on their ears for sound information.

      d emphasise the types of sounds elephants produce.

   3 Bats are similar to elephants in that they

      a communicate with one another.

      b travel great distances.

      c get 'hearing' information from different sources.

      d create mind maps of their locations.

   4 What does Dave say about shipping and whales?

      a The main problem for whales is physical damage by the propellers.

      b More research needs to be carried out into the impact of noise pollution.

      c Whales are the animals most severely impacted by water pollution.

      d Ships cause noise pollution that harms whales.

   5 At the end of the interview both speakers agree that

      a considering the hearing of animals in general, ours is relatively limited.

      b some reptiles have worse hearing than humans.

      c the damage caused by noise pollution needs to be rectified.

      d everyone can learn something from the series.

Vocabulary extension

3 **Complete the sentences with the correct prepositions from the box. There are two extra prepositions.**

at   between   ~~by~~   down   in   into   on   to (x2)   up

   1 Cats can hear very high-pitched sounds, but they are surpassed *by* the ability of bats.

   2 People who are colour-blind can sometimes not differentiate _____ the colours red and green.

   3 The lecturer went _____ depth about dogs' amazing abilities to smell.

   4 I would be grateful if you could pass _____ this information to your classmates.

   5 My ability to speak French is quite poor, as opposed _____ my sister who is completely fluent.

   6 I'll keep my ear _____ the ground about any vacancy in the company and will let you know.

   7 This new writing checker app picks _____ punctuation and grammar errors in my work.

   8 I've been asked to assist the science teacher _____ doing some research into the phenomenon.

Pronunciation

4 🔊 *36* **Read some sentences from the interview in Exercise 1. Count syllables in the collocations in bold. Is each syllable pronounced? Listen and check.**

   1 We **fully appreciate** how busy you are.

   2 I **freely admit** that my knowledge about such things is limited.

   3 It's **anecdotally reported** that they can't see.

ACTIVE PRONUNCIATION | Rhythm

In English, we speed up or slow our pronunciation so that it fits into the correct rhythm, e.g. these two collocations, *fully appreciate* and *freely admit*, have different numbers of syllables, but they take the same length of time to say.

The full sentences should take about the same amount of time to say.

I fully appreciate | how busy you are.

I freely admit | I don't understand.

To achieve the right rhythm, we need to use syllable stress correctly. With adverb + adjective/verb collocations there is usually one main syllable stress and one secondary.

---

5 🔊 *37* **Read the sentences. Find the stressed syllables in the collocations in bold. Listen and check. Then practise saying the sentences.**

   1 It is **widely believed** that the weather has an influence on our mood.

   2 It has been **anecdotally reported** that the forest fire was caused by a barbecue.

   3 The report has been **closely examined** for errors.

   4 The committee is **fully aware** of the number of complaints received.

   5 The rumour has been **hotly denied** by all parties involved.

6E SPEAKING

1 🔊 *38* Listen and repeat the phrases. How do you say them in your language?

> **SPEAKING | Evaluating ideas**
>
> It doesn't go far enough.
> That's all very well, but what if it caused other problems?
> It sounds a pretty half-baked theory to me.
> It sounds good in theory.
> I don't think they've thought this through.
> I think this idea has legs.
> There's a lot to be said for the second option.
> This idea has a lot going for it.
> It's a perfectly reasonable idea, but I don't think anyone will accept it.
> I take issue with some of the claims, namely those that diminish the importance of physical activity.

2 🔊 *39* Complete different reactions to the comments with the correct phrases using the words in bold. Listen and check.

> The cars reach ridiculous speeds outside our house and it's getting really dangerous! They're talking about putting up go slow signs.

> Oh, that ¹*doesn't go far enough*. They need to at least install cameras. **GO**

> ² _____, but do you think drivers will take notice? **PEREFCTLY**

> I ³ _____. What happens if they don't slow down? **THOUGHT**

> That's ⁴ _____ drivers don't want to slow down? **ALL**

> I ⁵ _____ about the accidents. It's all anecdotal. There are no actual records. **ISSUE**

> They're saying that if this doesn't work, they'll put in road humps – that will definitely slow down the traffic.

> I ⁶ _____. Drivers won't want to damage their cars. **HAS**

> This ⁷ _____. Could be the answer. **FOR**

> There ⁸ _____ physically restricting speeds like this. I like the idea. **LOT**

> It ⁹ _____, but drivers slowing down and then speeding up between humps will just add to the air pollution, won't it? **IN**

3 Complete the conversation with the words and phrases from the Speaking box.

Karl There have been loads of complaints about excess noise in our road. People are getting very stressed out.

Hannah Where's the noise coming from? Cars? Parties?

Karl Mainly late night parties in gardens. Our houses are very close together. The police just say to ask the people to keep the noise down, politely.

Hannah Well, that doesn't ¹*go far enough* – people like that don't listen. We had the same problem and they apologised and then just carried on! I've heard about an app they're developing that can record and assess the noise levels, so people can provide evidence to the authorities.

Karl It sounds good ² _____, but how are they going to check the authenticity of the recordings?

Hannah Oh, there'll be clever stuff built in.

Karl Yes, I guess. That's ³ _____, but what about the older people who suffer from excess noise? Not all of them have devices with apps on.

Hannah Well, they'll have to deal directly with the police, I imagine. But it will be good for the majority of people. Actually, I think ⁴ _____ legs. Using technology in the fight against noise pollution seems like a good idea to me!

Karl OK, I agree the idea ⁵ _____ it. Certainly better than trying to persuade people who are in a party mood to quieten things down. And there's a lot ⁶ _____ making the reporting completely anonymous to avoid spoiling neighbourly relations!

4 **ON A HIGH NOTE** Write a short conversation between two people discussing whether new plans for online medical consultations are a good idea.

6F WRITING AND VOCABULARY | An article

1 Give your article an interesting title.

2 Engage the reader immediately.

3 Speak directly to the reader.

4 Organise with clear paragraphing.

5 Vary sentence length.

6 Use complex sentences.

7 Use an appropriate style.

8 Use a range of vocabulary, for example a variety of adjectives.

9 Conclude in a memorable way.

SOUL MAN

Barack Obama loves his music, Frank Sinatra called him a genius, and Jamie Foxx won awards for playing him in a film. Who am I talking about? It is the ground-breaking African American singer and pianist, Ray Charles, one of the all-time music greats. Not only did Ray overcome prejudice and poverty to reach the top, but he also had to overcome blindness.

Ray's music will not necessarily appeal today to those whose preference is for fast, rhythmic tracks, but his influence on bands and musicians over the last decades is undeniable. His voice is unmistakable. Low, with a hoarse edge and full of soul, it can send tingles down even the firmest of spines. However, it was not only a remarkable voice that made Charles the legend that he is, it was also the way he integrated different genres of music. He blended rhythm and blues with gospel to become a pioneer of soul music in the 1950s. Later, in the 1960s, he played a part in mixing country music, rhythm and blues and pop. Such versatility and creativity went on to win Charles acclaim and legendary status.

Young Ray certainly did not have the easiest of childhoods. Born to a poor family in 1930, he developed glaucoma at an early age and had lost his sight by the time he was seven. At a school for the blind he was taught to play classical music on the piano through Braille music, which was an extremely difficult feat involving the use of one hand to read the Braille while the other hand played it. He later maintained that doing this gave him a prodigious memory. Ray came to prefer jazz and later set up bands, eventually becoming a successful recording artist. Over his career he won seventeen Grammy Awards.

The musician's life was not smooth, by any means. His personal life had its problems and his career faltered when electronic music and glam rock took the music scene by storm in the seventies and eighties. But he remains an inspiration to all of how perseverance and talent can overcome a multitude of obstacles. Jamie Foxx gives a mind-blowing performance of Charles in the biopic, *Ray*, and the film keeps the memory of a superb musician alive.

1 Read the article. Match sentences a–g below with call out points in the article 1–9 that they are examples of.

a ☐ On a final note – go and hear him sing live. Magic.

b ☐ So, you're sent a free ticket to a gig by someone you've never heard of.

c ☐ His music was absolutely groundbreaking and inspirational at the time.

d ☐ No question about it.

e ☐ His first performance is claimed to have taken place at the tender age of six years old.

f ☐ Talk of the Town!

g ☐ What would you do?

2 Rewrite the underlined parts of the sentences using the adjectives from the box.

confidence-building   jaw-dropping   ~~life-enhancing~~
record-breaking   thought-provoking

1 Such a course could <u>help you to improve your life considerably</u>. *be life-enhancing for you*

2 The cost of funding such a centre is <u>unbelievably expensive</u>. _____

3 The dancer won the award for <u>the eighth time, more than anyone ever</u>. _____

4 What people learn through such activities <u>helps them to believe in themselves</u>. _____

5 The topics covered in the article <u>certainly make you consider things in a new way</u>. _____

3 WRITING TASK Read the task below and write your article.

There is a youth club in your area that provides learning opportunities for young people to make good choices in life. It's a place where they can both learn and spend their free time off the street. The centre wants to bring in professional tutors to teach dance/well-being/mindfulness classes, but money is needed. Write an article describing the centre, its importance for the community and the new project. You want to raise the money through crowdfunding.

ACTIVE WRITING | An article

1 Plan your article.
- Give your article an interesting title.
- Think of an opening that will engage the reader.

2 Write the article.
- Think about how to organise your article in clear paragraphs.
- Use different sentence lengths for emphasis.
- Conclude in a memorable way.

3 Check that ...
- you have used a range of structures including compound adjectives.
- there are no spelling, grammar or punctuation mistakes.

UNIT VOCABULARY PRACTICE > page 73

1 6A VOCABULARY AND SPEAKING Choose the correct words to complete the sentences.

1 I'm auditioning for the school orchestra later this afternoon, so please *twirl* / *cross* your fingers for me.

2 My brother is extremely uncommunicative these days – whenever I ask him a question, he simply *furrows* / *shrugs* his shoulders and carries on with whatever he's doing.

3 When I told my grandmother that I was intending to go to drama school, she *folded* / *pursed* her lips in disapproval, as she thinks I ought to train to be a doctor like my father.

4 It was obvious to the group that Matt was nervous about giving his presentation as he *cleared* / *ground* his throat several times before starting.

5 If you watch people playing chess, you'll probably see them *wrinkling* / *stroking* their chins. It's a dead giveaway that they're thinking hard.

6 One sure way of making yourself look authoritative is to *steeple* / *drum* your hands when you're sitting opposite someone at a desk.

2 6A VOCABULARY AND SPEAKING Complete the conversation with the correct names of the body parts.

Isla Getting cold ¹*feet* about applying for this summer job! I might not have what it takes. What do you think?

Katy Off the top of my ² _____ I can't really say – as I've never worked somewhere like that. Just go to the interview and check out what it involves. If it looks like it's beyond you – don't get in over your ³ _____. Look for something else.

Isla I'm a bit worried that there won't be anything else out there.

Katy Hey – keep your ⁴ _____ up! You'll find something. Just don't be like my sister who turns up her ⁵ _____ at anything that involves cleaning! I've landed something really interesting for the summer, but my ⁶ _____ are sealed at the moment because Alice went for the job too and you know what she's like – when I got those trainers she wanted, she gave me the cold ⁷ _____ for a week.

Isla Congratulations! Perhaps now your mum will get off your ⁸ _____ about playing computer games all day long!

3 6B READING AND VOCABULARY Choose the correct words to complete the sentences.

1 I have a particular *rage* / *loathing* for anything that tastes of lemon.

2 We *endeavoured* / *ascribed* to finish the project in the allotted time.

3 If criminals show *remorse* / *contempt*, they sometimes get a lighter sentence.

4 Strenuous exercise will *inundate* / *exacerbate* the injury if you're not careful.

5 We should try not to *supress* / *wallow* our emotions.

6 It is natural to feel *awe* / *apprehension* before an exam.

4 6D LISTENING AND VOCABULARY Complete the opening of a story with the correct forms of the words from the box.

blare chime clink ~~crash~~ crunch rumble rustle screech

It was early evening and I was sitting on the beach listening to the waves ¹*crashing* on the sand. It was good to be alone after all the crowds of the afternoon at the beauty spot, with all their ² _____ bottles and ³ _____ of sandwich wrappings. I loved the peacefulness. A distant ⁴ _____ of thunder warned of the approaching storm and the church clock ⁵ _____ 6 o'clock, so I decided it was time to go home. I packed up my things, tucked my book under my arm and started to walk back to the car park. Suddenly there was a ⁶ _____ of brakes and a horn ⁷ _____, making me jump, and the water birds lift, screaming, into the sky. Heavy footsteps ⁸ _____ on the stones. 'Mark, you're needed at home – now!' my father's voice shouted urgently …

5 6D LISTENING AND VOCABULARY Complete the sentences with one verb in each gap.

1 We fully *appreciate* the time and effort you have put into writing this report.

2 This new beauty product allegedly _____ a painful skin rash if it is not applied with care.

3 The police have closely _____ the evidence and found no reason to arrest the suspect.

4 It has been hotly _____ by the spokesperson for the authorities that there was any misuse of public funds.

5 I would freely _____ that I have made a lot of mistakes regarding this matter in the past.

6 It has been anecdotally _____ that several of the contestants in the talent show ended up in hospital with food poisoning.

6 6F WRITING AND VOCABULARY Complete the compound adjectives with one letter in each gap.

1 We had to wait a ne*rve*- wracking ten days for the results of our tests.

2 They have made a s__ __ __ __ - chilling film from the novel, which could definitely give people nightmares.

3 A j__ __ - dropping amount of money was invested in the theatrical production and I doubt whether they will make their money back.

4 Following years of dedicated research, the team recently made a g__ __ __ __ __ breaking discovery, which should completely change the way new antibiotics are developed.

5 The council leader made a t__ __ __ __ __ __ - provoking remark on the radio this morning, which people have been commenting on all day.

6 Going to summer camp when you're a child can prove to be a c__ __ __ __ __ __ __ __ __ __ - building experience.

7 ON A HIGH NOTE Write an email to a friend about a recent experience that was extremely funny, including people's reactions.

1 **For each learning objective, write 1–5 to assess your ability.**

1 = I don't feel confident. 5 = I feel confident.

	Learning objective	Course material	How confident I am (1–5)
6A	I can use body-related collocations and idioms.	Student's Book pp. 78–79	
6B	I can understand the purpose of specific sections in an article and talk about emotions.	Student's Book pp. 80–81	
6C	I can use reporting verbs and impersonal reporting structures.	Student's Book pp. 82–83	
6D	I can identify specific details in a conversation and talk about sounds.	Student's Book p. 84	
6E	I can evaluate ideas when talking about stress.	Student's Book p. 85	
6F	I can write an article.	Student's Book pp. 86–87	

2 **Which of the skills above would you like to improve in? How?**

Skill I want to improve in	How I can improve

3 **What can you remember from this unit?**

New words I learned and most want to remember	Expressions and phrases I liked	English I heard or read outside class

GRAMMAR AND VOCABULARY

1 **Choose the correct words to complete the sentences.**

1 Bella ___ denied having eaten the cake.
a fully   **b** freely   **c** hotly

2 I hate it when people ___ their knuckles in class.
a creak   **b** crack   **c** clink

3 She has a deep ___ of films featuring violence.
a awe   **b** loathing   **c** rage

4 He ___ Henri's behaviour to a traumatic past event.
a ascribed   **b** inundated   **c** suppressed

5 The dentist warned me about ___ my teeth at night.
a crunching   **b** biting   **c** grinding

         / 5

2 **Complete the text with the words from the box. There are two extra words.**

anticipation ~~apprehension~~ contempt eye-watering life-enhancing nerve-wracking serenity suppress

So you're facing a challenge …

Should you be full of **1**_apprehension_ about starting a new school or job, you should relax and **2**_____ any negative emotions. Think about the experience with **3**_____ rather than anxiety. Do some breathing exercises and imagine a scene of **4**_____ with noises such as waves crashing on the shore. Persuade yourself that this experience could be **5**_____ as opposed to **6**_____, and you'll approach whatever comes in a positive way.

         / 5

3 **Choose the correct words to complete the sentences.**

1 I regretted not *to get / getting* in touch with him.

2 The yoga teacher urged us *to spend / spending* a set time every evening doing the exercises.

3 My English friend suggested we *visit / to visit* some tourist attractions while we were in London.

4 The students queried the time *were they given / they were given* to complete the exam tasks.

5 The author claims *researching / to have researched* the subject of his article thoroughly.

         / 5

4 **Use the prompts to complete the sentences.**

1 _____ (It / rumour / famous astronaut / give) a talk at college last week, but he didn't.

2 _____ (The first computer / think / design) by Charles Babbage.

3 _____ (Body language / know / reflect) a person's subconscious feelings.

4 Years ago _____ (it / believe / health issues / can / treat) only with certain herbs.

5 _____ (Charlie Chaplin / say / believe / laughter / be) a cure for everything.

         / 5

USE OF ENGLISH

5 **Complete the text with one word in each gap.**

The power of music

Watching highlights from a decade of headliners from the Glastonbury festival yesterday evening, I **1**_freely_ admit to **2**_____ completely stunned by the power music has to take you back in time. With their mind-blowing performance, Mumford and Sons took me back eight years. **3**_____ has been said that they ascribe their success to the crowds of fans who encouraged **4**_____ to return to Glastonbury year after year, and I can easily believe it. **5**_____ the top of my head, I cannot think of another band which has so completely dominated the Pyramid stage with such energy and connection with the cheering crowds as this south London group of talented musicians. They are rumoured to **6**_____ been invited to play at Glastonbury again next year and I, for one, desperately hope to be among those welcoming them back.

         / 5

6 **Complete the second sentence using the word in bold so that it means the same as the first one. Use between three and six words, including the word in bold.**

1 Sally signalled to me that she was happy when she came out of the oral examination room. **THUMBS**
Sally *gave me the thumbs up* when she came out of the oral examination room.

2 They have said that a new health centre will open in this area within the next few months. **ANNOUNCED**
It _____ be a new health centre in this area within the next few months.

3 In Eva's opinion it was not right to reach a decision before consulting everyone involved. **MAINTAINED**
Eva _____ not reach a decision before consulting everyone involved.

4 Lots of people have offered to help with the charity appeal online. **INUNDATED**
We _____ people willing to help with the charity appeal online.

5 The examiner told me that I should have paid more attention to my pronunciation. **CRITICISED**
The examiner _____ attention to my pronunciation.

6 I'm afraid this plan has not been considered carefully enough. **BAKED**
I'm afraid this is _____.

         / 5

         / 30

07 *The creative urge*

7A VOCABULARY AND SPEAKING

Fashion-related adjectives, vague language, fashion-related idioms and phrases

1 ★ Match the words from the box with the definitions. There is one extra word.

metallic navy neon ~~pastel~~ plaid scarlet sparkly

1 It's a pale, soft colour. *pastel*
2 It's the kind of pattern you usually see on a Scottish kilt. _____
3 It's a bright colour that seems to glow. _____
4 It looks like polished metal. _____
5 It's dark blue. _____
6 It's bright red. _____

2 ★ Complete the crossword.

Across

1 Cut short, for example, a pair of trousers cut to the ankle.
5 Brightly coloured and easily noticed.
8 Deliberately bigger than needed.

Down

1 Very thin transparent material.
2 With narrow folds of cloth.
3 Smooth and shiny material.
4 Two colours that look wrong together.
6 Soft leather with a slightly rough surface.
7 Expensive material with a soft thick surface on one side.

```
¹C R O P P E D
```

3 ★ Put the adjectives in order to complete the sentences.

1 She was wearing a pair of (corduroy / soft / flared) *soft, corduroy, flared* trousers.
2 He was wearing a(n) (trendy / suede / Italian) _____ coat.
3 She looked great in a (velvet / funky / navy) _____ skirt.
4 He always wore a (plaid / garish / satin) _____ shirt.
5 The uniform included a (navy / baggy / V-neck) _____ jumper.
6 She decided to wear a (chiffon / pastel / evening / blue / vintage) _____ dress.

4 ★ Complete the conversation with the words and phrases from the box. There is one extra word or phrase.

greenish ~~somewhere in the region of~~ stuff
stuff like that thingies whatsisname

Erin Is that another new pair of earrings? How many have you got now?
Lily Oh, it must be ¹*somewhere in the region of* a hundred pairs.
Erin What's your favourite pair?
Lily I have a gorgeous pair by that designer, er ²_____, you know the man who does amazing things with stainless steel.
Erin Oh, I've no idea. I don't really follow fashion design and ³_____.
Lily I know you're not a fashion victim or anything, but you do have a sense of style. I love those ⁴_____ on your cuffs, very stylish.
Erin The cufflinks? They're my Dad's actually.
Lily They're a great colour, kind of ⁵_____ and metallic.
Erin Thanks very much.

Flappers in the 1920s

James Dean

8 ★★ **Complete the online article with the words from the box.**

baggy clashing cropped flamboyant flared metallic neon pastel region rolled sense so ~~statement~~ tucked

5 ★ **Complete the sentences with one word in each gap.**

1 You don't need lots of clothes, just a well-thought-out capsule *wardrobe* in neutral colours.

2 She's such a fashion _____; she throws clothes away as soon as they're out of fashion.

3 A _____ neck can keep you nice and warm in the winter.

4 Office shoes should be practical rather than a _____ statement.

5 I wear what I like. I don't take any notice of the fashion _____.

6 She's wearing _____ trousers which only come halfway down her calves.

6 ★ **Match the two parts of the sentences.**

1 ☐ Some people think they clash, but

2 ☐ You need a necklace with that dress as

3 ☐ Roll up your jacket sleeves a bit

4 ☐ Why don't you untuck the shirt

5 ☐ Different pastel shades can

6 ☐ Those oversized metallic earrings

a so you can see the shirt cuffs underneath.

b a finishing touch.

c complement each other well.

d I think pink and red go well together.

e are really eye-catching.

f at the back and leave the front tucked in?

7 ★ **Choose the correct words to complete the sentences.**

1 You could *jazz* / *mix* up the outfit with a statement necklace.

2 I don't have much fashion *sense* / *knowledge*.

3 If you have clothes in neutral shades, it's easy to *match and mix* / *mix and match*.

4 I'm not a *slave to fashion* / *fashion slave*, but I am quite interested in it.

5 If you always *pair* / *complement* the same items together, try some new combinations.

6 According to the *fashion* / *fashionable* police, wearing socks with sandals is a crime.

How the young came to be the vanguard of fashion

At least for those who can afford it, making a fashion ¹*statement* is something which is far from new. But it is probably only in the last hundred years or ² _____ that young people have been in the vanguard of fashion, rather than following in their parents' footsteps.

In the 'roaring' 1920s, young women known as 'flappers' scandalised society with their ³ _____ 'bob' hairstyles and relatively short knee-length skirts. Evening wear was ⁴ _____, even outrageous, and a great deal of sparkly, ⁵ _____ fabric was used.

During the 1940s, young people were drawn into the workforce, meaning that by 1944 young Americans had somewhere in the ⁶ _____ of $750 million to spend. Advertising and marketing industries were quick to encourage young people to develop a ⁷ _____ of fashion. The term 'bobby soxer' was used to describe young girls who wore full ⁸ _____ skirts, or ⁹ _____ up jeans with pale ¹⁰ _____ -coloured jumpers and ankle socks.

By the 1950s, the youth market was even more important, partly as a result of the post-war baby boom, when the American teen population grew from 10 million to 15 million. Young film stars such as James Dean became fashion role models. Dean's classic look of a slightly ¹¹ _____ white T-shirt, ¹² _____ in at the waist of a pair of straight jeans remains influential to this day, as do many of the youth styles which followed. For example, the psychedelic and indeed often ¹³ _____ pairings of colours such as pink, purple and orange in the 1960s, the bright lime and shocking pink ¹⁴ _____ shades of the 80s, and the grunge look of the 90s, all of which are often seen in modern day fashion collections. The key role of the young in inspiring fashion movements is clearly here to stay.

9 ON A HIGH NOTE **What is more important to you, fashion or comfort? Say why. Describe your favourite outfit and say why you like it.**

7B GRAMMAR

Relative clauses, prepositional relative phrases, nominal relative clauses

1 ★ Rewrite the sentences to make them correct. Find an unnecessary word, a missing word or a punctuation error.

1 The building, which many considered so ugly is today a UNESCO World Heritage site.

   The building, which many considered so ugly, is today a UNESCO World Heritage site.

2 Is that the evening dress, which you bought in Paris?
   _____

3 I know someone designs flamboyant jewellery.
   _____

4 Alex is a slave to fashion which means she never has any spare cash.
   _____

5 I would love to go back to Madrid, in where we first met.
   _____

6 This is the reason for why I usually buy vintage clothing.
   _____

7 You need to talk to a designer specialises in wedding dresses.
   _____

8 The model, was dressed in a long metallic gown, strode down the catwalk.
   _____

9 The world of fashion, which he hoped to make his career, was very competitive.
   _____

10 1990 to 1992 were the years when, Alexander McQueen was at fashion college.
   _____

2 ★ Find the defining and non-defining relative clauses. Put commas where necessary.

1 The painter who created this piece had a fertile imagination.
2 Picasso who was born in Spain lived much of his life in France.
3 The people who bought this sculpture were happy to pay the high price.
4 The artist spent his childhood in Brazil which had a formative effect on his work.
5 Picasso who was only nineteen at the time hosted his first exhibition in Barcelona.
6 I saw a film called *Loving Vincent* which was about Vincent Van Gogh.
7 The painter who was self-taught was actually better than the other one.
8 The background which had a lush and dreamlike quality was inspired by the Botanical Gardens.
9 Peter who is a painter spends hours in his studio.
10 I'd like to see the new Taika Waititi film which was released on Friday.

3 ★★ Rewrite the sentences using reduced relative clauses where possible.

1 The students who were taught by Richard all became excellent artists.

   The students taught by Richard all became excellent artists.

2 Whose are those paintings which are exhibited in the first gallery?
   _____

3 The man who lives next door is a well-known artist.
   _____

4 A painting that had been lost for decades has just resurfaced.
   _____

5 They wanted £6 million for the painting, which was far too much.
   _____

6 Please let me have all the paintings that you have available.
   _____

4 ★★ Rewrite the sentences to make them more formal. Use the correct preposition and *whom* or *which*.

1 It's difficult having no one to talk to.

   It's difficult having no one with whom I can talk.

2 This is something we have already spoken about.
   _____

3 The music I listen to is usually quite calming.
   _____

4 A gallery is a place where pictures are displayed.
   _____

5 Georges Braque is an artist I know very little about.
   _____

6 After Picasso met Georges Braque in 1906, he developed the Cubist style of art.
   _____

7 Jarry was a person Rousseau could trust.
   _____

5 ★★ Complete the sentences using the prepositional relative phrases from the box. There is one extra phrase.

all three of whom   as a result of which   at which time
by which time   in which case   many of whom

1 Picasso painted his first self-portrait in 1896, *at which time* he was only fifteen.
2 The Cubists, _____ were well-known artists, used geometrical forms in their art.
3 Picasso died in 1973, _____ he had become one of the most famous artists in the world.
4 Goya, El Greco and Velázquez are some other famous Spanish painters, _____ have works in the Prado Museum in Madrid.
5 Velázquez gave King Phillip advice on which artists to buy, _____ the Prado now has an enviable collection.

6 ⭐⭐ Replace the underlined parts of the sentences with *whatever, whichever, wherever* or *whoever*.

1 <u>No matter what</u> they say, you are definitely talented. *Whatever*

2 You are lucky being able to visit the Prado <u>at any time</u> you like. _____

3 <u>No matter what</u> you do, don't give up painting! _____

4 We can go <u>any day which</u> suits you best. _____

5 I would love to meet <u>the person that</u> lives in that house. _____

6 Use <u>any</u> colour you want. _____

7 <u>The person who</u> painted that has real vision. _____

8 <u>Everywhere</u> he went, he took his art supplies with him. _____

7 ⭐⭐ USE OF ENGLISH Choose the correct words a–d to complete the text. Note the use of commas.

	a	b	c	d
1	who	which	whom	, who
2	which	which	many of whom	whom
3	, who	in which	with whom	who
4	which	who	whom	whose
5	where	when	which	of which
6	which	in which	when	who
7	for the	as	in	as a
8	which	whom	who	whose
9	who	which	where	, which
10	who	when	where	whom
11	which	of which	, which	in which

Forgotten Sisterhood

The Pre-Raphaelite Brotherhood was a group of artists formed in 1848 ¹__ were inspired by fifteenth century Italian art. As the name suggests, this group of artists were men, ²__ are well known to this day: Dante Gabriel Rossetti, John Everett Millais, William Holman Hunt. But what of the women ³__ were in their circle – sisters, wives, models, fellow artists whose names have largely been forgotten?

Perhaps the best known is Elizabeth Siddall, wife of Rossetti, artist's model and a painter in her own right, ⁴__ paintings show talent. As a woman, she was unable to study at art school, ⁵__ she could have learned more about technique. She was also a popular model for the Pre-Raphaelite Brotherhood. One of the most famous paintings featuring her as a model is Millais' Ophelia, ⁶__ she is shown floating in water. The story goes that modelling for this painting involved lying in a cold bathtub. Millais encouraged her to stay for long hours in the water, ⁷__ result of which, she became very ill with pneumonia.

Another of the Pre-Raphaelite 'sisterhood', Mary Evelyn De Morgan, was lucky enough to be one of the first women ⁸__ was accepted into the Slade School of Art ⁹__ was opened in 1871. Despite this, she used her middle name, Evelyn, throughout her career, because at that time it was a name which was commonly used by men as well as women, ensuring that her work could be judged on its merit, and not dismissed because she was female.

However, perhaps the most famous of the 'sisterhood', Christina Rossetti, was not a painter, but a poet. Sister to Dante Gabriel Rossetti, Christina was somewhat overlooked at the time ¹⁰__ her brother was far more famous. However, her reputation in modern times has eclipsed his. She has even been referred to as Britain's 'greatest woman poet' ¹¹__ is quite an accolade.

8 ON A HIGH NOTE Write a paragraph describing a painting you love or hate which you have found online. Try to use a variety of relative clauses.

1 Read a poem in which the sea is compared to a dog. Match stanzas 1–3 with adjectives a–c describing how the 'dog' is feeling.

Stanza 1 ☐   **a** sleepy
Stanza 2 ☐   **b** ravenous
Stanza 3 ☐   **c** restless

2 Read the poem again and answer the questions.

1 What does the poet say that the hungry dog is 'eating'? *the stones (which he calls 'bones')*

2 Do you think he is satisfied with his food? Say why.
_____

3 What is the sea doing when the dog 'shakes his wet sides over the cliffs'? _____

4 What nouns that describe parts of a dog's body can you find in the poem? _____

5 What verbs that describe noises a dog makes can you find in the poem? _____

6 What is the sea doing on quiet days? _____

3 What poetic devices are used in these extracts from the poem? Choose *A* for alliteration, *S* for sibilance or *O* for onomatopoeia.

1 the rumbling tumbling stones   A / S / O
2 and howls and hallos long and loud   A / S / O
3 he lies on the sandy shores   A / S / O
4 snuffs and sniffs   A / S / O
5 he scarcely snores   A / S / O
6 with his clashing teeth   A / S / O
7 the giant sea dog moans   A / S / O

Vocabulary extension

4 Write the verbs from the box, which were used in the poem, in the correct column.

bound   clash   gnaw   ~~howl~~   moan   roar   rock   roll
rumble   sniff   tumble

Sounds	Movements
howl	

5 Complete the sentences with the correct forms of the verbs from Exercise 4.

1 He _moaned_ with pain, 'I think I've broken my arm.'
2 She was making a dreadful noise, _____ two saucepan lids together.
3 We could hear the thunder _____ in the distance.
4 Quick as a flash, the fox _____ over the fence.
5 He tripped over and _____ all the way down the hill.
6 We could hear the eerie sound of the wolf _____ down the valley.
7 She _____ at the milk to see if it was out of date.
8 While his teeth were coming through, the baby liked _____ on any hard object he could find.
9 The plane _____ overhead, breaking the peace of the afternoon.

ACTIVE VOCABULARY | Animal sounds

The sounds made by animals are usually onomatopoeic. For example, *purr* for a cat or *growl* for a dog. Of course, these sounds are represented differently in different languages, and even in a single language there may be different words. For example, a dog's bark may be represented as *woof-woof*, *arf-arf*, *ruff-ruff* and *bow-wow*.

6 Match animals 1–10 with sounds a–j.

1 ☐ frog   **a** gobble
2 ☐ owl   **b** honk
3 ☐ turkey   **c** croak
4 ☐ elephant   **d** squeak
5 ☐ sheep   **e** bleat
6 ☐ goose   **f** screech
7 ☐ mouse   **g** neigh
8 ☐ horse   **h** trumpet
9 ☐ bat   **i** bray
10 ☐ donkey   **j** hoot

7 **ON A HIGH NOTE** Imagine you are by the sea, or in the middle of a jungle. Write a paragraph describing what you can see and hear.

The Sea

By James Reeves

1   The sea is a hungry dog,
    Giant and grey.
    He rolls on the beach all day.
    With his clashing teeth and shaggy jaws
    Hour upon hour he gnaws
    The rumbling, tumbling stones,
    And 'Bones, bones, bones, bones!'
    The giant sea-dog moans,
    Licking his greasy paws.

2   And when the night wind roars
    And the moon rocks in the stormy cloud,
    He bounds to his feet and snuffs and sniffs,
    Shaking his wet sides over the cliffs,
    And howls and hollos* long and loud.

3   But on quiet days in May or June,
    When even the grasses on the dune
    Play no more their reedy tune,
    With his head between his paws
    He lies on the sandy shores,
    So quiet, so quiet, he scarcely snores.

'Hollo' is a less common version of 'holler' meaning 'shouting loudly'.

7D LISTENING AND VOCABULARY

1 🔊 **40 Listen to three conversations and complete the sentences with one word in each gap.**

1 In the first conversation, the friends have _____ opinions about the art they saw.

2 In the second conversation, the woman is already positive about folk _____.

3 In the third conversation, the photographers start by talking about how they get their _____.

2 🔊 **40 Listen again and choose the correct answers.**

Conversation 1

1 Sam is trying to
  a suggest how to make the exhibition accessible.
  b challenge Becky's opinions of the paintings.
  c persuade Becky to go back to the exhibition again.

2 In Sam's opinion, what makes the exhibition stand out?
  a The novelty of the approach to portraiture.
  b The ambiguity of the portraits exhibited.
  c The quality of the painting portrayed.

Conversation 2

3 What do the speakers agree about folk art?
  a Artists can't express themselves in many ways.
  b Folk music is a valuable form of folk art.
  c It includes more than physical objects.

4 How does the woman feel about the programme?
  a Confused by the definition of folk art given.
  b Disappointed by the relative lack of explanation.
  c Taken aback by the conclusion.

Conversation 3

5 When talking about her artistic process, the woman
  a tries to justify her lack of consideration for others.
  b points out how easily she finds inspiration.
  c admits that she needs to take more breaks.

6 What does the man say about his earlier work?
  a That it was more focused than now.
  b That he doesn't have the same connection to it now.
  c That the work he does now is superior.

Vocabulary extension

3 🔊 **41 Complete the sentences from the recording in Exercise 1 with the words from the box. Listen and check.**

~~ambiguous~~ commercial intimidating intricate
profound tangible visceral

---

1 It's a bit more _ambiguous_ this way, less obvious.

2 I think it's really _____. It's like a window straight into the soul of the person.

3 It isn't limited to _____ items, such as pottery.

4 All those detailed and _____ patterns …

5 A lot of it is just _____, and factory produced.

6 Sometimes people find that a bit _____, or scary.

7 Your work certainly often has a really _____ impact, it can be like a punch to the gut.

4 **Match the adjectives from Exercise 3 with the definitions.**

1 Based on emotions, rather than reason or thought. _visceral_

2 Complicated or delicate. _____

3 Expressing more than one possible meaning. _____

4 Primarily intended to make money. _____

5 Making you feel nervous. _____

6 Able to be touched. _____

7 Very deep and meaningful. _____

5 **ON A HIGH NOTE Write a paragraph describing a photograph and the impact it has on you. Use the adjectives from Exercise 3.**

Pronunciation

6 🔊 **42 Listen to three pairs of words. What do you notice about the word stress in each pair?**

ambiguity – ambiguous
atmosphere – atmospheric
commerce – commercial

ACTIVE PRONUNCIATION
Word stress with certain suffixes

Adjectives are formed by adding a suffix to the root word. The suffixes *-eous*, *-ious*, *-ulous*, *-uous*, *-orous*, *-ic*, *-ive*, and *-ial* change the stress pattern in the root word and the stress usually comes in the syllable before the suffix.

i̇ndustry – indu̇st**rious**
mi̇racle – mirȧc**ulous**
cȧrnivore – carni̇v**orous**

---

7 🔊 **43 Write the adjective forms of the words, using the suffixes from the Active Pronunciation box. Find the stressed syllable in both words. Listen and check. Then practise saying the pairs of words.**

1 (my)stery _myst(eri)ous_
2 melody _____
3 analysis _____
4 benefit _____
5 confidence _____
6 advantage _____
7 nomad _____
8 aroma _____
9 courage _____

10 influence _____
11 miracle _____
12 instinct _____
13 ridicule _____
14 drama _____
15 president _____
16 glamour _____
17 humour _____
18 sense _____

UNIT VOCABULARY PRACTICE > page 85

7E SPEAKING AND VOCABULARY

1 🔊 44 **Listen and repeat the phrases. How do you say them in your language?**

SPEAKING | Describing a film

SUMMARISING THE PLOT

There's simply no other way to describe this film than to say that it's a work of art.

It's impossible to sum up this story; there's just too much going on.

It tells the superficially mundane story of a girl's coming of age and maturity, but in a completely unique way.

DESCRIBING THE PLOT IN DETAIL

The film kicks off with a realistic picture of family life.

Just as it starts to look as if the film is about everyday life, a fantastical, fairytale element is introduced.

To Chihiro's horror, they turn into a pair of giant animals.

There's a parallel plot involving the person who is rebelling.

Our heroine finds herself having to work in a strange bath house, which caters for bizarre monsters.

GIVING YOUR OPINION

I wasn't sure that I was really a fan of animation.

My expectations were low, and they were met.

It had me captivated from the very start.

It wasn't on a par with his previous film.

It was worth staying until the end.

It's no great surprise that this has become a cult film.

2 **Complete the sentences with the correct prepositions.**

1 _To_ his horror, he discovered that she had actually died 100 years earlier.

2 It's impossible to sum _____ this plot, it's just too complex.

3 The film kicks _____ with a very funny scene set in a restaurant.

4 It was OK, I suppose, but not _____ a par with his best work.

5 Is it worth staying up _____ 2 a.m. to see the new episode?

3 **Replace the underlined parts of the sentences with the correct phrases from the Speaking box.**

1 I can't put the plot into just a couple of sentences, it's too complex. _I can't sum up the plot_

2 Meanwhile, similar things are happening to another couple. _____

3 I didn't think I was an admirer of this genre, but I've changed my mind. _____

4 On the surface the story appears ordinary and everyday. _____ _____

5 I'm not surprised that it's done well at the box office. _____

6 I couldn't stop watching it from the moment the opening credits rolled. _____

4 🔊 45 **Complete the conversation with one or two words in each gap. Listen and check.**

Cameron What are you watching at the moment?

Leah I've recently got into watching an old TV series from the 90s, *Friends*. Have you ever seen it?

Cameron I have definitely heard of it. But what's it about exactly?

Leah Hmm. Well, it's pretty impossible to ¹*sum up* the plot, there's a LOT going on. Basically, it's about six friends in their twenties living in Manhattan who go through just about every life experience imaginable: love, marriage, children, heartbreaks, fights, new jobs and job losses and all sorts of drama. The series ² _____ with Rachel – a runaway bride – who leaves her fiancé at the altar and moves in with Monica, an aspiring young chef. We also get to know the third girl in the gang, Phoebe (I just love her!), who supports herself playing weird but hilarious guitar songs in the underground. There are also three guys – Ross, Chandler and Joey – all rather vivacious and funny characters. I'm not gonna lie: this sitcom had me ³ _____ from the very start. There are ten series and every single one is on a ⁴ ___ with the first one. It's no great ⁵ _____ that *Friends* has become an iconic TV show.

Cameron I'm not that into sitcoms, but I could give it a go one day.

Leah Definitely! Are there any box sets you're watching at the moment?

Cameron Yes, I'm working my way through *Tiger King*. It's a documentary which tells the superficially ⁶ _____ story of a guy running a wildlife park, but in fact it's full of drama and intrigue! You wouldn't believe everything that happens. There's ⁷ _____ no other way to describe it than to say that it's literally incredible.

Leah Ooh, I'll have to check that out next.

5 **ON A HIGH NOTE Write a short paragraph about your favourite TV series.**

7F WRITING | A letter to the editor

> Begin with an appropriate formal greeting.

> Inform the reader what your letter is in response to and briefly summarise your argument.

> Introduce your first point and support it with reasons and examples.

> Introduce your second point and support it with reasons and examples.

> If room, introduce your third point and support this with reasons and examples.

> Sum up with a strong point, and refer back to the original article you are responding to once more.

> Sign off appropriately.

Dear Editor,

I am writing in response to Jane Cleary's article, *Why the public library is obsolete*. While the article makes many valid points about the growth of online resources, it completely overlooks the benefits to society which the public library continues to offer.

The author mentions that the number of adults visiting libraries in person has declined from nearly fifty percent fifteen years ago, to around thirty percent today. While I would not dispute her figures, this still remains a very significant percentage of the population. It is also likely that a large proportion of this thirty percent are those who are most in need of the services that a library can provide.

Another key point which the article completely failed to address is that library services are free to all. There may well be far more access to books online than ever before, but the vast majority of these services are paid for. If free, I understand that they are often illegal file-sharing services. Libraries provide unrestricted and legal access to books for everyone, and this should not be dismissed lightly. After all, not everyone can afford to buy books.

We should also remember that children, who were not referred to in Ms Cleary's article at all, are vitally important library users. Libraries are often where children develop a love of books. They provide free story-telling workshops, recommendations and support for parents. In fact, a library is very often at the centre of a community and, as well as providing books and free Internet access, they also give out information on health and well-being and much more.

In conclusion, I strongly feel that saying that libraries are obsolete is tantamount to saying that society is obsolete. If we want to build literacy, imagination and a sense of community, we won't do better than through our local libraries.

Yours faithfully,

Jackie Price

---

1 Read the letter. Choose the argument that the writer does NOT make.

a Libraries provide a completely free service.

b Libraries help to support the homeless.

c Libraries help to support the local community.

d Libraries are particularly important for under-18s.

2 Replace the underlined parts of the sentences with suitable phrases. Then check your answers against the letter.

1 While the article <u>presents many convincing arguments</u> about the growth of online resources … m<u>akes</u> m<u>any</u> v<u>alid</u> p<u>oints</u>

2 It <u>utterly ignores</u> the benefits to society. c_____ o_____

3 While I would not <u>argue with</u> her figures, … d_____

4 This <u>continues to be</u> a very significant percentage. s_____ r_____

5 That's another key point which the article <u>totally avoided dealing with</u>. c_____ f_____ t_____ a_____

6 The point is that library services are <u>not paid for by any individual</u>. f_____ t_____ a_____

3 WRITING TASK Read the headline and subtitle from an article and write a letter to the editor of the newspaper expressing a contrary view.

> ### WHY BOOKS DESERVE TO BECOME OBSOLETE
> They're uncomfortable to use, take up space in our houses and are an environmental nightmare.

ACTIVE WRITING | A letter to the editor

1 Plan your letter.
- Look at the arguments in the headline and subtitle and think about why these might not be entirely valid.
- Think of any other arguments.

2 Write the letter.
- Write an introduction, referring to the original statement and stating your reason for writing.
- Put one main point in each paragraph.
- Use a relatively formal writing style.
- Finish with a strong conclusion.

3 Check that …
- you have used the correct letter writing conventions.
- there are no spelling, grammar or punctuation mistakes.

UNIT VOCABULARY PRACTICE

1 7A VOCABULARY AND SPEAKING Complete the text with one word in each gap.

THE COLOUR WHEEL

Some people seem to naturally just know which colours go well together, but for those of us who aren't sure whether a colour combination is trendy and [1]f*unky* or just [2]g_____, the colour wheel, which shows which colours work well together, can be a helpful tool.

Firstly, wearing monochromatic colours (the same colour in slightly different shades) can often look good. For example, pairing [3]p_____ blue with [4]n_____ blue.

Alternatively, you could choose to wear colours which [5]c_____ each other – those opposite each other on the wheel, for example, pink and green, or blue and yellow. You need to get the shade right, but this can look very [6]e_____-c_____. Similarly, colours next to each other on the wheel, known as analogous colours, also look good [7]p_____ together. Good examples would be pink and red, or blue and green, or pink and purple, though traditionally we have been told to avoid these [8]c_____ combinations. You can always tone down the look by wearing it with white or denim.

2 7C READING AND VOCABULARY Complete the sentences with the words from the box.

dappled   docile   downy   ~~gilded~~   luminous
opalescent   silken   tender

1 The *gilded* dome of the cathedral shone brightly.
2 The dog looks fierce, but he's actually very _____.
3 The moon was _____ that night and it was easy to see where we were walking.
4 The pony was _____ with white spots.
5 She gently stroked the baby's _____ head.
6 The _____ scales of the fish shone in the water.
7 She had long shiny, _____ hair.
8 He gave her a loving _____ smile.

3 7C READING AND VOCABULARY Complete the second sentence using the word in bold so that it means the same as the first one. Use between three and six words, including the word in bold.

1 We got up really early to catch the train. **LARK**
  We *were up with the lark* to catch the train.
2 I haven't stopped working all day. **BEE**
  I've been _____ all day.
3 His ideas are basically always the same. **PONY**
  He's a _____.
4 He always tries to avoid doing the washing up. **WEASEL**
  He always tries _____ the washing up.
5 The staff in this shop can't wait to start selling you stuff you don't need. **RATS**
  The staff in this shop are like _____ trying to sell you stuff you don't need.

4 7D LISTENING AND VOCABULARY Choose the correct words to complete the conversation.

Jack Have you been watching that reality TV show where they're all in separate flats in the same block and never actually meet except online?

Cara Isn't that a bit [1]*trashy / flamboyant*? I mean, it's not exactly intellectual, is it?

Jack No, definitely not. The living in separate flats thing is certainly [2]*grisly / gimmicky*. But I think they're trying to make a point about social media, and how you can't really know someone until you've met them in real life.

Cara That's true. I know someone who comes across as such a lovely person on social media, but in real life they're nearly always [3]*impenetrable / mediocre*, wearing a mask that makes it hard to fathom what they are thinking or feeling. But I still think it's a bit weird and [4]*creepy / vivacious* encouraging people to pretend they're someone else online in order to win a reality TV show.

Jack Oh, come on. It's only a bit of fun, it's all [5]*tongue-in-cheek / overrated*. It's just entertaining watching them playing stupid games and monkeying around.

5 7E SPEAKING AND VOCABULARY Match film genres 1–8 with short descriptions a–h.

1 ☐ biopic
2 ☐ disaster movie
3 ☐ epic fantasy
4 ☐ period drama
5 ☐ post-apocalyptic
6 ☐ psychological horror
7 ☐ rom com
8 ☐ gangster movie

a In this film, four wives who have never previously been involved in their husbands' businesses are pulled into a dark underworld when their husbands are sent to prison.
b This film is famous for the sweeping battle scenes between the ice monsters and the fire dragons.
c Jeanette had resigned herself to being single when her dog caused her to literally bump into Joe.
d This film is about the life of one of the most important figures in the South African anti-Apartheid movement.
e Ten strangers find themselves stranded in an isolated motel. But what is the secret which threatens each and every one of them?
f The film looks at the life of the servants downstairs, and the rich family upstairs, and finds that they may have more in common than they think.
g Trapped in a burning skyscraper, who will survive?
h Jim Blake wakes up after an operation to discover that while he was asleep, the world has changed beyond recognition.

6 ON A HIGH NOTE Describe the most outrageous thing you have ever worn.

1 **For each learning objective, write 1–5 to assess your ability.**

1 = I don't feel confident. 5 = I feel confident.

	Learning objective	Course material	How confident I am (1–5)
7A	I can use vague language and fashion-related words to talk about fashion.	Student's Book pp. 94–95	
7B	I can use relative clauses to add emphasis.	Student's Book pp. 96–97	
7C	I can understand metaphors in a text and talk about emotions.	Student's Book pp. 98–99	
7D	I can identify specific details in a conversation and talk about art.	Student's Book p. 100	
7E	I can describe the plot of a film and give my opinion when talking about films.	Student's Book p. 101	
7F	I can write a letter to the editor.	Student's Book pp. 102–103	

2 **Which of the skills above would you like to improve in? How?**

Skill I want to improve in	How I can improve

3 **What can you remember from this unit?**

New words I learned and most want to remember	Expressions and phrases I liked	English I heard or read outside class

GRAMMAR AND VOCABULARY

1 Choose the correct words to complete the sentences.

1 She was wearing a *navy / garish* neon orange dress.
2 It was pure *serendipity / kerfuffle* that I came across the plate in an antiques shop.
3 I'm afraid I must *make / take* issue with that point.
4 When Dan saw his mum talking to the head teacher, he took off like a *weasel / rat* up a drainpipe!
5 The voices became louder, then faded *away / off*.

/ 5

2 Complete the sentences with the phrases from the box. There is one extra phrase.

fertile imagination   finishing touches   jaw-dropping
one-trick pony   ~~tongue-in-cheek~~   well-rounded
with a twist

1 I wouldn't take what he said too seriously, it was probably *tongue-in-cheek*.
2 The _____ scale of this project is daunting.
3 I just need a few hours to put the _____ to my painting and then it will be ready to exhibit.
4 Try it with a little bit of cinnamon, it's delicious. It's apple juice, but _____.
5 Maths and Science are important, but we also need creative subjects for a _____ education.
6 This actor is a _____ – he plays the same character in every single movie.

/ 5

3 Complete the sentences with the correct relative pronoun and a preposition where needed. If no relative pronoun is needed, write –.

1 The avant-garde art movement, *which* began in the 1850s, started a cultural revolution.
2 Modern Art begins with Van Gogh, Cezanne, and Gauguin, all _____ were key to its development.
3 Cubism, futurism and surrealism were all movements _____ the artist pushed the boundaries of art.
4 The Impressionists argued that people do not see objects, but only the light _____ they reflect.
5 Modern Art was introduced to the USA through artists _____ moved there during World War I.
6 Pop artists such as Andy Warhol or David Hockney, _____ often incorporated commonplace objects into their works, were active in the late 50s and the 60s.

/ 5

4 Choose the INCORRECT word in each sentence.

1 That's the café *which / where / in which* the artists used to meet.
2 The work *– / that / what* they produced was awesome.
3 He gave an exhibition, *the success of which / whose success / that success* was inevitable.
4 She was the person *on whom the artist relied / whom the artist relied / who the artist relied on* for support.
5 Rousseau and Picasso, *both / both of whom / who both* lived in Paris, became quite close.

/ 5

USE OF ENGLISH

5 Complete the sentences with the correct words formed from the words in bold.

1 I have no idea what that film was about, it was completely *impenetrable*. **PENETRATE**
2 I find _____ horror films utterly terrifying. **PSYCHOLOGY**
3 The costumes in the film were stunning - really _____. **CATCH**
4 She had a beautiful _____ voice. **MELODY**
5 It might be _____ to get there early and be at the front of the queue. **ADVANTAGE**
6 Mary was an exceptional actor and had a lively and _____ personality. **VIVACITY**

/ 5

6 Complete the text with one word in each gap.

Olivia Colman

THE CROWN REVIEW

The Crown chronicles the reign of Queen Elizabeth II from her wedding in 1947 through all the major events of the twentieth century, and eventually, into the twenty-first century. It is said to be one of the most expensive TV shows ever made, with a budget of over $130 million, the [1]*lion's* share of which must have been spent on some of the most gorgeous and opulent sets I have ever seen.

The stellar cast includes Claire Foy, Olivia Colman and Imelda Staunton, all of [2]_____ play Elizabeth at different stages of her life, and their performances are on a [3]_____ - equally impressive.

I believe this is a box set [4]_____ has appeal for anyone who has an interest in twentieth century events, and even to those who do not usually like [5]_____ dramas.

Despite a largely sympathetic portrayal of the royal family, this is certainly not a show which caters solely for royalists. On the [6]_____, it explores the role of the royal family in some depth.

/ 5

/ 30

8A VOCABULARY AND SPEAKING

Permission and prohibition, phrasal verbs

1 ★ Choose the correct words to complete the mini-conversations.

Billy Did you know that Otto has been [1]*barred / proscribed* from the café because he had a row with a mate and broke some crockery?

Jane I can understand that – just because his father owns the café doesn't [2]*endorse / entitle* him to behave so badly!

Lia We've been [3]*authorised / condoned* to study in the library until ten o'clock the night before the exam. That's great, isn't it?

Penny Absolutely. Last year, the authorities wouldn't [4]*proscribe / endorse* proposals to allow students to stay on the school premises so late.

Norm They're really [5]*putting / clamping* down on absenteeism this term.

Marcus I know – the teachers won't [6]*sanction / outlaw* more than a couple of hours off for a doctor's appointment.

Cala I certainly don't [7]*entitle / condone* what the police say Turner has done, but surely they can't hold him for such a long time without charge?

Mina The law [8]*proscribes / sanctions* keeping someone in custody for longer than 48 hours. They'll have to let him go.

Lucas The college is trying to [9]*put / authorise* an end to students using information from unreliable websites in their assignments.

Tina Yes, I've got a list of the websites they've [10]*clamped / outlawed*.

2 ★ Match the two parts of the sentences.

1 ☐ The authorities need to clamp
2 ☐ Some countries are said to proscribe
3 ☐ The police are not authorised
4 ☐ In many countries women were not entitled
5 ☐ The company has just put an
6 ☐ In my opinion, the council should never condone

a keeping prisoners in solitary confinement for lengthy periods without due cause.
b misbehaviour in public places.
c to break up peaceful protests where there is no violence.
d end to excessive overtime for some of its workers.
e down on people using barbecues in the forest.
f to vote in general elections until relatively recently.

3 ★ Complete the headlines with the words from the box.

bars   clamp   condone   endorse   ~~outlaw~~   sanctions

> LOCAL AUTHORITIES TO [1]*outlaw* LARGE SPORTING EVENTS IN PUBLIC PARKS FROM NEXT WEEK

> GOVERNMENT TO [2]_____ DOWN ON TAX EVADERS IN NEXT FINANCIAL YEAR

> COMPANY [3]_____ EX-EMPLOYEE FROM PREMISES FOR THREATENING BEHAVIOUR

> THE COMPANY WILL UNDOUBTEDLY [4]_____ THE RECOMMENDATIONS PUT FORWARD BY THE COMMITTEE

> COUNCIL [5]_____ GROUPS OF VOLUNTEERS TO CLEAR LITTER FROM BEACHES

> LOCAL COUNCIL DOES NOT [6]_____ RUDENESS TO PARK KEEPERS

4 ★★ Complete the text with one verb in each gap.

GLADIATORS

Gladiatorial combats in ancient Rome were violent and barbaric events, [1]a*uthorised* and encouraged by the Emperor, who personally [2]e_____ the death of a beaten man by his opponent. Important families at the time were [3]e_____ to train their own gladiators, and in spite of calls to ban the practice by those who did not [4]c_____ it, the events continued, drawing bloodthirsty spectators who filled the Colosseum time after time.

The life of such a gladiator, Spartacus, was made into an epic film in 1960. He led a rebellion which wanted to [5]o_____ the practice. An end was finally [6]p_____ to the fights years later due to the impact of Christianity.

5 ★★ **Choose the correct words to complete the sentences.**

1 Marty ___ out with something interesting in class today – tell you later!

   a held   **b** set   **c** came

2 The council have decided to hold ___ on redeveloping the old library building.

   a out   **b** off   **c** over

3 Such inflammatory comments can set different sections of the community ___ each other.

   a against   **b** into   **c** between

4 I imagine the police will come down ___ on drivers who break the new speed limits in town.

   a tightly   **b** hard   **c** fast

5 It can be detrimental to people's mental health to ___ grudges against others for long periods.

   a hold   **b** set   **c** take

6 I don't think I'll be able to ___ in the good news about my university application for a while!

   a come   **b** take   **c** hold

7 Our teacher has taken ___ setting us vocabulary tests every Monday, and I'm not sure it's a habit I like!

   a on   **b** out   **c** to

8 The government has to ___ about changing some of these old laws soon.

   a come   **b** set   **c** take

6 ★★★ **Complete the sentences with the correct forms of the phrasal verbs from the box.**

come down hard   come out with   hold anyone back
hold it against   hold off on   set about
set families against   set forth   take in   ~~take to~~

1 My friends and I have _taken to_ running for an hour every day after school. It's good fun.

2 The college _____ on anyone they find has copied essays from a website.

3 We've been advised to _____ starting the new club until funding has been agreed.

4 No one will _____ you if you decide not to donate monthly.

5 Social status should not _____ from achieving their dreams.

6 We need to _____ reorganising the schedules for next term's tournaments.

7 It's hard to _____ the news about the number of redundancies announced by the factory.

8 The civil war _____ each other.

9 The author _____ her controversial views about the world in her latest book.

10 Mark has an unconventional attitude to life, but he often _____ some good ideas.

7 ★★★ **USE OF ENGLISH Complete the conversation with one word in each gap.**

Adam I was reading an article about parental discipline over this last century. It was quite hard to **1**_take_ in how strict parents used to be.

Felix You're right. My grandfather sometimes **2**_____ out with some unbelievable things about his childhood.

Adam Really? Like what?

Felix Well, he said his parents weren't that strict, but when he was about ten his dad remarried, and Grandad's new stepmother **3**_____ an end to all that! She immediately **4**_____ about changing all the rules and came **5**_____ hard on him if he broke any of them.

Adam Your poor grandad. Well, my grandmother was **6**_____ from going to the cinema unless it was with her parents or brother until she was sixteen! So, she **7**_____ to persuading her brother (with chocolate!) to say he was taking her, but then letting her go with her friends.

Felix A whole different world then.

Adam And the article says that many girls had stricter rules than boys. This actually used to **8**_____ siblings against each other in those days and many girls held a **9**_____ against their parents for years because of the unfairness.

Felix But in those days, girls were **10**_____ back from doing a lot of things. Luckily, we live in different times. We have a lot more freedom. My parents weren't that strict with us. Unless we **11**_____ to exploiting the freedom – then they'd **12**_____ down for a few weeks.

Adam Yes, I think that's the case for most families!

8 ON A HIGH NOTE **Write a paragraph about something you rebelled against when you were younger. How do you perceive your behaviour now? Explain why.**

8B LISTENING AND VOCABULARY

1 🔊 **46 Listen to a lecture about the history of fitness training. Tick the activities that are mentioned.**

a ☐ balancing   e ☐ sprinting   i ☐ shooting

b ☐ crawling   f ☐ boxing   j ☐ stretching

c ☐ swimming   g ☐ wrestling   k ☐ dancing

d ☐ throwing   h ☐ gymnastics

2 🔊 **46 Listen again and complete the sentences with no more than three words in each gap.**

1 The lecturer uses the word _widespread_ to describe the availability of fitness centres today.

2 The lecturer says that one natural skill was compromised because farmers started using _____.

3 According to the lecturer, the sports in the first organised competitions had their origins in _____.

4 The nickname of one of the pioneers of modern-day sports gymnasiums was the _____.

5 For Jahn the most important reason for becoming fit was _____.

6 The centres in Paris and Brussels differed from previous centres in that they were _____.

7 The speaker points out that these commercial centres aimed at helping people obtain an _____.

8 Future gyms will need to address the problem of encouraging people with _____.

Vocabulary extension

3 Complete the collocations in bold from the recording in Exercise 1 with the correct forms of the verbs from the box.

address   conform   engage   hone   lay   ~~strive~~

1 For those who _strive_ **for a perfect body** shape, going to the gym is a necessity.

2 Parents can _____ **the foundations** for a child's future attitude to exercise by introducing them to cycling and other routine exercise.

3 Some athletes _____ **their bodies** to the perfect shape for their particular sport.

4 Schools need to _____ **the physical requirements** of their students as well as their mental ones.

5 In the past, _____ **in combat** meant that soldiers had to train in many different ways.

6 Students are sometimes excluded if they do not _____ **to the standards** of behaviour.

Pronunciation

4 🔊 **47 Read some sentences from the lecture in Exercise 1. Find the stressed words in the underlined phrasal and prepositional verbs. Listen and check.**

1 People are often unwilling to <u>stand out from</u> the crowd as looking different.

2 This desire to <u>conform to</u> popular standards concerning appearance includes attitudes to keeping fit.

3 But have we always been so <u>concerned about</u> our levels of fitness?

4 The need for a whole range of physical skills <u>went up</u> dramatically …

5 Early man was naturally fit. He didn't need to <u>work out</u>!

6 They often <u>took up</u> training for competitions.

ACTIVE PRONUNCIATION
Stress in phrasal and prepositional verbs

In two-part phrasal verbs:

• we usually give the main stress to the particle and secondary stress to the verb.
How many staff do we need to **take on**?

• the particle is usually not stressed if there is a pronoun between the verb and the particle.
We didn't **take** _him_ **on**.

• the particle is usually not stressed if It is followed by a noun.
We didn't **take on** _Jasper Barnes. He was inexperienced._

• we can give equal stress to the verb and particle if we want to give special emphasis to the verb.
We must **take on** _some more staff._

• the particle may receive less stress when there is an important noun between the verb and particle.
Did you **take** _Sue Peters_ **on**? _She gave a great interview._

In prepositional verbs, the stress is always on the verb.
You must **focus on** _your strengths._

In multi-word phrasal verbs, the main stress is on the first particle and secondary stress is on the verb.
Let's **hold off on** _the decision._

5 🔊 **48 Find the main and secondary stress in the underlined phrasal and prepositional verbs. Listen and check. Then practise saying the sentences.**

1 The seminar should be really interesting. I'm <u>looking forward to</u> it.

2 The college <u>doesn't approve of</u> students who wear expensive jewellery to class.

3 People used to <u>laugh at</u> the eccentric man, but he had one of the best brains in the country.

4 I'll be driving my car past your house later. <u>Look out for</u> me!

5 Controversial new policies can <u>set</u> people <u>against</u> each other.

6 Please don't <u>involve</u> me <u>in</u> your argument.

7 Which celebrities do you really <u>look up to</u>?

8 I have to <u>cut back on</u> chocolate. I eat way too much.

9 I didn't <u>look up</u> the word. Sorry!

UNIT VOCABULARY PRACTICE > page 97

8C SPEAKING

1
49 Listen and repeat the phrases. How do you say them in your language?

SPEAKING | Hyperbole and understatement

HYPERBOLE

- **Using extreme numbers/amounts**
  I've spent **about a million years** wearing school uniform.
  This jacket weighs **a ton**!
  I've been there **tons of times**!
  It cost my parents **a small fortune**.

- **Using extreme adjectives**
  gigantic (rather than *big*)
  ancient (rather than *old*)
  ravenous (rather than *hungry*)
  soaked (rather than *wet*)
  incinerated (rather than *burnt*)

- **Using superlatives**
  the tiniest diamond you've ever seen

- **Using the word *literally* (when something isn't true)**
  It's **literally** the most ridiculous thing I've ever heard!

UNDERSTATEMENT

- **Using 'softeners'**
  a bit/slightly/kind of/rather complicated

- **Using phrases with *not/no***
  not exactly/terribly/entirely
  not the most reliable/ **not the** strong**est**
  no big deal

2
Rewrite the sentences using hyperbole or understatement.

1 This suitcase is extremely heavy.
   This suitcase weighs a ton.

2 A new bicycle is going to be very expensive.
   _____

3 I got 95% in the exam.
   _____

4 I left the chicken in the oven far too long and it was black when it came out.
   _____

5 I have never handed in an assignment late before.
   _____

6 We got very wet walking to college this morning.
   _____

7 Changing my phone contract is not going to be a problem.
   _____

3
50 Complete the conversation with the words from the box. Listen and check.

big entirely exactly fortune ~~literally~~ million
most (x2)

Angelo Have you seen the new train timetable that has just been posted on the website?

Sofia Sorry. I've ¹*literally* just set foot in the door and I haven't been online yet.

Angelo It's the ²_____ ridiculous thing ever. There's no 8.30 train running anymore.

Sofia What! But there's been an 8.30 train for a ³_____ years!

Angelo That's what they're saying. They want us all to use the 8.45.

Sofia But a season ticket for the 8.45 costs a small ⁴_____ ! They can't do that!

Angelo I know how you feel. The 8.30 wasn't ⁵_____ cheap either.

Sofia Well, this certainly isn't the ⁶_____ logical change they've come up with. I imagine the 8.45 will be packed with work commuters too.

Angelo I'm not ⁷_____ sure whether I'll go for the 8.45 or the 8.00 and just hang around.

Sofia Some people will say it's no ⁸_____ deal, but I think there should be more trains rather than less!

4
Complete the mini-conversations with one word or a phrase in each gap

Ashley Is that an old computer?
Yang Old? ¹*It's ancient*!

Azize You must be hungry after that long session at the gym.
Ryu You're right. ²_____!

Clive You look exhausted. Would you like to lie down?
Lenny Exhausted? I suppose I am ³_____.

Laura Are you looking forward to the competition at the weekend?
Eric I'm ⁴_____ it, but it will be good to see how fit I am.

Zac Hey, do you understand question 4 in our homework?
Marie I've ⁵_____ just opened my notebook. Give me a moment to read it through.

Max Do you think we'll win the sprint relay this afternoon?
Leo Not in a ⁶_____! Our team is NOT very fast at all.

5
ON A HIGH NOTE Write a paragraph about how a change in some aspect of your life (a rule, a law, a routine) has affected you.

8D READING AND VOCABULARY

1 Read the two texts quickly and answer the questions.

1 What did the sailor appreciate about travelling and living on a boat for a year?

2 What spoilt the child's attitude to school and home?

2 Read both texts again and choose the correct answers.

Text 1

1 Look at gaps 1–4. Where does the following sentence fit best?

'Deeper than I can imagine, this never-ending sea, no one in sight, or radio range.'

a gap 1   **b** gap 2   **c** gap 3   **d** gap 4

2 The writer uses the word 'crumb' in Paragraph 1 to

a contrast the size of her boat with others.

b indicate how the colour of her boat stands out from the sea.

c emphasise her feeling of insignificance.

d show how she felt when she lost her way.

3 The writer was attracted to the notion of solo sailing because

a she had previously lived near the Devon coast.

b it provided a special way of seeing and meeting people.

c it was a family tradition to be on the water.

d she no longer enjoyed her work.

4 Why was the writer amused by a comment by someone in Portugal?

a She heard the same comment over and over again.

b It showed her reputation had preceded her.

c It implied she'd had a lot of problems.

d The information was wrong.

Text 2

5 The writer makes a correction in Paragraph 1 regarding

a visitors' opinions of Evan's house.

b Evan's relationships with others.

c Evan's interests outside the house.

d Evan's family and background.

6 What do we learn about Evan's parents?

a They want to help their son.

b They lead good social lives.

c They regret their son not having sports or music interests.

d They are concerned about appearances.

7 When Evan was attending school, he

a was a target for bullying.

b did not mix a great deal.

c was intent on studying hard.

d concentrated on business studies.

8 Which is NOT mentioned as being taken for granted by Evan?

a The upkeep of his parents' property.

b Lack of intrusion on his personal space.

c His future role in life.

d His good looks.

Vocabulary extension

3 Complete the sentences with the highlighted adjectives from the texts.

1 The new medicines could save many patients from _untold_ distress over the coming years.

2 An _____ squirrel came right up to our kitchen window yesterday to check out what was happening.

3 Our hotel room's _____ view of the ocean made it worth paying extra for.

4 He gave a _____ nod when I joined the meeting, but he barely acknowledged me otherwise.

5 The house had the _____ number of rooms to accommodate a family with three children, but its location did not meet their expectations.

6 People cannot afford to be _____ about having a job as you never know what's round the corner.

ACTIVE VOCABULARY | Idioms with *take*

The verb *take* is used in many idioms.

take someone/something for granted

take issue with something

Sometimes the phrase has both a literal and an idiomatic meaning, (e.g. ***take*** hold of).

I ***took*** hold of the railing as I went up the steps. (literal)

an idea that ***took*** hold the previous summer (idiomatic)

---

4 Match the underlined words and phrases in sentences 1–8 with their meanings a–h.

1 ☐ We need to take stock of the current situation and then think about making plans.

2 ☐ Blake took umbrage at what I said and gave me the cold shoulder for days.

3 ☐ Working ten-hour days can take its toll on you after a few weeks.

4 ☐ Don't take the moral high ground here – I did nothing wrong.

5 ☐ What's your take on what's just happened?

6 ☐ Take whatever he says with a pinch of salt – you know you can't trust him.

7 ☐ I think we just need to take five and then come back to this refreshed.

8 ☐ My sister never takes anything at face value – she always thinks there's a catch of some description.

a was offended, showed resentment at

b don't necessarily believe

c accepts something without question

d understanding

e think you're a better person in a situation

f have a bad effect on

g stand back, look and evaluate

h have a short break

5 ON A HIGH NOTE Write a short paragraph about a time when you did something on your own that you were proud of. Write why you did it and how you felt.

UNIT VOCABULARY PRACTICE > page 97

Setting sail
one woman's year alone at sea

1 It is black in the Bay of Biscay, just stars above, and below, the canyons. We're but a crumb out here, floating beyond the continental shelf where it drops from 300 m to near 5,000 m. **1__** And silent, but for the waves rushing against my little boat, *Isean*. Stars shoot overhead, but they'll have to try harder for my attention. I'm staring down, where dolphins are magically lit by phosphorescence. One wonderful creature spins beside me, a trail of stars in its wake. I'm in a trance, my arm trailing the water. The sails luff, I've gone off course and look skywards for the Plough – I'm using stars, rather than a compass for my bearings. Later, I will somehow fall asleep while dolphins breach by my window.

2 I can hardly believe I'm here, headed for Spain on my own boat. I wasn't even expecting to cross the Channel. **2__** I'd quit my job to sail around Britain, an idea that took hold the previous summer, sailing in Devon and Cornwall. It wasn't just the beauty of the coastline, the gentle pace – collecting mussels, swimming with seals – it was the unique perspective. Sailing alone into harbours seeking shelter, I was invited in, not local nor tourist, but part of an ancient seafaring tradition. I found myself at home chatting with Brixham trawlermen, watching old people in Fowey swing-dancing to *Erasure*.

3 I'd wanted an escape from London and my exit was clearly marked – to sea. It had sounded sensible but intimidating. I had a basic qualification – a day skipper's licence – but didn't consider myself experienced. Still, I'd learn along the way, and find crew for longer passages.

3__ If I made Brittany, I'd be happy with that as a winter adventure. A thousand miles later, I blew into Portugal. A year on, I'm in Italy, and still haven't come home.

4 I'd worried about being lonely in France. I needn't have. Brittany is the epicentre of sailing and everyone was interested in my journey. 'You are taking on the *nose of Brittany*!?! By *yourself*? In this *little boat*?' This reaction became common, so rare are solo female sailors. I laughed when someone in Portugal introduced themselves, 'I heard about you in Spain'. I've had so much respect along the way (and size does matter – I love when sailors emerge from enormous yachts, all thumbs-up in recognition of the challenge of sailing a small boat – *Isean* is under 8 m). And I've had untold support – there's this international community of self-sufficient problem-solvers on the water, almost always ready to help, because everyone knows what it's like to be in trouble at sea.

5 **4__** And for every challenge, there are many more unforgettable moments. Sailing towards Africa's mighty Jebel Musa – the Pillars of Hercules, marking the continents of Africa and Europe. There was the morning I was joined by a pod of pilot whales, and swordfish, a silver vision of pure muscle surging out of the sea. And watching the red moon rise from a quiet bay, or sleeping alfresco under a meteor shower. My back garden is perfectly clear water – pipefish and turtles my nosy neighbours. My fiery orange sunsets are unobstructed, my starry skies unpolluted by light. Every single day, I feel lucky to call this wild, unbiddable, impossibly beautiful sea my home.

UPSIDE DOWN

1 He'd led a privileged life. At least that's what everyone was telling him now. Inherited money had meant growing up in a spacious country mansion, the envy of all his school friends, or perhaps more truthfully, his school acquaintances. A garden the size of a town park isolated the family from inquisitive neighbours and protected them from noise and road pollution. Not that Evan had ever really exploited the potential of the grounds, content to look out on the wildlife and the changing colours of the leaves but not venture into the undergrowth looking for hidden streams or making dens. He wasn't an adventurous child. And muddiness was discouraged in his household.

2 Proving to have no interest in sports or learning an instrument – notably unathletic with no notion of rhythm or melody, he was left in peace with his technology and beloved games. He had token classmates for overnight stays but none he really wanted to talk to, and none that particularly wanted to talk to him. It wasn't his choice, but his parents' who

insisted, as it seemed to be the thing to do, showing that they were doing their parental bit to encourage their son to socialise. As far as Evan was concerned, he suffered enough uninspiring social contact at school. There he endeavoured to stay in his own little bubble, considered a loner, minding his own business and doing whatever was necessary to meet school regulations and gain the requisite grades that would grease his passage through the education system and out the other end. It was taken for granted that he would take over his family's estate in due course.

3 He had always taken for granted so many things: the abundance of space inside and outside his home, never knowing or caring who kept those lawns and flower beds looking so beautiful or who tidied and cleaned his rooms; having all he'd ever wanted without needing to ask, and peace and quiet, untroubled by demands on his company by any member of his family.

Privileged. Spoilt. Complacent.

That is until suddenly he wasn't.

Articles

1 ★ Complete the sentences with *the* or *ø* (no article).

1 ☐ We're travelling to *the* USA next week for a three-week holiday.

2 ☐ _____ beauty of his painting is unquestionable.

3 ☐ _____ bee is an amazing insect as aerodynamically it shouldn't be able to fly.

4 ☐ This animal is one of _____ most solitary mammals that is known to exist.

5 ☐ It's _____ constant need to follow trends that I can't understand.

6 ☐ All lawyers and judges should aim to deliver _____ justice.

7 ☐ We're going to be studying pack animal behaviour at _____ college next week.

8 ☐ Learning to play _____ violin can be hard on both the player and the ears of the person listening.

2 ★ Complete the rules with *the* or *ø* (no article). Then match eight of them with sentences 1–8 in Exercise 1.

a when there is only one, it is unique: *the*

b when referring to a place, e.g. school for its purpose: _____

c with seas and rivers: _____

d when referring to a whole group or species: _____

e when a relative clause makes something 'known': _____

f generally with an abstract noun: _____

g when something has been mentioned before: _____

h when the context makes it clear what we're referring to: _____

i with abstract nouns and places to be specific: _____

j when a superlative makes it unique: _____

k with plural names for countries and mountain ranges: _____

l with newspapers, inventions and musical instruments: _____

3 ★ Choose the correct options to complete the sentences.

1 Did you have *the* / *ø* fun at the exhibition you went to yesterday?

2 *A* / *The* new President has promised to make *the* / *ø* changes to help *the* / *ø* unemployed.

3 *The* / *ø* cat is far more independent than *the* / *ø* dog and will spend much of its time outside.

4 We watched *a* / *the* documentary in *the* / *ø* class last week about *the* / *ø* foxes and how they are becoming urbanised *the* / *ø* animals.

5 I joined *a* / *the* new group on social media today which shares *the* / *ø* photos from windows in *the* / *ø* different countries.

6 That's *a* / *the* presenter I was telling you about who narrated *a* / *the* TV series about *the* / *ø* Everest.

7 I'd prefer *a* / *the* larger of the two wolf pictures to accompany the article for the website.

8 Which of *the* / *ø* politicians in the photograph is *ø* / *the* president?

9 I would love to visit *ø* / *the* Philippines – I've been told they're *the* / *ø* beautiful islands.

10 My dad has never been outside *ø* / *the* Europe for work or pleasure, which I think is *a* / *the* great shame.

4 ★★ Complete the conversation with *a/an*, *the* or *ø* (no article).

Chloe I see there have been a couple of new additions to your class. It's unusual to see **1** *ø* new students joining halfway through the term, isn't it?

Maddie You're right. But these guys' family moved from **2** _____ Birmingham because of their dad's job and so they had to change **3** _____ schools. They're really nice. They're twins and you'd think they'd have the same personalities, but they don't at all. **4** _____ boy, Alex, is a bit of **5** _____ loner while his sister, Alice, is **6** _____ real social butterfly!

Chloe Is he like that through choice, do you think? Or maybe he just finds it hard to make friends? **7** _____ disruption, like living in a new place, can be difficult to deal with.

Maddie I'm not sure. I think they've both dealt with **8** _____ disruption caused by moving pretty well. No, I think he just likes being on his own a lot.

Chloe And Alice has **9** _____ very strong character. You can see **10** _____ leadership in everything she does! **11** _____ presentation she gave in class yesterday was excellent and she was full of **12** _____ confidence that comes from **13** _____ experience. She must be used to **14** _____ public speaking or acting.

Maddie Then she'll be up for doing **15** _____ school play at the end of term. I guess I'll meet her at **16** _____ auditions being held in May!

5 ★★ Replace the underlined parts of the sentences with the correct phrases using *the*.

1 We live next door to <u>a family called Barker</u>. *the Barkers*

2 <u>Poor people</u> are always the first to suffer when the economy has problems. _____

3 <u>Owls are nocturnal birds</u> although young owls can be seen during the day. _____

4 Both men fought bravely, but <u>Phil showed exceptional courage</u>. _____

5 <u>Oak trees</u> can live for hundreds of years.

_____

6 ★★ Find and correct the mistakes in each sentence.

1 (The crows are) such an intelligent bird. This morning I saw (the) adult crow chase away a cat that was lurking close to (the) obviously newborn chick. *The crow is, an, an*

2 The human beings need to belong to the social groups, as is evident from a range of terms we have to describe groups, such as congregations, audiences and so on.

_____

3 A loyalty shown by members of this group is particularly encouraging. _____

4 Brian Turner is leading voice in a campaign I mentioned previously to provide more signed performances for deaf in the theatrical productions nationwide.

_____

5 Krays were the infamous pair of brothers who terrorised parts of the London in mid-1900s.

_____

6 We are studying the animal behaviour in the class at the moment. _____

7 ★★ Complete the sentences with one word in each gap.

1 In the last test, I turned over two pages instead of one and I did the *same* thing yesterday!

2 Our teacher is the _____ of person who would spend more time with each student if he could.

3 If you feel the _____ to get a second opinion, please feel free to do so.

4 My grandfather used to love being the life and _____ of any party or family gathering.

5 I would definitely say I was a sociable person, just not in the _____ the article describes.

6 On the _____ of current evidence, I do not feel we can draw any real conclusions.

8 ★★★ Complete the text with *a/an*, *the* or *ø* (no article).

To be or not to be ...
a pack member?

Whether animals live in packs or herds, or lead solitary existences has a variety of reasons, at ¹ *the* heart of which is ² _____ survival. However, when forming groups, animals have to balance ³ _____ costs of sharing against ⁴ _____ benefits. With a group there is usually more competition for mating, and at times for ⁵ _____ food, but on the plus side protection is offered against predators; ⁶ _____ likelihood of a fish in a shoal being eaten is far less than if it were alone. ⁷ _____ group animals can develop co-operative defence strategies such as ⁸ _____ musk ox in ⁹ _____ Arctic, which form circles against ¹⁰ _____ wolves, or ¹¹ _____ ground squirrels in California that call to alert others to danger. Groups of animals also appear larger than they really are to predators, which can result in ¹² _____ hesitation that allows the prey just enough time to escape. Of course, groups of predators are more efficient hunters; ¹³ _____ lions and hyenas are two such examples although the cost of sharing the kill has to be considered. On balance, it seems that chasing down prey in ¹⁴ _____ pack has better results than the lone wolf or lion!

9 ON A HIGH NOTE Write a short paragraph about a situation you've been in with a large crowd of people, and say whether it was a good or bad experience. Explain why.

DOES INDIVIDUALISM BRING HAPPINESS?

Use objective language.

Use more formal vocabulary choices.

Use complex sentences rather than compound ones.

Use full forms and not contractions or abbreviations.

What is meant by the word 'individualism'? In truth, individualism is not a simple notion and can be interpreted in many ways. However, it is generally accepted that individualism refers to the idea of placing a focus on a person's individuality, in other words, on their independence and self-reliance. In today's world it has become normal for individuals to have independence in most areas of their lives, not relying on others for assistance. People tend to live their lives in their own way, making their own decisions and having only themselves to blame should those decisions prove to be wrong. The question is – does this make them happy?

The number of people who wish to become independent and self-reliant adults has increased over time. We have moved from a society where traditions and values encouraged interdependence of families, and the true individualists were often those with artistic leanings. These poets, artists and writers were often labelled as rebellious and eccentric, their lifestyles being very different from the socially accepted norm. However, there were sometimes downsides to the lives of these people. The freedom they sought could also bring loneliness and depression.

In modern society, we can see both types of lifestyle side by side. Older generations still maintain traditional values whereas the young are becoming ever more independent in their relationships with their parents, partners and even colleagues. Marriage has become less common and divorce has risen as individuals within a marital relationship seek to express their freedoms. The rise of gender equality has meant that women are no longer dependent on their male partner for income and can expect equality in their home lives too.

In deciding whether individualism can bring happiness, we need to consider each person, their character, their background and their expectations. Many of us are happy to make our way unfettered through life, enjoying the freedoms that this brings, while others yearn for support and an opportunity to share their lives and decisions more closely with others. Much depends on a person's upbringing and the role models they have had in childhood. We cannot generalise; one person's freedom may prove to be another's loneliness; one person's love of commitment may prove to be another's prison.

1 Read the essay. Match the highlighted words and phrases from the essay with their synonyms.

1 to tell the truth *in truth*

2 depending on each other _____

3 in a marriage _____

4 characteristics _____

5 help _____

6 want something a lot _____

7 unrestricted _____

2 Choose the complex sentence in each pair.

1 **a** Whereas on the one hand we might like the idea of being free, on the other we need the support of people close to us.
   b On the one hand we might like the idea of being free, but on the other we often need the support of someone close to us.

2 **a** He was a popular artist and enjoyed his solitude, and because of this he was often considered eccentric.
   b Being a popular artist who enjoyed his solitude, he was often considered eccentric.

3 **a** Were people to live very isolated lives, they might become less caring individuals.
   b People could live very isolated lives and therefore become less caring individuals.

3 WRITING TASK Read the task below and write your opinion essay.

In some schools, students are involved in decisions about new rules that govern school life. Write an essay in which you present your opinions on this topic, referring to:
- the importance in having a say in what affects us.
- the need to have enough information.
- the value of objectivity.

ACTIVE WRITING | An opinion essay

1 **Plan your essay.**
- Make notes which address the points referred to in the task.

2 **Write the essay.**
- Begin with an effective introduction where you indicate what you will be considering.
- Remain objective throughout.
- Use a range of formal vocabulary items.
- Use complex sentences.
- Give a concise conclusion where you summarise points and give your opinion.

3 **Check that ...**
- you haven't used contractions, abbreviations or colloquialisms.
- there are no spelling, grammar or punctuation mistakes.

UNIT VOCABULARY PRACTICE

1 8A VOCABULARY AND SPEAKING **Complete the sentences with one word in each gap.**

1 Have you been a*uthorised* to park in this parking bay?

2 After the incident at the house, the police b_____ anyone from entering, apart from their own officers.

3 This card e_____ you to a free coffee every morning for two weeks at our café.

4 The college will not c_____ antisocial behaviour of any kind on the premises, and all incidents will be dealt with thoroughly.

5 The practice of using asbestos and other dangerous materials in construction work was o_____ a very long time ago.

6 The proposal to erect a statue honouring the college's first principal was e_____ by the governors.

7 The council is endeavouring to c_____ down on people who dump litter and waste in local beauty spots.

8 The government has s_____ reducing fees for hospital parking across the country.

2 8A VOCABULARY AND SPEAKING **Complete the sentences with the correct forms of the verbs** *come, set, hold* **or** *take.*

1 Centuries ago, the authorities used to *come* down hard on anyone caught stealing even the smallest food item.

2 I _____ forth my ideas regarding after school catch-up classes at the staff meeting yesterday.

3 The reactions of the authorities to the protest march were so extreme that I couldn't _____ it in.

4 My brother _____ to wearing jeans to work and I have a feeling he'll be told off about it soon.

5 The political rally was going well and was well controlled, but I couldn't _____ my brother back from shouting at the MP right at the end.

6 The college has _____ about canvassing students on their reactions to the new timetable.

3 8B LISTENING AND VOCABULARY **Complete the blog with the adjectives from the box.**

arched chubby dimpled full glossy pearly rosy silky tight willowy

Recently looking through an old photograph album of my grandmother's, I was struck by how turning each page showed subtle changes in her appearance and clothes. She had movie-star looks in her teens with **1**arched eyebrows, **2**_____ lips and **3**_____ , curly hair. If the photos hadn't been taken in black and white, I am sure her cheeks would have been **4**_____ and her teeth **5**_____ and sparkling! Her figure was a little **6**_____ and she had a **7**_____ chin, but moving over the page into her twenties she had clearly lost weight and was **8**_____ and athletic-looking! It was interesting to see too, how fashions changed. From full **9**_____ skirts to shorter **10**_____ ones. It is so good to have a pictorial record of her life in a book like this. With online galleries these days, it's not quite the same, really.

4 8B LISTENING AND VOCABULARY **Choose the correct words to complete the sentences.**

1 After a good five-kilometre run, my skin always looks *sparkling / glowing.*

2 When people aren't well, their hair often appears *lank / sleek* and lifeless.

3 My grandfather was never very *full / muscular* or athletic. I wouldn't say he looked *chubby / weedy*, but he definitely had a pretty *soft / lean* figure.

4 My Spanish friend is very attractive with *arched / luminous* eyes, *olive / chubby* skin and *sparkling / sleek* dark hair.

5 8D READING AND VOCABULARY **Choose the correct words to complete the sentences.**

1 If you're having a celebration, invite Luke – he always proves to be the life and ___ of the party.
   a soul   **b** heart   **c** animal

2 On first impression, I thought Kelly was a bit ___, but later she relaxed and turned out to be very friendly and helpful.
   a self-sufficient   **b** introspective   **c** standoffish

3 I'm certainly not a party ___ and much prefer a low-key affair to a big raucous occasion.
   a butterfly   **b** animal   **c** player

4 Some people are quite happy to be alone and enjoy their own ___ , rather than socialising all the time.
   a team   **b** company   **c** selves

5 I'm not sure I would describe Carrie as being ___ , but she is often rather quiet and thoughtful.
   a gregarious   **b** social   **c** introspective

6 For some people, appearing to be ___ and individualistic is really just a façade and underneath they want to be helped.
   a reserved   **b** self-sufficient   **c** gregarious

6 ON A HIGH NOTE **Write a short paragraph about someone you know who enjoys being different from others. Describe the person and his/her attitude, with examples.**

1 For each learning objective, write 1–5 to assess your ability.

1 = I don't feel confident. 5 = I feel confident.

	Learning objective	Course material	How confident I am (1–5)
8A	I can use words and phrasal verbs to talk about permission and prohibition.	Student's Book pp. 108–109	
8B	I can identify specific details in a radio programme and talk about beauty.	Student's Book p. 110	
8C	I can use hyperboles and understatements when talking about rules.	Student's Book p. 111	
8D	I can compare different styles of texts.	Student's Book pp. 112–113	
8E	I can use articles to express different meanings.	Student's Book pp. 114–115	
8F	I can write an opinion essay.	Student's Book pp. 116–117	

2 Which of the skills above would you like to improve in? How?

Skill I want to improve in	How I can improve

3 What can you remember from this unit?

New words I learned and most want to remember	Expressions and phrases I liked	English I heard or read outside class

GRAMMAR AND VOCABULARY

1 Complete the sentences with one word in each gap.

1 Toddlers and young children sometimes _come_ out with the most outrageous and funny things!
2 It's not good for a person's mental health to _____ grudges for a long time.
3 I used to want to be out with my friends all the time, but now I _____ my own company and read a lot.
4 I think the school should _____ off on making uniforms compulsory for the time being.
5 The new speeding restrictions should _____ an end to cars accelerating along this stretch of road.
6 Can't you see that by spreading these rumours she is trying to _____ us against each other?

/ 5

2 Choose the correct words to complete the conversation.

Tedra How would you describe her eyes?
Eric I would say they were [1]*sparkling / pearly / silky*.
Tedra And her physique?
Eric Unquestionably [2]*dimpled / lank / lean*.
Tedra What about her behaviour toward others?
Eric Definitely [3]*introspective / antisocial / self-sufficient*.
Tedra And her manner?
Eric She always seemed [4]*rosy / sanctioned / standoffish*.
Tedra Was she a [5]*gregarious / social / glowing* butterfly?
Eric No, I'd say she was a loner.

/ 5

3 Complete the sentences with the correct words formed from the words in the box.

arch athlete gloss glow muscle ~~weed~~

1 My cousin used to be a really _weedy_-looking boy, but he's much more muscular now.
2 Tonya's _____ eyebrows must be plucked.
3 The nurse looks quite thin, but he's very _____ and can lift even heavy patients easily.
4 Many shampoos claim to produce sleek, _____ hair, but few really do.
5 She used to have a(n) _____ physique when she was competing, but not now.
6 People keep on paying me compliments on my _____ complexion.

/ 5

4 Complete the sentences with a/an, the or ø (no article).

1 Rebels like Robin Hood have been immortalised in _ø_ folklore.
2 The boater is a type of hat worn as part of a uniform at many private schools in _____ UK.
3 He hates _____ conformity of any sort.
4 The pack mentality of _____ species such as wolves enables them to survive harsh conditions.
5 The detective went to _____ prison last week to interview _____ inmate.

/ 5

USE OF ENGLISH

5 Choose the correct words or phrases a–d to complete the text.

REBELS AND SOCIETY

Is it possible to be a true rebel who despises conformity? When we look back through the centuries, we see clearly that there have constantly been groups of people who have not wanted to conform to societal norms, for whatever reasons. Some because they believe that society is [1]___ doing what they really want. Others because they want to be different. In general, society does not [2]___ the behaviour of those who live on its fringes. However, what is interesting is that groups who believe they are leaving conformity, like [3]___, are in fact becoming conformist in another way. They are following their own trend. Being [4]___ is not individualistic, but a common characteristic among many such groups and [5]___ becomes just one of many who dislike company in general. In other words, aren't rebels just changing one conformity for another?

1 **a** setting them against **b** holding them back from **c** taking them in **d** coming down hard
2 **a** entitle **b** authorise **c** condone **d** outlaw
3 **a** the hippy **b** a hippy **c** hippy **d** hippies
4 **a** standoffish **b** social **c** sanctioned **d** introspective
5 **a** a party animal **b** a loner **c** a team player **d** a herd animal

/ 5

6 Complete the second sentence using the word in bold so that it means the same as the first one. Use between three and six words, including the word in bold.

1 Understanding the implications of the new regulations was not easy. **TAKE**
It was difficult _to take in what_ the new regulations meant.
2 A baby hummingbird took its first flight and I watched it through the window. **HAD**
Through the window I watched _____ taken its first flight.
3 Jacquie and I are both writing letters in protest against the cuts. **SAME**
I'm writing a letter in protest against the cuts, and _____ thing.
4 There's a need for the government to take action against people using mobile phones while driving. **DOWN**
The government should _____ mobile phones while driving.
5 You can usually find Liam at the centre of any social gathering. **LIFE**
Liam _____ of any social gathering.
6 I strongly believe there is no excuse for animal abuse. **CONDONED**
I strongly believe _____.

/ 5

/ 30

9A **VOCABULARY AND SPEAKING**

Adjectives and expressions related to disbelief and surprise, word families

1 ★ Complete the sentences with the words from the box.

aback beats blew bowled defied else ~~goes~~
pull scratching taken

1 The way he's flexing his body just *goes* against all the rules.

2 It _____ me how anyone can come up with such creative ideas.

3 We were _____ over by the brilliance of the group's performance.

4 I was slightly taken _____ when the conjuror asked me to come up on stage to be part of his act.

5 Don't be _____ in by all the hype surrounding the show – it's nowhere near as good as the producers claim.

6 When the artist painted the canvas in ten minutes flat – well, that was something _____!

7 The talent of the young theatrical group just _____ me away.

8 They showed the winner of the strongest man competition and he was pulling a bus! It just _____ belief.

9 Trying to understand how to assemble the flat pack cupboard really got me _____ my head.

10 The organisers want to involve every single person in the village in the summer show. It's going to be amazing if they manage to _____ it off.

2 ★ Complete the adjectives in the conversation with one letter in each gap.

Leo As you recommended, I watched the second in the *Big Talent* series yesterday, and you were right. Some of the entries were amazing, especially the magic act with the young couple. The trick with the cards was [1]mes*m e r i s i n g* – I couldn't take my eyes off how quickly his fingers were moving! It was [2]baff__ __ __ __ for the judges too.

Sara I know – and how he managed to transfer the photograph into a woman's bag was completely [3]mys__ __ __ __ __ __ __. Mind you, I also really admired the acrobat – his whole act was [4]riv__ __ __ __ __ – I couldn't look away, and when he balanced on the seat of tiny chair on the top of the pile of ten chairs with just one hand – well, it was a [5]hea__ __ - __ __ __ __ __ __ __ __ moment.

Leo The dance act was good too. It's [6]min__ - __ __ __ __ __ __ __ __ how high they manage to jump, and the speed they turn at. I thought the background video of the skier plunging down the mountainside was quite [7]bre__ __ __ __ __ __ __ __ __.

Sara I'm glad you enjoyed it. I thought it was your sort of thing. What I also love is the end of each show where the acts are waiting for the judges' decision. There's always that long pause! It can be quite an [8]ele__ __ __ __ __ __ __ __ moment as all the acts are hanging on the next words, knowing they could change someone's life!

3 ★★ Find and correct one mistake in each sentence.

1 Well, it just goes ⟨by⟩ all the rules – you leave revising until the last moment and get a distinction. *against*

2 How my mobile phone ended up in the science lab cupboard is quite breathtaking. _____

3 It was touch-and-go on the stage just now, but I think we managed to take it off. _____

4 My mother manages to do a full-time job, an evening job and look after three kids – she is really something different! _____

5 This tiny spider produces an enormous web in minutes – it just defies reality. _____

6 Don't sit rubbing your head over the question. I'll check for an answer online. _____

4 ★★ Complete the pairs of sentences with the words in bold.

1 UNREAL / UNREALISTIC
a It felt really *unreal* to be watching my childhood hero on stage at last.
b It's _____ to think that a trainee magician could perform such illusions so soon.

2 UNIMAGINABLE / UNIMAGINATIVE
a The examiner was disappointed that so many of the submissions were _____.
b The number of people involved in creating the special effects was _____.

3 ILLUSORY / DISILLUSIONED
a The performer was _____ by the reception to his show and cancelled the tour.
b The effect of fire was _____, created by clever lighting.

4 DECEPTION / DECEIT
a The article uncovered the celebrity's _____ about the charities he claimed to have contributed to.
b The conjuror's _____ was so clever that no one realised how he performed the trick.

5 EXPLANATORY / INEXPLICABLE
a There were some _____ notes on the tricks at the back of the book.
b For me it is _____ how the trick took in so many people!

5 ★★ Match sentences 1–6 with sentences a–f to make logical continuations.

1 ☐ We're hoping the new theatre facilities will be ready for the end of term play.
2 ☐ People believe that the authorities will invest more money into the project.
3 ☐ You won't need my help in setting up the new stage lighting system.
4 ☐ Many people have offered to contribute money to the project.
5 ☐ There are rumours that the theatre company avoided paying any tax last year.
6 ☐ I was blown away by Martine's performance in the production last night.

a If fraud is proven, there could be severe repercussions.
b Unfortunately, I think their hopes are illusory. It will never happen.
c But it's unrealistic to expect more than fifty percent of them to come through with a donation.
d I also thought that the guy who played the fool was extremely convincing.
e However, in reality, I've a feeling it's going to be more like six months.
f Explanatory notes came with it, so it won't be at all difficult.

6 ★★★ USE OF ENGLISH Complete the conversation with the correct words formed from the words in bold.

Tia I've just read an article about how they managed to de-age the actors in *The Irishman* – that brilliant film with Robert De Niro and Al Pacino.

Petra I saw that – ¹*incredible* (**CREDIBLE**) film. And I wondered about the ageing thing. I think it was most people's ²_____ (**ASSUME**) that they used make-up and clever computer stuff. But even in the hands of a great artist, a character wearing a lot of make-up can appear ³_____ (**REAL**). The audience are buying into a ⁴_____ (**DECEIVE**) – they know what they see isn't actually true, but they want to believe in the illusion.

Tia Exactly, and you're sort of right. To get the same actor looking the right age over five decades, naturally, it requires some very ⁵_____ (**IMAGINE**) cinematic approaches. Martin Scorsese wanted his actors to move about as naturally as possible, so this technical wizard, Pablo Helman, VFX supervisor, spent an ⁶_____ (**IMAGINE**) amount of time developing a method using a special type of camera.

Petra Well, it certainly works! I don't really want to know how – audiences like me love the ⁷_____ (**EXPLAIN**). It's movie magic and we don't want to be ⁸_____ (**ILLUSION**)!

7 ★★★ Complete the blog review with one word in each gap.

FAVE FILM BLOG

So, best film I've seen this week? OK, not a hard choice, this one – in fact, no other contenders whatsoever! It ¹b*eats* me how I missed it first time round. I'm talking about *The Prestige* with the superb Hugh Jackman and Christian Bale, who always play their roles so ²c_____. Made in 2008, it appears not to have aged at all. The film revolves around a deep rivalry between two illusionists and evolves into a story of pure revenge. Centre stage in this film are the tricks themselves. They are ³b_____ to audiences in the film who are ⁴t_____ in by the audacious tricks again and again. And they are ⁵r_____ to us – the audiences at home, as we see how the tricks are daringly ⁶p_____ off. But the tour de force toward the end of the film is the development of a completely ⁷i_____ trick in which a man is seemingly transported from one place to another within a second. It is an ⁸e_____ moment in the film, and that is a very apt adjective because electricity is at the heart of the illusion. Is this true magic? We all know that appearances are ⁹d_____. In this case they truly are, but the real ¹⁰d_____, when it is finally revealed, ¹¹d_____ belief.

8 ON A HIGH NOTE Write a short review for the school website about a film, a TV series or a play that you have seen recently with unbelievable special effects or illusions.

9B GRAMMAR

Uses of *will*, *will* vs *would*

1 ★ **Choose the correct words to complete the sentences.**

1 Finally! Tickets are available for the new production at the Globe Theatre. Pass me my phone and I 'll *book / be booking* a couple now for the opening night.

2 Katya will *be calling / have called* me later on to check on our progress, so I can ask her about your query then.

3 My dad will *be / have been* forty next weekend, so we'll *have / be having* a big party.

4 You can discuss everything with Danny when you see him this evening. He'll *be telling / have been told* about the decision at the afternoon meeting, and he'll *have had / have been having* time to calm down!

5 In a month's time I know I'll *sit / be sitting* here too scared to open the email with my results in!

6 If enough tickets are sold, we *'ll make / make* a significant profit after expenses.

7 I'll *be / being* very careful when I'm editing the film you've just finished, so don't worry – I do have some experience, remember.

8 A break at 5.30 will *be / be being* very welcome. I'll have *worked / been working* on the script all afternoon.

2 ★ **Match questions a–g with sentences 1–8 from Exercise 1. There is one extra sentence.**

Which sentence includes …

a ☐ a promise?

b ☐ a fact?

c ☐ the completion of an activity?

d ☐ an expectation?

e ☐ an immediate decision?

f ☐ the result of a condition?

g ☐ an imagined future event?

3 ★ **Match sentences 1–6 with uses of *will* a–f.**

1 ☐ I've been expecting Ralph for half an hour. That will be his car now. He'll be checking his phone before coming in.

2 ☐ There's no point calling Helen to change your takeaway order – they'll have picked it up already.

3 ☐ Most days he'll get to the studio at about 6.30 ready for a two-hour make-up session.

4 ☐ He will leave his bicycle on the drive. I've tripped over it time after time.

5 ☐ She will take on difficult rescue dogs.

6 ☐ The website won't load. Who can I get to help?

a a way of describing regular typical behaviour

b as an alternative to *refuse* in the present form

c an insistence on doing something that is viewed negatively

d a certainty about something in the present involving a form of deduction

e irritating typical behaviour

f a certainty about something in the recent past involving a form of deduction

4 ★★ **Complete the conversation with the correct forms of the words in brackets and *will*. Use the full form when necessary.**

Alex Hey, do actors have little rituals they need to go through before a performance?

Caleb You'll have heard about some famous sports stars, like Nadal, who ¹*will always put* (always/put) his water bottles in the same positions and touch his shirt on court? Well, actors are the same.

Alex Ah, so do you have any rituals?

Caleb Oh, just a few! On the second and following nights of a show I ² _____ (do) my make-up and put on my costume, etc. in exactly the same order as the first night! But there's a guy I often act with – he ³ _____ (try) to park in exactly the same parking place every night. Once he actually went five times to check out the car park because his favourite spot had been taken when he arrived.

Alex Wow! Well, if he ⁴ _____ (have) such an odd ritual …!

Caleb Exactly! And he ⁵ _____ (not choose) another space when we start a new play because he thinks changing his ritual is bad luck.

Alex I hear that there's one person who everyone moans about because of a habit he has backstage?

Caleb Yes, that ⁶ _____ (be) Marty – he ⁷ _____ (whistle) when he's backstage and all actors know that you must NOT whistle backstage. It's almost as dangerous as quoting from the Scottish play.

Alex Oh – you mean Shakespeare's *Macb…*

Caleb DON'T say it!

5 ★★ Replace the underlined parts of the sentences with the correct forms of *will*.

1 My brother <u>keeps refusing to</u> turn down his rock music and it's driving me up the wall. *won't*

2 Don't worry about reminding Callum to learn his lines. <u>I'm sure he spent</u> all afternoon on them. He is so reliable. _____

3 If he <u>insists on changing</u> his mind at the last moment, no wonder people don't trust him. _____

4 On most performance nights I <u>usually arrive</u> at the theatre about six, do my make-up and then relax with a book before curtain up. _____

5 He <u>tells</u> the same old jokes at parties and they aren't funny anymore. _____

6 Can we please get a move on? <u>I'm sure the director's waiting</u> for us to start the read through. _____

7 She <u>is adamant about taking on</u> extra work and then she ends up stressed. _____

6 ★★ Choose the correct forms to complete the sentences.

1 I didn't call Zac to ask for his help because he would ___ at that time.
   a be driving   **b** have driven   **c** have been driving

2 I ___ the tickets online if I were you.   .
   a would buy   **b** will buy   **c** will be buying

3 He insisted that we ___ enjoy the play.
   a will   **b** would   **c** would rather

4 In his show last year, after the opening trick, the illusionist ___ for a volunteer from the audience.
   a will ask   **b** would ask   **c** would be asking

5 He always promises that he ___ on time, and is always late!
   a will be   **b** would be   **c** is being

6 I would ___ it in the same way as you have, but your approach has definitely worked!
   a not be doing   **b** have done   **c** not have done

7 ★★★ Replace the underlined parts of the sentences using *would*.

1 <u>My thoughts are</u> that the teachers will definitely agree to the scheme.
   I *would think/would have thought*

2 <u>It's my preference</u> to wait until after the meeting before making a final decision.
   I _____

3 <u>It is for you to decide</u>.
   That _____

4 <u>Our real desire is for</u> this to be over soon.
   We _____

5 <u>You will have my gratitude if you can</u> keep this secret for the time being.
   I _____

6 <u>My expectations are</u> that the production will receive critical acclaim.
   I _____

8 ★★★ Complete the blog with the verbs from the box and the correct form of *will* or *would*.

agree   choose   go   have   not shut   put   say   stand   ~~stuff~~

Tidiness and me

I know I'm not the tidiest of people. I ¹ <u>*'ll stuff*</u> books and pens randomly into my school locker and then of course, the locker door ² _____! And I'm the total opposite of my best friend, Mia. Without looking now, I just know that her locker ³ _____ tidy piles of papers and pens in it and her lunch box ⁴ _____ neatly beside her bottle of water. Not only this, she ⁵ _____ all her friends' photos in rows! The thing is she ⁶ _____ on and on about how far below her standards I fall in terms of neatness – as though it were a real failing! Personally, I ⁷ _____ that I'm probably more normal than she is, but there's no way she ⁸ _____! Well, if I ⁹ _____ a complete opposite as a best friend, I shouldn't really complain!

9 ON A HIGH NOTE Write a short paragraph about the habits, past and present, of a friend or family member.

9C SPEAKING

1 🔊 *51* Listen and repeat the phrases. How do you say them in your language?

2 Complete the mini-conversations with the correct words from the Speaking box.

Ann My **¹**_gut feeling_ is that he's going to resign pretty soon.

Becky That's a possibility. Personally, I think it's **²**_____ he'll try to struggle on.

Amal I'd say it's **³**_____ that they'll build flats on the old site.

Celia But I **⁴**_____ that would involve getting planning permission.

Gilly I **⁵**_____ that Ethan will get the award.

Aisha I don't know. There's **⁶**_____ that Jake might beat him to it.

Milo Anna **⁷**_____ furious when she realised her bike had been stolen.

Sue She was already in a bad mood, so it **⁸**_____ things any better!

3 Rewrite the sentences to speculate about an event in the time given in brackets.

1 They may well decide not to come. (past)
They may well have decided not to come.

2 I presume that would involve a lot of research. (past)
_____

3 I'd say it's pretty certain that he's gone away for a well-needed break. (future)
_____

4 It's highly likely that she's overslept. (future)
_____

5 There was always the chance that he would refuse. (future)
_____

6 She must have been waiting to see how we would react. (present)
_____

4 🔊 *52* Complete the conversation with the correct words from the Speaking box. Listen and check.

Leila I love looking through old family photo albums, don't you? It's a shame we've got out of the habit these days.

Jack Yeah, well ... Oh, that's brilliant – I'm **¹**_guessing_ that was your parents' wedding?

Leila Yes. It **²**_____ have been taken just before the ceremony. Mum's looking nervous.

Jack I **³**_____ imagine everyone is a bit nervous before getting married. And those two young boys? I **⁴**_____ they're your cousins, Tony and Will? They've still got those cheeky grins!

Leila And did you know Will is getting married in April?

Jack Really? Will that be here in Manchester?

Leila No one's sure. His girlfriend is Portuguese, so the wedding could **⁵**_____ be in Portugal.

Jack A big beach wedding?

Leila Well, it **⁶**_____ be on the beach, but as for 'big' ... they're saving for a house so my **⁷**_____ feeling is that it will be a small one. It might be that we all pay for our own travel and accommodation – that is if it's abroad. But there's **⁸**_____ the chance that they'll tie the knot here after all.

Jack Being April, it's **⁹**_____ likely that they'd get rained on here in the UK! Portugal would be a much better option!

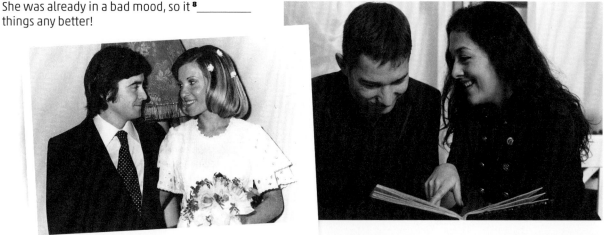

9D LISTENING AND VOCABULARY

1
🔊 53 Listen to five people talking about memory and tick the things that are mentioned.

1. ☐ a job they had
2. ☐ a type of animal
3. ☐ a holiday
4. ☐ a piece of music
5. ☐ a childhood event
6. ☐ the name of a book
7. ☐ some singers

2
🔊 53 Listen again. What does each person say about the memory? Match speakers 1–5 with sentences a–h. There are three extra sentences.

Speaker: 1 ☐ 2 ☐ 3 ☐ 4 ☐ 5 ☐

a Negative events can be blanked out.
b Some memories are triggered at unexpected times.
c Dreams are built on memories both recent and distant.
d Certain items linger longer than desired.
e No one has fully explored the workings of memory.
f Remembering incorrectly is not down to a bad memory.
g Memory can enhance or alter certain things that happened.
h Memory does not store some things.

3
🔊 53 Listen again and match speakers 1–5 with how they illustrate their comments about memory a–h. There are three extra options.

Speaker: 1 ☐ 2 ☐ 3 ☐ 4 ☐ 5 ☐

a Asking someone to specifically forget something.
b Recording some memories in a diary.
c Multitasking during a conversation.
d Giving a detailed example of a sequence of events.
e Recalling a word related to the one required.
f Recounting something you want to remember.
g Feeling emotional when reminded of something.
h Solving a particular difficulty by using memories.

Vocabulary extension

4
Complete the sentences with the correct forms of the verbs from the box, which you heard in the recording in Exercise 1.

cease   linger   ~~override~~   rectify   retrieve   well up

1 The taste of garlic in the food was so strong that it _overrode_ all the subtle flavours.
2 My mother's perfume is lovely and it _____ in a room long after she's gone.
3 My computer crashed yesterday and it took me ages to _____ the file I had been working on.
4 However many times I see the trick, I never _____ to be amazed by it.
5 When he heard the news, his eyes immediately _____.
6 This is down to me, and I need to _____ the situation as soon as possible.

5
ON A HIGH NOTE Write a short paragraph about your strangest dream.

Pronunciation

6
🔊 54 Listen to some sentences from the recording in Exercise 1. Which sounds are missing when the sentence is read quickly?

1 An hour after waking it's gone.
2 It would take a lot of time to do that.
3 It's baffling.
4 Hands up! It's my own fault.

ACTIVE PRONUNCIATION
Extreme elision* in fast speech

We often lose syllables or sounds when we speak quickly, contracting words.

It is dark. = It's dark.   *I cannot do it. = I can't do it.*

However, we often go further and sometimes miss complete words, or make a token attempt at the initial vowel, but do not carry it through. Compare the following sentences.

I'd say it's pretty certain that he'll come.
I'd say spretty certain that he'll come. (lost *it*)
I presume that would involve a lot of money.
I presume thated involve a lot of money. (lost most of *would*)
I bought some artwork.
I bought smartwork. (lost most of *some*)
How did she reply?
Howd she reply? (lost most of *did*)

* elision – the omission of a sound or syllable when speaking

---

7
🔊 55 Listen and in each pair tick the sentence that you hear. Then practise saying the sentences.

1
a ☐ I'm trying to remember. Sorry it's gone.
b ☐ I'm trying to remember. Sorry sgone.
2
a ☐ What did you tell her when you saw her?
b ☐ What ju tell her when you saw her?
3
a ☐ There weren'tny students in the class.
b ☐ There weren't any students in the class.
4
a ☐ Where you taking us?
b ☐ Where are you taking us?
5
a ☐ But it's not that I've forgotten.
b ☐ But snot that I've forgotten.

8
🔊 56 Listen to a person speaking quickly and write down what he says. Pause after each sentence to give yourself time to write.

9
🔊 57 Listen to the sentences from Exercise 8 spoken more slowly and check your answers.

UNIT VOCABULARY PRACTICE > page 109   105

1 Read an advert for a competition and four teachers' reactions to it. Then complete the information in the advertisement.

2 Read the comments again and match questions 1–4 with teachers A–D.

Which teacher ...

1 ☐ has a different opinion to the others regarding the value of such a competition?

2 ☐ shares Ms Fable's view on the role of imagination in a child's life?

3 ☐ has a different view to Mr Fairy on who should be able to benefit from entering the competition?

4 ☐ has a similar view to Mrs Tales on the type of person best suited to assessing the entries?

Vocabulary extension

3 Look at the highlighted collocations and expressions in texts A–D and complete the sentences with one word in each gap.

1 Not being picked for the first team might _dampen_ others' enthusiasm for the game, but not Mikey – it just spurred him on to do better.

2 When the romantic novelist tried her _____ at writing a mystery story, it wasn't very successful.

3 If you have any comments or suggestions, please let us know – we appreciate receiving _____ and constructive criticism.

4 I have just ordered a book about writer's block – it's filled with 748 ideas about how to _____ your imagination so I do hope I'll finish this essay soon!

5 Getting some negative feedback may, unfortunately, _____ your creativity.

6 If it's difficult to come up with ideas for an essay, sometimes it's good to just shut your eyes and let your thoughts _____ free. Something will always pop into your mind.

ACTIVE VOCABULARY | Phrases with *play*

There are many English phrasal verbs and idioms that use the verb *play*.

Using the imagination definitely **plays a vital part** in children's early development.

The importance of this should never be **played down**.

4 Complete the collocations in bold with the words from the box.

ball cards down ~~ear~~ innocent part time up

1 I haven't had a chance to consider all the options, so I'll just have to **play it by** _ear_ in the meeting.

2 You shouldn't **play** _____ your role in getting the production on stage – if it weren't for you, it wouldn't have gone on.

3 The council can't make up their minds about the proposed plans for the school – so all these delays are just a sign that they're **playing for** _____.

4 I saw you taking the last piece of cake from the tin – so don't **play the** _____ with me!

5 If you **play your** _____ **right**, you could end up with a really good job in television.

6 When the children **play** _____ in class, I usually give them some writing or colouring to do, to calm them down.

7 Early exposure to books and stories **plays an important** _____ in developing a child's creativity.

8 My brother wanted to reduce his hours at work, but the company refused to **play** _____, saying the hours were in his contract.

5 ON A HIGH NOTE Write a short paragraph about the type of stories you would write if you were a professional writer, giving your reasons and some examples.

COMPETITION: National ¹*Writing* Competition

Entrants must be aged between 7 and ²_____ years.
Judges will be a panel of five top children's ³_____.

TOPICS: animals; ⁴_____; mountains

For more details on dates, judges, word counts, etc. check out our website.

A MR FAIRY

Children love stories, and they love making them up. I thoroughly support those who say that creativity needs to be encouraged at an early age. The importance of this should never be played down. This can hold them in good stead for the future as it has been shown that a person's intelligence can be enhanced by being creative. So, I was delighted to read about the proposal to set up a story writing competition for children under thirteen. The suggestion is to have established, reputable writers sit alongside non-professional judges to read and assess the stories. For older students, a significant number of opportunities already exist. In my class of mid-teens, my students are regularly given time to do creative writing and it's a task they enjoy, where they can let their imaginations run completely free. Everybody shares results, but no one is pressured into telling their stories if they are not comfortable with this.

B MRS TALES

What an excellent idea to give children's creative writing a focus such as this competition does. As far as I'm concerned, it's important for children to have a reason for writing, which means having a reader in mind when they write – whether this is a classmate, parent or, as in this case, a panel of judges who are respected authors themselves. I would hope that each entry receives some feedback so that the children can improve on their writing abilities in the future. My only comment to the organisers is that I feel the upper age limit is too low as this does not allow early teens to try their hand at writing. I shall definitely circulate the competition information amongst the teaching staff and expect a large number of entries.

C MS FABLE

Using the imagination definitely plays a vital part in children's early development and I am in favour of encouraging the use of play both inside and outside the classroom. A central part of this for pre-teens is considered to be inventing stories, however far-fetched, sometimes in role-play games or later, in writing. I do not quibble with this, but I am not convinced that children should be putting their efforts up against others to be judged. Each child's story is individual and is special to them, and putting it forward for appraisal risks making story-writing a gradable exercise, like Maths or Science tests and as such could prove to dampen enthusiasm rather than boost it. Regular story writing is already part and parcel of a primary school teacher's weekly programme and its benefits cannot be exaggerated.

D MR REED

I find the proposal for a writing competition an interesting one, particularly if this becomes a regular annual, or even monthly event. Students within this age group would find feedback from people whose own books they have most probably read themselves, informative and encouraging, and the organisation should be praised in having persuaded authors such as those cited to become involved without payment. While not everyone would benefit from having their work assessed by a critical eye as this may stifle their creativity, I am sure that it would outweigh any disadvantages. The entrants' teachers could stave off any potential disillusionment or disappointment by pointing out the positive points in the work, should those not be included in any feedback. The topics listed in the proposal, particularly 'space', are appropriate and should easily spark students' imagination.

9F WRITING | A proposal

Give your proposal a title.

Give headings to make the proposal clear to read.

Give an introduction where you say why you are writing the proposal.

Explain the current situation.

Outline the benefits your proposed plan would bring.

Use formal and objective language.

Make recommendations for action.

Give a final reason to explain why this would be a good idea.

Proposal for inter-school participation in an annual theatrical production

Introduction
The purpose of this proposal is to outline the benefits of staging an annual theatrical event that would involve a range of schools in the area.

Current situation
As it stands, each school or college in this area puts on their own annual production, usually at the end of the autumn term, which involves students, teachers and technicians from within each school. Both staff and students put a significant amount of time and effort into these productions, and they are generally extremely well received by the audiences. No one doubts the value to all participating students of such productions. However, each production is limited in some way by the facilities at each individual school. The stage size, the range of lighting, cost of costume hire, and the number of seats in the auditorium all restrict schools from taking on more extravagant productions, meaning that they are unable to offer their students a more exciting and profitable experience.

Benefits of inter-school projects
[1]Should all the local schools work together to put on an annual theatrical event, it would provide [2]countless benefits. Firstly, it would enable the production to be staged at the town theatre, with its large stage and auditorium and its advanced technical facilities. All these factors would allow a more adventurous production to be staged, with larger cast numbers and the use of special effects. The budgets from each school would be pooled to fund the project and students could also [3]engage in promoting the production, [4]ensuring full houses and maximum return on the investment.

Recommendations
I would recommend contacting the drama departments in local schools to suggest meeting to discuss the possibilities of collaborating in this way. This kind of cooperation would [5]maximise the financial investment each school contributes to its annual productions and provide a wide pool of talent within the student population and the teaching staff to draw upon. In addition to this, it will provide valuable hands-on experience for students, allow them to meet and work with new people and [6]strengthen bonds between the schools.

1 Read the proposal. Match words and phrases a–f with underlined parts 1–6 from the proposal with a similar meaning.

a ☐ get involved in
b ☐ make stronger
c ☐ a lot of
d ☐ make the most of
e ☐ if
f ☐ making sure

2 Choose the correct words to complete the sentences.

1 The aim of this proposal is to *address* / *enable* the financial issues involved in …
2 When considering options, our *purpose* / *priority* is to ensure continuity.
3 A *key* / *confident* aspect of the proposal is …
4 I would *ensure* / *urge* you to consider this proposal favourably.
5 My hope is that you will give this your full *priority* / *consideration*.

3 WRITING TASK Write a proposal.

Your college has decided to redevelop the social space used by students so that it provides both a relaxing and functional area for students. You have been asked to submit a proposal outlining some ideas about what the redeveloped space should offer students in terms of different types of areas, facilities and equipment, and recommendations on how this could be achieved.

ACTIVE WRITING | A proposal

1 Plan your proposal.
- Think about what students need from a social space at school, e.g. space to relax/chat/work.
- Make notes about what to include in each paragraph: introduction, current situation and recommendations.

2 Write the proposal.
- Give it a title.
- Give headings to your paragraphs.
- Use an objective, formal style.
- Use language for recommending and persuading.

3 Check that …
- all the relevant information is there.
- there are no spelling, grammar or punctuation mistakes.

UNIT VOCABULARY PRACTICE

1 **9A VOCABULARY AND SPEAKING Choose the correct words to complete the sentences.**

1 I was *blown / bowled* away by my cousin's violin solo in the school orchestra performance last week.
2 The effort put into the construction of the new exhibition centre is *unimaginative / unimaginable*.
3 The owner left a useful *explicable / explanatory* note about how to use the kitchen equipment.
4 The width of the river at this point is quite *deceptive / deceitful* – it's much narrower than it looks.
5 I think we were all taken *in / aback* by his reaction to the news about the theatre closure.
6 I never cease to be *captured / captivated* by the view from my friend's fifteenth floor apartment.

2 **9A VOCABULARY AND SPEAKING Choose the correct words a–d to complete the text.**

MASTER OF ESCAPOLOGY

The name Harry Houdini is synonymous with escapology. He was a master conjuror and escape artist and some of his escapes completely defy **1**___. Many audiences experienced **2**___ moments as the seconds on the clock that the great man needed to escape from water, or even milk, without drowning ticked by. Indeed some of his feats were **3**___ even to other experienced escapologists. However, Houdini was also an excellent showman and knew exactly how to heighten tension before eventually **4**___ off an apparently miraculous trick that went **5**___ all the rules. Indeed certain exploits of his still have experts scratching their **6**___ today.

1 **a** reality **b** imagination **c** assumption **d** belief
2 **a** mind-boggling **b** breathtaking
  c heart-stopping **d** unrealistic
3 **a** baffling **b** disconcerting **c** deceptive **d** illusory
4 **a** taking **b** blowing **c** pulling **d** bowling
5 **a** before **b** out of **c** away **d** against
6 **a** ears **b** brows **c** heads **d** noses

3 **9D LISTENING AND VOCABULARY Complete the sentences with the words from the box to make adjective-noun collocations.**

~~definitive~~ graphic ingenious light recurring well-documented

1 No one could give me a(n) *definitive* answer to my questions about how the effects are created.
2 There are some _____ experiments that took place in the UK two years ago.
3 Unfortunately, I've always been a(n) _____ sleeper and even morning birdsong wakes me up.
4 In the film they showed that the illusionist used a(n) _____ technique to take the audience in.
5 People sometimes get _____ dreams because of a trauma they've suffered.
6 At the beginning of the book there is a(n) _____ description of the houses devastated by the storm.

4 **9E READING AND VOCABULARY The underlined adjectives are in the wrong sentences. Swap them so that they appear in the correct place.**

1 A far-fetched expert gave a fascinating talk on the topic this morning. *reputable*
2 Your theory raises some reluctant questions. _____
3 My sister is very intriguing in her aim to get into university. _____
4 Unfortunately, the teacher is too elaborate to allow us the necessary time out of class to continue the research. _____
5 The plans are really reputable and will never come to fruition. _____
6 The plan is quite single-minded with plenty of detail, but I think it could work. _____

5 **Choose the correct verbs to complete the conversation.**

Oliver At last the police are going to **1***make / open* an investigation into the series of burglaries in our block of flats.

Ella That's good. But they need to **2***have / take* an open mind. We **3***put / made* detailed mention of all our opinions in the letter we all signed, but they **4***disregarded / opened* the possibility that it was an outside job, and **5***opened / raised* questions about how far we trusted our own neighbours!

Oliver Well, everyone's known everyone here for years. When I said that I'd seen the same couple of guys hanging around – guys who I know live way across the river – they **6***ridiculed / defied* the idea, and said it was far more likely to be someone from the block.

Ella Let's hope they make progress and **7***lie / lay* to rest that silly idea.

6 **ON A HIGH NOTE Write a short paragraph about a clever crime that you have read or watched a film about, saying why it was so clever and why it fooled the authorities.**

1 **For each learning objective, write 1–5 to assess your ability.**

1 = I don't feel confident. 5 = I feel confident.

	Learning objective	Course material	How confident I am (1–5)
9A	I can use adjectives and expressions to describe disbelief and surprise.	Student's Book pp. 124–125	
9B	I can use *will* and *would* to express attitude.	Student's Book pp. 126–127	
9C	I can make speculations about the past, present and future.	Student's Book p. 128	
9D	I can tell the difference between a fact and an opinion.	Student's Book p. 129	
9E	I can identify specific details in a comment and talk about unexplained events.	Student's Book pp. 130–131	
9F	I can write a proposal.	Student's Book pp. 132–133	

2 **Which of the skills above would you like to improve in? How?**

Skill I want to improve in	How I can improve

3 **What can you remember from this unit?**

New words I learned and most want to remember	Expressions and phrases I liked	English I heard or read outside class

GRAMMAR AND VOCABULARY

1 Complete the sentences with one word in each gap.

1 The creative use of special effects in the film was mind-b_oggling_.

2 My mother has always been a l_____ sleeper and will wake at the quietest sound in the house.

3 You may think it's far-f_____, but I truly believe that one day humans will live on Mars.

4 The latest winner of the Turner art prize was very unconventional and raised a few e_____!

5 There was a heart-s_____ moment in the film when the car nearly went off the cliff.

6 Ryan Gosling gave an absolutely r_____ performance – I couldn't stop watching!

/ 5

2 Match the two parts of the sentences.

1 ☐ In his report the expert made detailed

2 ☐ It is important to raise

3 ☐ It is advisable that people who have vivid

4 ☐ When I watch these crime thrillers, it beats me

5 ☐ I can't understand why some people will go

a to any lengths to get on TV for even a short time.

b how quickly all those laboratory tests are done.

c awareness of the need to recycle plastic waste.

d dreams do not eat food just before bedtime.

e mention of the type of tyre prints near the crime scene.

/ 5

3 Complete the text with the words from the box. There are two extra words.

conclusively   deceptively   definitive   disillusioned
far-fetched   inexplicable   lay   ~~put~~

IT'S A MYSTERY

There is very little mystery in most people's lives today, which is why, experts believe, we love reading about them. Does Atlantis exist? Why is the Bermuda Triangle considered dangerous? Why was the Mary Celeste discovered deserted? All questions in answer to which various theories have been **¹**_put_ forward. But do we really want to prove **²**_____ what happened to the Ark of the Covenant? Do we want to **³**_____ to rest the rumours that abound about buried treasure that is waiting to be found? Surely the truth is that we delight in the **⁴**_____ explanations and the fact that science and technology, however advanced they become, cannot give **⁵**_____ answers to every mystery there is. I believe that a need for the unbelievable and **⁶**_____ is truly part of our nature.

/ 5

4 Complete the sentences with *will* or *would* and the correct forms of the verbs in brackets.

1 Don't bother phoning him as he _will be_ (be) on his way over here right now.

2 Can't we go any faster? Jack _____ (wait) for over an hour at the station by now.

3 You can turn up the volume as high as you like – Kelly _____ (not wake up) however loud it is.

4 Thanks for the offer. It _____ (be) very kind of you to give me a hand with the lifting.

5 Every day I got back from school, the dog _____ (wait) for me at the front gate.

6 Whenever I'm trying to explain things, she _____ (look) out of the window in silence.

/ 5

USE OF ENGLISH

5 Complete the second sentence using the word in bold so that it means the same as the first one. Use between three and six words, including the word in bold.

1 I was completely amazed when they read my name out as the winner of the contest. **BOWLED**

It completely _bowled me over when my name_ was read out as the winner of the contest.

2 She's got this irritating habit of leaving her books all over the table after studying. **LEAVE**

She _____ the table after studying.

3 Giving him some time to relax before sending him to work might be a good idea. **GIVE**

I _____ relax before sending him to work.

4 The new primary school teacher is excellent and the children are never shouted at. **VOICE**

The new primary school teacher _____ the children and she's an excellent teacher.

5 Watching TV so late at night is bound to make you feel tired in the morning. **WILL**

If _____ at night, it's no surprise that you're tired in the morning.

6 The decision surprised some people. **EYEBROWS**

The decision _____.

/ 5

6 Complete the text with the correct words formed from the words in bold.

DREAMS MAY COME TRUE?

It is incredible how many people have **¹**_recurring_ (**RECUR**) dreams and seriously believe that they are in some way **²**_____ (**PROPHECY**). Most of our instincts are to say that this would be an impossibility, but are we right to **³**_____ (**REGARD**) the idea entirely? There have been some reports that a **⁴**_____ (**REPUTATION**) expert has admitted that dreams that are seen to be predicting something should not be **⁵**_____ (**RIDICULOUS**), but are in fact the mind's way of putting together an outcome to a dilemma, or an event in progress. This may not be a **⁶**_____ (**DEFINE**) answer, but it's not a far-fetched fantasy either.

/ 5

/ 30

111

10A VOCABULARY AND SPEAKING

Work-life balance collocations and idioms

1 ★ Choose the correct words to complete the sentences.

1 It can often prove difficult to strike the right *connectivity / balance* between work and leisure time.

2 For students who study hard all the time this will definitely pay *returns / dividends* in the future.

3 At first, I didn't grasp the *signification / significance* of what the teacher was saying.

4 People need to learn how to juggle the *unremitting / unacceptable* demands of work and family.

5 We need to be able to draw a *line / target* between our work and private life.

6 If you don't meet your work *balances / demands* during the week, you may have a stressful weekend.

7 *Consistent / Constant* connectivity can be of great benefit or a great burden these days.

2 ★ Complete the mini-conversations with the correct forms of the verbs from the box.

draw grasp juggle maintain pay ~~strive~~

Kurt Without an ambition, it can be hard to focus at work.

Uma Yes, you need to have something to ¹*strive* for.

Marcus Alex is looking very tired these days.

Mina Yes, he's been ²_____ the unremitting demands of two part-time jobs lately.

Anika I know I need to be consistent in my studies and have regular study periods, but I'm such a terrible procrastinator!

Tina Just think that it will ³_____ dividends in the long run and your life will be stress free.

Lucy I do admire Ethan's work ethic.

Will Yes, he's managed to ⁴_____ a balance between work and study.

Zac Kenny didn't do well at the job interview yesterday. He never checks out the companies beforehand.

Eric Yes, he needs to ⁵_____ the significance of preparing well.

Laura Elena seems to be answering work calls all over the weekend. It's too much.

Roma Yes, she needs to ⁶_____ a line between work and personal life.

3 ★★ Complete the text with the correct verbs and collocations.

I have been in work now for a couple of years and here's the advice I would have given my teenage self.

You've got many years of hard studying ahead of you, so applying yourself to your studies now will ¹p*ay* d*ividends* when you go to college. Try to identify some aims and ambitions for the future and ²s_____ for them. You'll find yourself ³j_____ unremitting d_____ from school and your social network, but you need to ⁴s_____ the right b_____ between work and play – both are important in the right measures. Some students forego social activities in favour of working non-stop, but they're not ⁵g_____ the significance of the part relationships play in our lives. A good support system to see us through the college years is a must so we need to ⁶m_____ a b_____ and develop hobbies to give us wider experiences. ⁷C_____ c_____ will be a challenge and provide a continual distraction, so try to ⁸d_____ a l_____ between when you're available to chat and when you need to focus. It's going to be a hard but a fascinating decade. Good luck!

4 ★★ Match the two parts of the sentences.

1 ☐ It is never advisable to throw

2 ☐ Sometimes you can work

3 ☐ If you're looking at a blank screen with no ideas, it may be time to call

4 ☐ Most companies give you time to learn

5 ☐ When he took on the job, he didn't sign

6 ☐ It's time to change a job when it starts to intrude

7 ☐ It can be difficult to meet

a up to be working all weekend and every evening.

b it a day and go home.

c targets with a manager constantly looking over your shoulder.

d the ropes when you start a new job.

e your socks off and get nowhere.

f on family life and leisure time.

g a sickie because someone may find out.

5 ★★ Find and correct one mistake in each sentence.

1 I've run out of ideas, so I'll just ~~sign~~ it a day. *call*

2 Some people call a sickie whenever they feel just a little tired. _____

3 My parents never let their work strike on our family life when I was growing up. _____

4 The manager has asked me to help a new recruit throw the ropes this week. _____

5 I've just checked my contract and I definitely didn't strive up for all this overtime. _____

6 If you start up a new business, you'll have to pay your socks off for the first year at least. _____

6 ★★ Match the underlined parts of the sentences with idioms a–h with a similar meaning.

1 ☐ Would it be OK if I <u>quickly went down</u> to the cafeteria for half an hour?

2 ☐ Sometimes it can be hard to <u>do everything that is asked of you at work</u>.

3 ☐ <u>It is highly anticipated</u> that Rita will pass all her exams with the highest grades.

4 ☐ I know it's difficult, but you have to be <u>honest</u> about your other commitments.

5 ☐ It's important in meetings for each person to <u>give an opinion</u> about the issues discussed.

6 ☐ It has been a difficult time at work, but I'm not about to <u>resign</u>.

7 ☐ The company doesn't usually expect employees to work on a Saturday; this will <u>happen only once</u>.

8 ☐ Getting work experience in the office gave me a <u>really positive feeling about what the work was like</u> and I've decided to apply for a full-time position there.

a it's a given	**e** have their say
b throw it all in	**f** upfront
c real taste for the job	**g** be a one-off
d meet your work demands	**h** popped down

7 ★★ Complete the sentences with the correct form of the idioms from Exercise 6.

1 There's no question about whether Marie will be offered the job. It *is a given*.

2 Don't worry! You'll be able to _____ at the school council meeting next Friday.

3 This job is taking it out of me. I dislike the constant connectivity and I'm tempted to _____.

4 The manager has asked me to stand in for him while he's away next Monday. It's _____, but it shows that they value my work.

5 I fear that the work on this project is beyond my capabilities. I ought to be _____ about it so they can bring someone else in.

6 It's obvious that Tom is struggling to _____ at the moment and I think he needs a break.

7 Could you _____ to the snack bar and bring us all some sandwiches, please?

8 Shadowing someone at work can sometimes give you a _____, or it can put you off forever!

8 ★★★ Complete the conversation with the correct idioms using the words in bold.

Jesse I haven't seen you since the weekend. How did the first day at the restaurant go?

Tom I'm still recovering! It took me an hour or so to ¹*learn the ropes* (**ROPE**) – like the systems in place for food and drink orders and taking payments from the customers – then I ² _____ (**SOCKS**) off waiting tables for a whole afternoon and evening shift, without a break. I couldn't even ³ _____ (**DOWN**) the road for a breath of fresh air. I didn't get home until after midnight. Quite honestly, I didn't ⁴ _____ (**UP**) for a part-time job that was so full on.

Jesse Wow! That's a long day. ⁵ _____ (**GIVE**) that working in a restaurant is hard, but when I did some waiting work last summer, the hours were much shorter. You need to be upfront with the manager about how many hours you can work – remember you have college on weekdays.

Tom I know. However valuable it is, I can't let this experience ⁶ _____ (**ON**) my time for studying too severely. I know I need to get some money in my pocket, but if the next shift is anything like the last then I may well ⁷ _____ in.

Jesse Try to ⁸ _____ (**SAY**) first – and see how they react before you ⁹ _____ (**DAY**). Last Saturday might have been ¹⁰ _____ (**ONE**).

Tom Good thinking. I'll wait.

9 ON A HIGH NOTE Write a paragraph about a part-time job you had and what the experience was like. If you have not had one, would you like to try? Say why.

10B GRAMMAR

Gerunds and infinitives

1 ★ Match the two parts of the sentences.

1 ☐ Olga is really good at
2 ☐ Kelly is going to volunteer
3 ☐ Josie is desperate
4 ☐ Jesse is nervous about
5 ☐ Megan didn't mention
6 ☐ Billy's decision
7 ☐ Shaun neglected
8 ☐ My dad contemplated

a to start working soon.
b seeing Jamie last week.
c to tell me about the meeting.
d changing jobs a few years ago.
e to help out at her local animal rescue centre.
f taking his Maths exam next week.
g to get some work experience was a good idea.
h prioritising her workload.

2 ★ Complete the sentences with the correct forms of the verbs from the box.

be able   call   discuss   do   finish   know   lay off
~~leave~~   make   not ask   think

1 Despite *leaving* half an hour earlier than usual, we reached work ten minutes after the start of the meeting.

2 It's time _____ the decision about which of the new recruits will stay on for the second month.

3 There'll be nothing _____ after _____ this work, so you should _____ it a day.

4 I apologise for _____ for permission to take a break. I did it without _____.

5 We are delighted _____ to let you _____ that the decision _____ staff has been reversed.

6 The teacher has forbidden us _____ the test with anyone in case of cheating.

3 ★ Choose the correct words to complete the text. In one case both words are possible.

4 ★★ Complete the sentences with the correct passive forms of the verbs in brackets.

1 Despite *being made* (make) locally, these products are continuing to rise in price.

2 I'm happy _____ (offer) overtime any weekday evening.

3 You risk _____ (cheat) out of a lot of money if you click on links like these.

4 Everyone needs _____ (reassure) that they are not being taken for granted at work.

5 After _____ (give) an agenda for the day, trainees will be directed to the relevant rooms.

6 To attract investment, it's important for your work _____ (see) by the right people.

5 ★★ Use the prompts in brackets to complete the conversation. Sometimes more than one answer is possible.

Emilia Hi! Are you coming to the work fair next weekend? Mike **1** *happened to be studying* (happen / study) in the library when I went there last night and he **2** _____ (offer / drive / us).

Elena That's kind of him! But I was lucky **3** _____ (give / a ticket) for the concert in Green Park on Saturday. **4** _____ (After / tell) that there were none available, I'd expected **5** _____ (have to / go) to the careers fair! Then a friend **6** _____ (need / sell) her ticket – she'd bought it **7** _____ (without / check / date), but she **8** _____ (order / go) to the fair by her dad! I know it **9** _____ (be / important / explore) all career options **10** _____ (before / make) decisions about university degrees and so on, but my brother found the right career for himself without ever needing **11** _____ (go) to a single fair.

Emilia You're right. And you've already been to a couple. Have a wonderful time. The bands **12** _____ (supposed / be) on top form at the moment!

Baking your way to success

When Ellie was six, she pretended to be her mother and managed **1** *to spend / spending* over a hundred pounds on toys shopping online. Later, she decided **2** *to earn / earning* some extra money and had the idea of **3** *sell / selling* cakes and biscuits she'd made at home. Ellie's little business was extremely successful and she ended up **4** *to make / making* a lot of money and **5** *to invest / investing* it back into her baking. As she grew older, she dreamed about **6** *to start / starting* her own real business and contemplated **7** *to study / studying* business management at university. However, she was tempted **8** *to leave / leaving* school early to try **9** *to go / going* it alone. Her teachers eventually persuaded her **10** *to take / taking* a degree and continue to develop her business ideas in her free time.

Ellie found that studying and running a business at the same time was hard **11** *to do / doing*. The long hours compelled her **12** *to give up / giving up* studying and **13** *to work / working* for herself full time. This proved **14** *to be / being* the right decision. Ellie is now a successful entrepreneur and she advises other budding entrepreneurs **15** *to do / doing* the same as she has done. She believes that if you happen **16** *to have / having* a particular dream, you need **17** *to follow / following* your heart.

6 ★★ Complete the pairs of sentences with the words in bold.

1 TO HAVE TO TELL YOU / HAVING TOLD

a I regret *to have to tell you* that your application has been unsuccessful, but thank you for sending it in.

b I regret _____ so many fibs during my interview.

2 TO RAISE / RAISING

a This means _____ some questions about the issue in the next meeting.

b I mean _____ some questions about the issue in the next meeting.

3 TO BE / BEING

a I try _____ objective when it comes to checking my work through a second time.

b I tried _____ objective when I was checking my work through a second time, but it didn't help as I couldn't see my own mistakes.

4 TO TALK / TALKING

a In the video clip the advisor goes on _____ about the consequences of deciding to change career.

b In the video clip the advisor goes on _____ about the consequences of deciding to change career for quite a while.

5 TO SAVE / SAVING

a I forgot _____ my work before closing down the computer and I lost all my changes.

b I forgot _____ my work before closing down the computer and it was a relief to see that I had.

7 ★★★ USE OF ENGLISH Complete the second sentence using the word in bold so that it means the same as the first one. Use between three and six words, including the word in bold.

1 It was the director who decided to lay off ten people from the workforce. **MAKE**

It was the director's *decision to make* ten people from the work force redundant.

2 From reading the email chain, I think he's been scheduling meetings without letting everyone know. **APPEARS**

From reading the email chain, he _____ scheduling meetings without letting everyone know.

3 I'm really glad that they've chosen me to represent the college in the debating competition. **BEEN**

I'm really glad _____ to represent the school in the debating competition.

4 When you finish college, do you think you'll work here or abroad? **ENVISION**

On _____ here or abroad?

5 If you're famous, people will always recognise you in the street. **AVOID**

If you're famous, you _____ in the street.

8 ★★★ Complete the text with the correct forms of the verbs in brackets.

SMART JOBS FOR LAZY PEOPLE

How do you imagine your future work life ¹*unfolding* (unfold)? Are you thinking about a nine-to-five office job which could prove mundane and repetitive and result in your ²_____ (work) your socks off for little recompense, or could you imagine ³_____ (give) the chance to sit back, chill out and earn money for ⁴_____ (do) precious little? If the answer is the latter, then it's likely that you would be looking at ⁵_____ (work) from home, and perhaps ⁶_____ (become) a professional expert or consultant. I confess to ⁷_____ (advise) to follow this route by more than one friend! I was amazed ⁸_____ (learn) that some experts are known ⁹_____ (choose) their careers specifically because they can charge ridiculous amounts of money for a consultation that takes a very short time. Of course, it goes without ¹⁰_____ (say) that you first need ¹¹_____ (have) some expertise! However, this could be simply in something that you find interesting and fun, but which may seem difficult or not worth ¹²_____ (worry) about for others. So, stop ¹³_____ (reflect) on how you can have a relaxing and enjoyable working life by not ¹⁴_____ (put) in too much time and effort, and get out there and promote your expertise! You might make a small fortune.

9 ON A HIGH NOTE Write a short paragraph about what people have advised you to do for a future job or career and how you have viewed their advice and why.

10C READING AND VOCABULARY

1 **Read the title of the article. What do you think it refers to? Read the article quickly and check.**

  a twenty-five new types of jobs before the year 2025

  b twenty-five interesting jobs that young people can do under the age of twenty-five

  c twenty-five jobs that one person did before he/she was twenty-five

2 **Read the article again and match questions 1–7 with paragraphs A–F. One paragraph may be chosen more than once.**

Which paragraph …

  1 ☐ mentions ways of telling others about lessons learned?

  2 ☐ explains a common approach to finding a career?

  3 ☐ mentions how to understand what a job entails before applying?

  4 ☐ mentions a fear of change?

  5 ☐ suggests a range of motivations for job seekers?

  6 ☐ mentions a dissatisfaction with a good job?

  7 ☐ refers to how employment used to be viewed?

3 **Complete the notes with no more than three words in each gap.**

  1 Many people don't seek alternative employment because they are too *financially committed*.

  2 The title of the text refers to _____ that Emma Rosen developed to advise young people on choosing a career.

  3 In Emma's opinion, the Internet is limited in what we can find out about the everyday _____ of particular jobs.

  4 Her experience revealed that she was _____ doing a job that she'd previously thought interesting.

  5 Emma refers to a new way of looking at job prospects as a _____.

  6 The writer believes that what we want from a job differs from one _____ to another.

Vocabulary extension

4 **Replace the underlined parts of the sentences with the correct forms of the highlighted phrases from the text.**

  1 The restaurant <u>did everything it could</u> to improve customer experiences. *went all out*

  2 You need to <u>avoid narrowing your choices</u> when it comes to thinking about finding a new job. _____

  3 I found out about the job <u>myself</u> by shadowing a friend who was already in the role. _____

  4 <u>Regarding your progress this year</u>, I would say that you've done an excellent job. _____

  5 If you <u>are able to do a variety of things</u>, your chances of getting a good job increase. _____

  6 This job is <u>in great demand</u> and it might be difficult to get shortlisted. _____

  7 It took me ages to <u>get to the end of</u> all the work I'd missed. _____

  8 You need to <u>aim</u> high if you want to succeed in your career. _____

ACTIVE VOCABULARY | Idioms with *day*

There are many idioms and phrases in English using the word *day*. Many of these are linked to the topic of work.

call it a day – stop working on something

Let's **call it a day**.

day-to-day – happening every day as a regular part of life or routine

My **day-to-day** responsibilities include dealing with customers and checking stock.

5 **Match phrases and idioms 1–6 with their meanings a–f.**

  1 ☐ at the end of the day

  2 ☐ in this day and age

  3 ☐ make my day

  4 ☐ not give someone the time of day

  5 ☐ have a field day

  6 ☐ all in a day's work

  a just part of my normal routine

  b not consider even saying hello

  c in these times

  d enjoy/make a big thing out of something

  e make me feel happy

  f when everything has been considered

6 **Complete the sentences with the correct forms of the phrases and idioms from Exercise 5.**

  1 The press will *have a field day* if they find out about the scandal!

  2 _____, it will be my decision.

  3 Nobody writes letters surely _____!

  4 The boss congratulated me on the report, and it _____.

  5 Don't thank me – it's _____.

  6 I've had a lot of problems with him in the past and now I wouldn't _____.

7 **ON A HIGH NOTE** Write a short paragraph explaining which five jobs you would like to try out and why.

UNIT VOCABULARY PRACTICE > page 121

Twenty-five before twenty-five!

A So, are you one of the lucky ones as far as your career goes? Have you always known what you were destined to do, set your sights on a particular goal, achieved it and are now content in your choice of career? Unfortunately, this doesn't happen to many of us. A relatively normal path is to slog through our years of education, find out which subjects we're better at than others, follow that subject through to college and university and then look for a job in a related field. We may be lucky and end up doing something we love and are suited to, but sadly, this is often not the case. We find ourselves in a work environment we're not particularly happy to be in, engaged in tasks that are not actually that engaging and too financially committed to risk branching out and finding something new.

B A new way of looking at career choices has been highlighted by Emma Rosen in her recent book *The Radical Sabbatical*. Emma had studied for and was set for a potentially prestigious career in the civil service, having been given a highly sought-after position, only to realise that it wasn't what she had been expecting. Instead of sticking with it and continuing in a role that she wasn't entirely happy with, she decided to do something quite radical and endeavour to shape her own future by spending some time trying out a variety of other jobs, in order to find out which suited her best. This turned into a project to promote career fulfilment for young people and better career education, to which she gave the name *Twenty-five before twenty-five*, the age limit she gave herself, and the number of jobs she intended to do.

C Emma started by making a list of jobs she had been attracted to while she was growing up which ranged from archaeologist to publishing editor. Then she went all out to achieve her aim and work her way through the list. On her journey she gained insights into new approaches to finding a career that she has since shared in talks and interviews, and which make up a significant part of her book. It includes some sections recounting her experiences as well as others which give advice to young people embarking on their career paths.

D One of the main points Emma wants to make is about finding out in real terms what a future job involves, and she is adamant that this can only be done by either experiencing the job first hand – through a work placement – or by talking to people in detail about the roles they carry out and how their industry in general is doing. Checking jobs out online is all very well but limited in what you can learn about the day-to-day realities of the actual job, with its upsides and downsides. According to Emma, many jobs are apt to be glamorised by the marketing and by hearsay. For example, working as an archaeologist had sparked her excitement, but while doing that job in Transylvania as part of her project, she found it back-breaking and dirty work. Similarly, working in TV production had always appealed, but the reality showed her an outdated, hierarchical system that she was not comfortable to be working in.

E Something else Emma is keen to promote is the idea of a portfolio career – where a person has many strings to their bow. The days are gone when people chose one career which would see them through a lifetime of work. Today she advises that young people should start off by keeping their options open and considering five or six different potential careers as opposed to just one or two. This increases the number of job opportunities and allows people to be more objective in their decisions. In addition to this, she advocates considering a range of ways of working that can enable people to do multiple jobs, some at the same time. She cites the example of doing a nine-to-five job for a few days a week and working on an online or creative business at the weekends.

F Clearly, how we view our future career depends on the individual. Some strive for security, some for success, some for contentment, some for adventure. Emma's priorities were to make a difference and to be autonomous, and her advice is considered fascinating and well worth looking at. Could YOU list twenty-five jobs you'd like to give a go? What would they be? Let's have your lists on the website!

10D LISTENING AND VOCABULARY

1 🔊 *58* **Listen to an interview about working from home. Tick the points that are NOT mentioned.**

1 ☐ travelling   **5** ☐ efficiency
2 ☐ salaries   **6** ☐ meetings
3 ☐ distractions   **7** ☐ self-discipline
4 ☐ social activities   **8** ☐ taking breaks

2 🔊 *58* **Listen again and choose the correct answers.**

1 The purpose of the documentary is to
  a encourage more people to work from home.
  b present pros and cons of working from home.
  c outline the lives of several different workers.
  d compare and contrast various ways of working.

2 According to Ron, an advantage to choosing your own working hours is that people
  a do not have to work such long hours.
  b earn significantly more money.
  c avoid work colleagues they do not get on with.
  d approach work with a clearer head.

3 What does Ron say about online meetings?
  a Participants need to adopt different rules.
  b People should control their expressions and gestures.
  c They are less likely to be productive.
  d Certain members may be ignored.

4 Ron advises people working from home to
  a dress the same as they do for going to work.
  b pay attention to health and safety regulations.
  c learn how to maintain their IT themselves.
  d keep the same working hours as in the office.

5 What is true about the presenter?
  a She may need to work from home in the future.
  b She is good friends with her current colleagues.
  c She agrees that there are distractions at work.
  d She lacks enough self-discipline to work from home.

Vocabulary extension

3 **Complete the sentences with the words from the box , which you heard in the recording in Exercise 1.**

> board   company   dark   line   oil   ~~paint~~

1 I don't mean to *paint* the wrong picture – I love my job, it's just that I have too much on my plate.
2 If you decide to move out of the city, you have to take on _____ all the implications regarding job opportunities.
3 People who choose a particular _____ of work need to accept what it entails, e.g. regarding hours.
4 I know it's disappointing not to get a promotion, but you're in good _____ – my brother missed out too – and he's been in his job for five years!
5 Please don't keep me in the _____ about the plans – I need to know in order to organise my week.
6 He's been burning the midnight _____ recently, trying to get the project finished.

4 **ON A HIGH NOTE Write a short paragraph about whether you would like to work from home. Say why.**

Pronunciation

5 🔊 *59* **Read the extract from Ron's interview in Exercise 1 and mark where you think pauses (//) should be. Listen and check.**

> A lot of people enjoy the interaction of being around other people // physically. However, mandatory working from home may soon be on the cards, meaning people won't always have the choice. And there are considerable benefits of remote working. First and foremost is that there is no longer the need to commute. Commuting takes time, costs money, causes pollution and can be stressful. At home you only need to travel from one room to another! Just think about it. Your working hours are much more under your control. You have flexibility. Not only can you get up later – meaning your brain is brighter and less tired – but you can also put in hours when it suits you. In my book, some people work better in the evening, so sitting down to work later in the day would suit them better – in some cases, even burning the midnight oil!

ACTIVE PRONUNCIATION | Pausing

When we speak, we insert pauses for different reasons. They are used:

• to add emphasis to key points – pausing before saying something important.
• to signpost a change in topic or tone.
• to clarify the meaning. Full stops, commas and dashes in written language need to be replaced with pauses in spoken language to allow listeners to follow our lines of thought more clearly.
• after words or phrases used to order discourse.
• as a mental filler. Instead of using fillers such as *um* ..., *er* ..., we can use pauses while gathering our thoughts.

---

6 🔊 *60* **Mark pauses (//) in the sentences. Listen and check.**

1 Quite honestly, // I have absolutely no idea.
2 What I want to say is that I would be only too happy to work from home.
3 It's an interesting point. And then there are all those people who literally cannot work from home.
4 To start with, students need to be given a variety of experiences while they are still studying.
5 It's crazy the time we waste. Think about travelling to the station, waiting on the platform, sitting on the train ... And then there's the journey – maybe only short, but still taking time – from the station to your workplace.

UNIT VOCABULARY PRACTICE > page 121

1 🔊 **61** Listen and repeat the phrases. How do you say them in your language?

SPEAKING | Toning language down

Choose adjectives or rephrase in ways that are less abrupt or have a more positive connotation.

inconsiderate – unkind

confrontational – likes to face problems

REPHRASING NEGATIVE COMMENTS

I wouldn't say that. I think it's more a case of them taking time to evaluate your work.

I'd be more inclined to say that it's a challenge.

That's one way of putting it.

Surely, that's an exaggeration. He's just getting up to speed.

I don't think that's particularly helpful. It might be better to point out that you need more time.

That's a bit harsh, don't you think?

It might be a little challenging at times, but generally speaking, it could be worse.

I admit it seems rather complex.

2 Complete the mini-conversations with the correct phrases from the Speaking box.

Becky The targets Mr Rains wants us to meet are simply laughable!

Sam ¹*I'd be more inclined* to say they're a little ambitious.

Nick Our football team hasn't got a hope of winning the next match.

Ann ²_____, don't you think?

Sue I'm never going to get a reply from the company.

Mia ³_____that. They'll probably be in touch soon.

Jamie Every electronic device I've got is playing up. No gadgets are built to last these days.

Scott I think ⁴_____ of us buying the cheaper ones on the market.

Lia This course is impossible. It's way too difficult for us.

Jim ⁵_____ at times. But it will be fine.

Kurt My advice is to throw it away and buy a new one. It's rubbish.

Ludger I don't ⁶_____. I'm sure I can salvage something.

Pierre This is utterly ridiculous. I can't understand a thing!

Lucy I ⁷_____ complex. But I think we need to think it through.

Lenny He hasn't got a clue what he's talking about.

Zac That's ⁸_____ it. I'd say he just needs to read up on the subject more.

3 🔊 **62** Complete the conversation with the correct phrases, using the words in brackets. Listen and check.

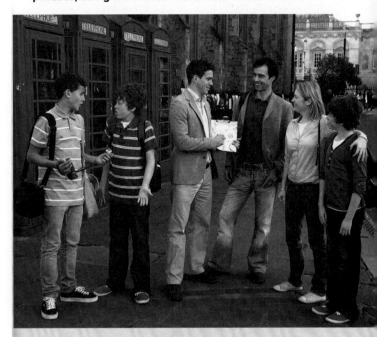

Alisha Have you seen this job advert? They want someone who can speak three languages. That's ridiculous. No one speaks three languages!

Ivan ¹*I admit it* (**ADMIT**) seems rather excessive for a tourist guide.

Alisha And it says you have to be available for eight hours every day except Wednesdays. That's asking for the moon!

Ivan ²_____ (**WAY**). The hours do seem a little long.

Alisha And here – just look at this – you need to have high grades in every subject. That is totally over the top.

Ivan ³_____ (**SAY**). They just want applicants who are relatively bright.

Alisha But it's a holiday job, I ask you! Another requirement is a detailed knowledge of the city geographically and historically. Nobody will have that knowledge unless they're at university!

Ivan ⁴_____ (**EXAGGERATION**). Lots of people who live here know a lot about our area.

Alisha Maybe. This advert is just putting my back up. And the salary is ridiculous. It's peanuts! They just want to rip everyone off. I bet they charge the tourists huge amounts for the guide.

Ivan ⁵_____ (**CASE**) them trying to make as much money as they can during the short summer season.

Alisha Well, no one in their right mind would apply for this. No one is that gullible.

Ivan ⁶_____ (**INCLINED**) say that only a few will have the necessary requirements. And they should be able to command higher fees.

Alisha Exactly. So, you DO agree!

UNIT VOCABULARY PRACTICE > page 121 | 119

Clearly state the topic of the report.	**REPORT ON CAREERS CONFERENCE AT TRUMPTON COLLEGE**
Outline what will be included.	**Introduction** The aim of this report is to evaluate the benefits of attending the annual careers conference at Trumpton College and to make recommendations as to whether future students should be encouraged to go.
Give headings to individual sections.	**Attendees** All Year 12 students were advised to attend the conference, which was held at Trumpton College over the weekend of the 24–25 May. The College is easily accessible by train so overnight accommodation was not required. As a result, a large number of students from our school attended on both days.
Use formal and objective language throughout.	**Conference organisation** The organisation of the conference was impressive. There was a well-balanced programme of talks and demonstrations, and more serious and in-depth lectures were alternated with the lighter 'hands-on' workshops and exhibitions. This ensured that maximum attention from the audience was maintained. There was also sufficient time in the schedule to allow interaction between groups of students from different educational establishments, as well as opportunities to mix socially with the speakers.
Describe events succinctly.	**Speakers** An excellent range of speakers covered topics of interest to our students. There were educational psychologists, experts on job applications and of course, representatives of different professions. What was impressive was that they were not intent on giving us an idealised picture of a job or career, but also went into detail about their own personal experiences in different roles, without glossing over any negatives. Inevitably some speakers were more articulate than others, but this is only to be expected at a conference.
Avoid repetition.	
Link the conclusion with the rest of the report.	**Recommendations** The vast majority of our students who attended the conference reported that they thoroughly enjoyed their experience and maintained that they had learned a great deal from the speakers and exhibitions. Clearly, hearing about a variety of possible career paths can open our eyes to previously unconsidered opportunities and it is vital for students to be equipped with as much information as possible before making life-changing decisions and embarking on a career. It is highly recommended that future students can access this same experience next year.
Make clear recommendations with justifications.	

1 Read the report. Replace the underlined words and phrases with formal equivalents from the report.

1 Three students from my class <u>went to</u> the recent seminar about different working practices. *attended*

2 <u>I think it is a great idea if</u> students can get individual careers advice on a regular basis. _____

3 Dan is <u>better at speaking</u> than I am. _____

4 There was <u>definitely enough</u> time to write up the report before class. _____

5 They <u>didn't set out to give</u> us the wrong information to buy particular products. _____

2 Choose the correct words to complete the sentences.

1 The *plan / purpose* of this report is to outline the benefits of the course.

2 This report will *serve / manage* as a record of the period of work experience.

3 This report sets *out to / about* describe the course.

4 *Overall / Precisely* the experience was beneficial.

5 If these recommendations are *placed / implemented*, the quality of the course will improve.

3 WRITING TASK Read the task below and write a report.

> Your school asked students in your class to organise a few days shadowing a relative or family friend at their workplace and to write a report on the experience. The report should include information about who you shadowed, for how long and what the experience was like. Finish with an evaluation of how useful the work shadowing was, and whether you would recommend it to future students.

ACTIVE WRITING | A report

1 Plan your report.
- Think about who you might shadow, what this person's work involves and what you might learn.
- Divide your notes into clear sections for a report.

2 Write the report.
- Give it a title.
- Give each section a heading.
- Give a clear evaluation and recommendation.
- Use formal and objective language.

3 Check that ...
- you have included all the points in the task.
- there are no spelling, grammar or punctuation mistakes.

1 10A VOCABULARY AND SPEAKING Complete the mini-conversations with the correct idioms and collocations using the words from the box.

call/day draw/line have/say intrude target/meet throw/all

Bill We've been working on this for four hours. I'm shattered! Aren't you?

Lucy I certainly am. Let's **¹**_call it a day_.

Nina I'm not sure whether to go to the drama club meeting after school. It will go on quite late.

Phil They're going to discuss upcoming productions. I think it's important for you to **²**_____.

Lena I think some parents help their children too much with their homework sometimes.

Meg Yes, it's important to **³**_____ between helping and cheating!

Noah My dad's been so busy recently we've hardly seen him.

Luke Mine too – he's got loads of **⁴**_____ at work and he's doing a lot of overtime.

Vicky I seem to be getting assignment after assignment these days. I never get any free time.

James It's hard, isn't it? Are you ever tempted to **⁵**_____ and get a job?

Gina I hear your sister has resigned from her job?

Nick Yes, it started to **⁶**_____ her family time, so she decided to leave.

2 10C READING AND VOCABULARY Complete the sentences with the words from the box.

apt calling cards covet destined envision spark

1 What do you _envision_ yourself doing in five years' time?

2 Some people _____ the idea of starting their own business, but it is a lot harder work than it looks.

3 It's on the _____ that many current jobs will disappear over the next decade because of advances in technology.

4 Employers are _____ to select applicants who have a certain amount of work experience in addition to the relevant qualifications.

5 If a prospective job does not _____ your excitement, it may turn out to be the wrong choice for you.

6 It is said that becoming a nurse or a teacher is a _____ and people who choose these careers do so from a desire to help others.

7 Sometimes it takes a long time to find the job that you feel _____ to do – but it will be worth the wait.

3 10C READING AND VOCABULARY Choose the correct words a–c to complete the text.

One of my relatives has actually **¹**__ her dream of having a book published – at the age of seventy-five! She had always thought it was just a **²**__ dream that she would never achieve, but she's done it! She's been a teacher all her working life and **³**__ down her talent at story-telling, thinking she was not really very special. But last year she decided to look back at some old diaries she'd written in 1940s England. She said in doing so she really **⁴**__ back the years and saw the potential for a novel. Her husband, my uncle, has been very **⁵**__ of her. It shows what you can do if you **⁶**__ your mind to it!

1 **a** made   **b** realised   **c** developed
2 **a** glass   **b** ball   **c** pipe
3 **a** played   **b** toned   **c** pushed
4 **a** folded   **b** recorded   **c** rolled
5 **a** kind   **b** supportive **c** loyal
6 **a** set   **b** imagine   **c** give

4 10D LISTENING AND VOCABULARY Match the two parts of the sentences.

1 ☐ If you make good notes during class, it will hold
2 ☐ People who feel themselves stuck
3 ☐ When you're in charge of a project, the buck
4 ☐ You shouldn't expect a good job just to land
5 ☐ Having run her business for ten years, my mum took
6 ☐ It often pays to work
7 ☐ When my dad's files got deleted, he blew
8 ☐ I was about to register when I realised I wasn't cut

a in your lap without actively going out and looking.
b in a rut at work should check out new opportunities.
c out to be an engineer and changed my course.
d you in good stead for when it comes to revising.
e your way up in a company, as you benefit from the experience.
f a back seat and let someone else be in charge.
g a fuse and shouted at the computer!
h stops with you when there are problems.

5 10E SPEAKING AND VOCABULARY Choose the correct words to complete the sentences.

1 If I'm being _brutally_ / _violently_ honest, I would say this report was rushed and needed more thought.

2 I like people who are upfront because at least you know where you _appear_ / _stand_ with them.

3 Our teacher never minces his _language_ / _words_ – if he doesn't like your work, he'll say so.

4 You really need to tone _off_ / _down_ your language – sometimes you come across as really rude.

5 It's OK to _speak_ / _tell_ your mind, but please try not to upset too many people.

6 ON A HIGH NOTE Write a short paragraph about your hopes and dreams for a future career, including where you see yourself in ten years' time.

1 **For each learning objective, write 1–5 to assess your ability.**

1 = I don't feel confident. 5 = I feel confident.

	Learning objective	Course material	How confident I am (1–5)
10A	I can tell the difference between formal and informal registers when talking about work.	Student's Book pp.138–139	
10B	I can use gerunds and infinitives.	Student's Book pp.140–141	
10C	I can identify specific details in an article.	Student's Book pp.142–143	
10D	I can draw inferences from the interview and talk about leadership qualities.	Student's Book p.144	
10E	I can tell the difference between positive and negative connotations and talk about honesty.	Student's Book p.145	
10F	I can write a report.	Student's Book pp.146–147	

2 **Which of the skills above would you like to improve in? How?**

Skill I want to improve in	How I can improve

3 **What can you remember from this unit?**

New words I learned and most want to remember	Expressions and phrases I liked	English I heard or read outside class

GRAMMAR AND VOCABULARY

1 **Complete the sentences with the words from the box. There are two extra words.**

back   bush   ~~fuse~~   have   mince   mind   seat   tone

1 My brother nearly blew a *fuse* when he realised I'd borrowed his car to go to the party.
2 It puts my mum's _____ up if we play loud music.
3 The boss didn't _____ his words when he found Tina had thrown a sickie.
4 It's a question of taking a back _____ for a while and letting someone else do the hard work.
5 You won't achieve anything unless you really set your _____ to it.
6 Everybody needs to _____ their say before we make a decision.

/ 5

2 **Complete the sentences with the correct words formed from the words in bold.**

1 If you are *upfront* about the problems you're facing, the manager will understand. **FRONT**
2 The head teacher is absolutely _____ in taking forward these new policies. **RESOLVE**
3 My family were extremely _____ while I was doing my university final exams. **SUPPORT**
4 There is no need to be so _____ – I wasn't criticising, simply making a point. **DEFEND**
5 Being _____ never gets you anywhere, it just exacerbates a bad situation. **CONFRONT**
6 I can't stand _____, offensive sports fans. **MOUTH**

/ 5

3 **Choose the correct words to complete the sentences.**

1 After checking through the homework, the teacher went on *to give / giving* us our next assignment.
2 Did you happen *to see / seeing* my new book?
3 If I do this online course, it will mean *to set / setting* aside an hour or two on Saturday mornings.
4 Don't avoid *to confront / confronting* any weaknesses you might have – that's the way to make progress.
5 I can't help *to wonder / wondering* why our teacher chose to come to work at our school.

/ 5

4 **Complete the sentences with the correct forms of the verbs in brackets.**

1 Set out early or you'll risk *being held up* (hold up) by the traffic.
2 When I got to the building, I remembered _____ (ask) to use the back entrance, so I went round.
3 From Jon's email, he appears _____ (work) on an interesting project for a while and wants our help.
4 I can't imagine _____ (teach) to drive by my father – we'd argue all the time!
5 I was quite upset _____ (not give) the chance to resit the exam. I know I could have passed.
6 He's used to _____ (not be) in the limelight.

/ 5

USE OF ENGLISH

5 **Choose the correct phrases (a–d) to complete the text.**

IT'S NEVER TOO LATE!

Lynn Ruth Miller was 71 when she became a stand-up comedian, and in an interview at the age of 86, the lady was still bubbling over with enthusiasm and proud **¹**__ a dream at such an advanced age. Her experience of life seems **²**__ her in good stead for those golden years, and she advised everyone **³**__ to give into the passiveness of retirement, but to embrace it. She remembered **⁴**__ by her mother to prepare to be a good wife and mother, and she had certainly not been expected **⁵**__ fame as perhaps the oldest stand-up in the world!

1 **a** of been realising   **b** being realised
    c of having realised   **d** of realise
2 **a** holding   **b** to have held
    c to hold   **d** to be held
3 **a** not being tempted   **b** not tempting
    c not having tempted   **d** not to be tempted
4 **a** being told   **b** to be told
    c to have been told   **d** telling
5 **a** achieving   **b** to be achieved
    c achieve   **d** to achieve

/ 5

6 **Complete the second sentence using the word in bold so that it means the same as the first one. Use between three and six words, including the word in bold.**

1 My friend Sara is very curious and doesn't like it if people don't include her in a conversation. **BEAR**
    My friend Sara is very curious and *can't bear not being included* in a conversation.
2 It is important to be able to give your opinion in a meeting. **MIND**
    It is important to be able to _____ in a meeting.
3 You have to raise your hand during a video conference or no one will notice you. **IGNORED**
    If you don't raise your hand in a video conference, you'll end _____ by everyone.
4 Dividing your time equally between work and family life is not always easy. **STRIKE**
    It can be hard _____ between work and family life.
5 For some people, following an academic career is not the right thing. **CUT**
    Not everyone _____ an academic career.
6 She'd really like to have my job. **COVETS**
    She _____ job.

/ 5

/ 30

123

PHRASAL VERBS

be taken aback: I was quite taken aback by how little knowledge the students had.

blend in: I try to blend in when I'm travelling abroad.

blow sb away: I saw a performance by this company in London a while back and I was blown away by it.

blow up (in one's face): Cheating in an exam may blow up in your face.

bowl sb over: He was bowled over by her beauty.

branch out: He's thinking about branching out into One-of-a-kind ugly accessories.

break into: After selling my products in Europe for five years, I decided to break into the Chinese market.

break out: Three men have broken out of a top-security jail.

breeze through sth: I've always breezed through exams, really.

call on sb/sth: My aim as a tennis coach is to help people learn to play tennis, calling on their own natural abilities.

cater for sb/sth: She finds herself having to work in a strange house, which caters for bizarre monsters.

check in on sb/sth: I decided to find myself a partner who would check in on me from time to time.

clamp down on sb/sth: The authorities felt they had no choice but to clamp down on him.

click with sb: When we know it, it's easier to be ourselves and to find the tribe that we really click with.

come about: His success came about through many years of hard work.

come across: We may come across more negatively than we realise.

come down (by): I suppose I could come down by £40 a month.

come down on sb: I think parents shouldn't come down too hard on teenagers.

come out with sth: What they've just come out with is a bad idea.

come up against: Unfortunately, he came up against a few problems.

confide in sb: I've never felt able to confide in my sister.

crack up: Everyone in the class just cracked up.

cram in/into: Trying to cram too many different tasks in/into the same couple of hours is quite challenging.

curl up: Marcus enjoys curling up with a good book.

cut back on sth: The school had to cut back on its spending.

cut down on sth: I just can't cut down on chocolate!

drum sth into sb: The time teachers spend drumming information into their students could be better employed in teaching them how to think.

fade away: Apart from anything else, it fades away in a few weeks, when the building gets dirty again.

fall back into: I was amazed at how easily I fell back into the old routine.

fall out: I didn't want to fall out with her.

flood back: Seeing him again brought all the memories flooding back.

free up: If we don't spend too much time memorising facts, that frees up our time.

get away: We want to get away every weekend this summer.

give in to sth: Don't give in to the temptation to argue back.

go against sth: No one dared to go against the rules.

hand sth down: Nature refers to hereditary factors, everything handed down to us biologically from our parents.

hand sth in: It isn't an excuse for not handing in your essays on time.

hang out with: If we are a Real Madrid supporter, we hang out with like-minded people.

head off: When these birds fly for the first time, they head off out to sea alone.

hold off on: Parents should hold off on criticising what teenagers have said until they've really listened to them.

hold sb back: Teenagers whose parents hold them back may eventually lose confidence in themselves.

hold sth against sb: If parents are too strict, their kids may hold it against them later on.

kick in: The painkillers kicked in and he became sleepy.

kick off: The film kicks off with a realistic picture of modern Japanese family life.

knock off sth: We had to knock quite a lot off the price before we could sell our house.

knock sth up: Could you knock up a fabulous birthday cake?

let down: She wanted to get off the bike and go home, but she knew she couldn't let down her team.

lift off: One officer reported seeing the lights lift off into the sky.

line up: Little did Billy know when lining up for the race that day how his life was going to change.

live up to sth: The documentary did not live up to my expectations.

pass up: I got a chance to work for a start-up, but decided to pass up on the opportunity.

play sth down: I did a lot of street dancing in my early teens, but I was apt to play down my talent.

plough on: Julia ploughed on with the endless exam papers.

plump for: What kind of car would you ideally plump for?

pull sth off: It beats me how they pull it off again and again.

put sb off doing sth: Having to cram the facts into my head like that really put me off learning altogether.

put sth aside: An experiment asked participants how much of their income should be put aside.

put sth off: People tend to put things off because they are lazy.

put sth up (for sale online): My dad put some old vinyl records up for sale online.

puzzle over sth: The sighting raises some questions which we have been puzzling over for years.

reel sth off: Anyone could probably reel off the standard list: salt, sugar, bitter and sour.

run out of steam: I get started on something with loads of enthusiasm and then, after a few weeks, I run out of steam and stop.

rustle up: I'll rustle up a couple of steaks on the barbecue.

sail through: Adam sailed through his final exams.

set about doing sth: It is natural for teenagers to set about trying to do things differently from their parents.

set forth: Parents should let teenagers set forth their views, even if they don't agree with them.

set in: When boredom sets in, the healthy habits waver.

set out to do sth: Parents might have worried when their children set out to spend three days camped out in a muddy field.

set sb against: Arguing about this can set teenagers and parents against each other.

set up: My family set up this business 100 years ago.

shake sth off: If we remind another person of someone disagreeable, this association will be hard to shake off.

shoo sb out/away: There were so many flies – we tried to shoo them away.

sign up for sth: I decided to sign up for the school hockey team.

sort sth out: She went to a psychiatrist to try to sort her problems out.

spring up: Fast-food restaurants are springing up all over town.

stock up: There has been a move away from stocking up on essentials.

stumble across: Researchers have stumbled across a drug that may help patients with this disease.

sweat out: I prefer to do something that makes you sweat out the stress – like lifting weights.

take on: Be careful you don't take on too much extra work.

take sth in: He watches the older kids just taking it all in.

take to doing sth: When I was a teenager, I took to wearing jeans with loads of holes in them.

trawl through: I'll have to trawl through all my lecture notes again.

wear sth out: I wear out my thumbs on fast and furious video games.

weasel out of sth: He's now in court trying to weasel out of $25 million in debts.

win over: Even when our parents had said no initially, he could always win them over.

wind down: Just listening to the click of the needles helps me wind down.

PREPOSITIONS

PREPOSITIONS IN PHRASES

AGAINST
against one's best interest: The sunk-cost fallacy often leads us to do things which are really against our best interests.

AT
at a disadvantage: Introverted people seem to be at a disadvantage, but all is not lost.

at no time: At no time were we offered an apology of any kind.

at sb's expense: Marcus noticed the girls might be having fun at his expense.

at sea: I'm completely at sea with the new computer system.

at top speed: The tube hurtled round a bend at top speed.

at the end of the day: At the end of the day, the children really won't be any bother, they're quite self-sufficient.

BY
by nature: Even though I'm pretty strong and hard-working by nature, I do get exhausted and fed up sometimes.

by the skin of one's teeth: We managed to catch the plane by the skin of our teeth!

FOR
for the time being: For the time being, she is living with her father.

IN
(be) in a fix: One day it's not going to work and I'll still be in a fix when I get up!

(be) in two minds: I'm in two minds here. There are pros and cons for each solution.

(live) in each other's pockets: Their families would live in each other's pockets.

in a frenzy: The women were screaming, and in a frenzy to get home.

in a nutshell: OK, that's our proposal in a nutshell.

in any case: In any case, you should avoid scalding hot soups that get cold fast and deep-fried food that may become soggy.

in awe: I was just in awe, really.

in complete agreement over sth: Scientists are in agreement over the benefits of this procedure.

in debt: His father was a metalworker, who was constantly in debt.

in edgeways: You can't get a word in edgeways!

in evidence: The police are always in evidence at football matches.

in excess of: The coach was in excess of thirty minutes late.

in line with: When we know this, we can consider whether the choices we make are in line with these values.

in motion: It was poetry in motion.

in no way: In no way am I responsible for his actions.

in point of fact: In point of fact, these industries are estimated to have generated around $250 billion worldwide last year.

in sight: I don't binge and eat everything in sight – just a few pieces of cheese or a handful of crisps will be enough.

in the long run: Moving to Spain will be better for you in the long run.

in the strongest terms: I would like to express in the strongest terms, how deeply disappointed we were.

ON
(be) on a steep learning curve: We've been on a steep learning curve since the beginning of the course.

(be) on the lookout for sth: I'm always on the lookout for a good book.

on a larger scale: Should it be adopted on a larger scale in other places, it could reduce our dependency on pesticides.

on a par with: The wages of clerks were on a par with those of manual workers.

on balance: I think on balance I prefer the old system.

on condition that: Anything could be on the table on condition that it's healthy and fresh.

on fire: You're on fire today, Sam! You're always the driving force behind the crazy adventures.

on full alert: Your senses are suddenly on full alert.

on one's lonesome: They're just as happy on their lonesome most of the time.

on the cards: Whatever our abilities, there is always a fulfilling career on the cards.

on the contrary: On the contrary, there are clearly many benefits.

PREPOSITIONS AFTER NOUNS
aptitude for: I don't really have that much natural aptitude for studying.

awareness of: The most important rationale for buying local goods is the growing awareness of climate change.

(be) nuts about sth: They've always been nuts about music or horses or fashion.

campaign against: Jameela Jamil has been leading a campaign against airbrushing photos.

congratulations on: Congratulations on a superb performance!

contempt for: No one wants to be greeted in shops by surly staff showing contempt for the customer.

dedication to: Should you demonstrate dedication to work, we may offer you a permanent position.

demon for: I know I'm a demon for drumming my fingers on the desk when I'm impatient, and people get really irritated with me.

dependency on: This technique could reduce our dependency on pesticides.

difference to: Watching these videos is like a form of therapy and can make a real difference to people's lives.

downside to: There are undoubtedly some downsides to shopping in supermarkets.

drawback to: In spite of these benefits, there are some clear drawbacks to shopping locally.

emphasis on: In Japan there is a lot of emphasis on politeness.

increase in: There has been a three percent increase in tips left by diners.

insight into sth: The experience gave me an insight into the learning processes in young children.

investigation into: The results of the investigation into the collision will not be known before March.

permission for sth/to do sth: The students have been given permission to leave early.

preference for: There will always be a preference for those things which they are accustomed to.

rationale for: The most important rationale for buying local goods is the growing awareness of climate change.

reason for: The reasons for these depressing figures are easily explicable.

reasoning behind: The reasoning behind that is that it'd be more of a long-term solution.

requisite for: Constant grinning should not be a requisite for a job involving interaction with clients.

research into: There's been a lot of research into first language acquisition.

respect for: Having good table manners means that you have respect for the people sitting with you.

scope for sth: However, as they grow older, the scope for dreaming extends too.

slave to: I'm a slave to fashion.

PREPOSITIONS AFTER ADJECTIVES
apt to do sth: Our dreams are apt to change at various stages of our lives.

barred from: She also campaigned to allow for women to vote who were barred from voting at that time.

blasé about sth: We're so used to films that feature incredible special effects that we've become blasé about it.

bound for (London): The train was going eastwards, bound for a place she had never heard of.

critical of sb: I wouldn't want someone being too critical of me, but it's really helped me to keep on track.

dependent on sth: Do we really want to be so utterly dependent on technology?

destined to: They may not be destined to become famous themselves, but we can learn a lot from these kinds of role models.

destructive to sth: The dialogue created an inner environment of stress that was ultimately destructive to the goal of hitting the ball well.

entitled to: One day it was announced that girls were no longer entitled to education.

forced into doing sth: Had this ancient Chinese tradition not been rediscovered, farmers would be forced into using a whole range of pesticides.

inclined to do sth: I'd be more inclined to say that it's a challenge – and we rise to challenges, don't we, Joe?

inundated with/by sth: 'How to become a happier you' is a hot topic at the moment and we are being inundated with advice and tips.

parallel to sth: Hold your left foot parallel to your right foot.

pertinent to sth: This cycle is very pertinent to many of the stress reactions we experience in everyday life.

perturbed about: More and more people are perturbed about products having been manufactured under terrible working conditions.

reliant on sth: We need to retain our ability to function without being reliant on technology.

supportive of: My parents were extremely supportive of my choice.

upfront about sth: John likes to have his say and he always speaks his mind – he's always upfront about things.

willing to do sth: If we want to achieve anything, we have to be willing to step out of our comfort zone.

PREPOSITIONS AFTER VERBS

adapt to: The brain is quick to adapt to the new normal, and discard any skills it perceives as unnecessary.

apply oneself to sth: I now apply myself to one task at a time.

ascribe sth to sth: It would seem logical to ascribe a racing heart and raised blood pressure to nervousness and apprehension.

associate sth with sth: Your brain associates this place with sleep and rest.

audition for: You said you'd audition for the play.

authorise sb to do sth: He authorised her whole family to be set free.

backfire on: Trying to make your partner jealous by flirting with other people can easily backfire on you.

ban from: I was banned from going out with my friends for a couple of weekends.

bar sb from (doing) sth: She also campaigned to allow for women to vote who were barred from voting at that time.

be all down to sth/sb: I'm a midnight snacker, and it's all down to the power of my dreams.

benefit from: Many thousands have benefited from the new treatment.

blame for: The report blames poor safety standards for the accident.

bombard with: We're continually being bombarded with information, advice, warnings and threats relating to healthy eating.

cluster around: Everyone was clustering around the info boards.

comment on: People were always commenting on his size.

compliment sb on sth: Bob complimented me on my new hairstyle.

conceive of: This implies that the languages spoken by the Inuit mould the way they conceive of the world.

concern oneself with: We need to concern ourselves with maintaining a good state of emotional health.

conform to: We can forgive her for not conforming to the twenty-first century attitudes half a century beforehand.

congratulate sb on sth: Who is the first person you would tell about an achievement, so they could congratulate you on it?

contrast with: The texture is amazing, and it contrasts really well with the gold satin blouse and the earrings and so on.

contribute to: Research indicates some factors which can contribute to the experience.

cram for: If you take a holiday, you'll be in a better mental state to start cramming for your exam.

criticise for: He has been criticised for incompetence.

deduce from: We can probably deduce from this that they don't feel the need to quantify precisely in the way that many of us do.

deflect sb from sth: Nothing can deflect me from reaching my goal.

devote sth to sb: When you shop locally, you can devote some of your time to your family and friends.

divert sb/sth away: The magician made a big noise to divert the audience's attention away.

entice into: Don't let anyone entice you into eating more than you had planned.

entitle sb to (do) sth: Membership entitles you to the monthly journal.

fall prey to: Our decision-making ability can be dramatically improved by recognising when we may be falling prey to this fallacy.

fiddle with sth: She was at her desk in the living room, fiddling with a deck of cards.

float away: He could feel himself floating away from everyone and everything.

gape at: What are all these people gaping at?

glisten with: The boy's back was glistening with sweat.

gorge oneself on sth: Ducks gorge themselves on the insects and weeds which would otherwise destroy his crops.

head for (a place): Well, what I do is head for the kitchen, rustle up what I've just seen on the screen – and then feel awful afterwards.

impose sth on sb: She has imposed her tastes and values on him.

interact with: Lucy interacts well with other children in the class.

intrude on: It was the way it intruded on my personal life that was the problem.

lobby for: Who lobbied for women to be allowed to vote in elections?

moan at: I moan at him because he purses his lips when he's irritated.

munch on: Barry sat munching on an apple.

ooze with: Create the perfect picture of a gooey chocolate cake, oozing with light, fluffy cream.

pass sth on to sb: He didn't pass any of this information on to the kids so they wouldn't worry.

persist with: If you have already invested time or money in something, you should persist with it no matter what.

pile with: The room was piled high with boxes.

ponder over: The university board is still pondering over the matter.

pop into: It could be that a picture just pops into her brain and that's the start of a painting.

pride oneself on sth: Choco Shoe prides itself on excellent customer service.

prompt sb to do sth: In the 1950s, a more athletic body came into fashion, and prompted men to start working out.

rebel against: Maybe it's time for both men and women to rebel against being held to external beauty standards.

refer to: Nurture refers to the influence of our environment.

reflect on: It's a good idea to reflect on the pros and cons and the possible outcomes of a situation.

sneak into (a place): What places did you sneak into when you were young?

soar through: What fascinates me is the sudden acceleration of speed as the rocket soars through space.

sort sth into (piles): Please sort the books into piles.

strive for: We must continue to strive for greater efficiency.

subscribe to: My dad subscribes to the theory that employees should always talk about what's bothering them.

succumb to: We wanted to hear what can trigger people's appetites – when and why they succumb to temptation.

turn into: One of our childhood passions might just turn into a lifelong hobby or even a career.

yearn for: Do you yearn for some naughtily unhealthy American burgers or deep-fried chicken?

yield to: Finally, she yielded to temptation and helped herself to a large slice of cake.

WORD BUILDING

PREFIXES

Prefix	Examples
anti- (= against)	anti-bullying, anti-hacking
co- (= with, together)	co-working, co-pilot
extra- (= more than normal)	extra-special, extra-large
inter- (= between)	international, Internet
multi- (= many)	multi-sensory, multi-talented
over- (= more than expected)	overweight, overload
re- (= again)	re-establish, re-read
self- (= me)	self-confident, self-aware

Prefixes that give an opposite meaning

Prefix	Examples
dis-	disabled, disagree
il-/ir-	illegal, irregular
im-/in-	immature, insecurity
mis-	misjudged, misbehave
non-/un-	nonsense, unacceptable

SUFFIXES

Noun suffixes

Suffix	Examples
-age	marriage, package
-al	proposal
-ant/-ent	assistant, president
-ation/-ion/-ition	communication, rebellion, definition
-cian/-ian	musician, librarian
-dom	freedom
-ence/-ance	defence, appearance
-er/-or/-ist	voyager, sailor, artist
-hood	childhood
-ice	practice, notice
-ing	meaning, revising
-ism	sexism, mechanism
-ment	government, improvement
-ness	weakness, goodness
-ship	relationship, friendship
-sis	analysis, emphasis
-tion/-sion/-cion	obstruction, suspension, suspicion
-ty/-ity	eighty, reality
-ure	pressure, culture

Adjective suffixes

Suffix	Examples
-able/-ible	habitable, horrible
-al	informal, social
-ed	exhausted, relaxed
-ic	artistic, ecstatic
-ing	interesting, matching
-ive	active, productive
-ful/-less	useful, useless
-ous	generous, nervous
-ory/-y	contradictory, chatty
-ly	curly, likely

Adverb suffixes

Suffix	Examples
-ly	effectively, probably

Verb suffixes

Suffix	Examples
-ate	complicate, congratulate
-en	shorten
-ify	clarify, identify
-ise/-ize	victimise, realise
-ute	commute

PRONUNCIATION TABLE

Consonants

p	pair, complete, appear
b	box, abbreviation, job
t	tennis, waiting, attend
d	degree, wedding, word
k	kiss, school, think, section
g	girl, again, luggage, ghost
ʧ	check, match, future
ʤ	judge, page, soldier
f	feel, difficult, laugh, physical
v	verb, nervous, move
θ	third, author, bath
ð	this, father, with
s	saw, notice, sister
z	zone, amazing, choose, quiz
ʃ	ship, sure, station, ocean
ʒ	pleasure, occasion
h	habit, whole, chocoholic
m	meaning, common, sum
n	neat, knee, channel, sun
ŋ	cooking, strong, thanks, sung
l	lifestyle, really, article
r	respect, correct, arrival
j	year, use, beautiful
w	window, one, where

Vowels

ɪ	information, invite
e	sentence, belt
æ	add, match, can
ɒ	not, documentary, wash
ʌ	love, but, luck
ʊ	footwear, look, put
iː	reading, three, magazine
eɪ	race, grey, break
aɪ	advice, might, try
ɔɪ	boy, join
uː	two, blue, school
əʊ	coat, show, phone
aʊ	about, now
ɪə	appear, here
eə	pair, various, square
ɑː	dark, father
ɔː	bought, draw, author
ʊə	tour, pure
ɜː	hurt, third
i	happy, pronunciation, serious
ə	accessory, actor, picture
u	situation, visual, influence

SELF-CHECK ANSWER KEY

Unit 1
Exercise 1
1 tight-fisted 2 frank 3 strong-willed 4 smart cookie 5 live wire 6 soft touch
Exercise 2
1 plump 2 wet 3 thin 4 line 5 Much
Exercise 3
1 have been walking 2 will have walked 3 had been walking 4 had walked 5 will be walking 6 was walking
Exercise 4
1 've been trying 2 haven't had 3 're feeling 4 'd already made 5 was feeling 6 'm forever making
Exercise 5
1 oversimplification 2 vulnerabilities 3 discretion 4 spontaneity 5 sincerity
Exercise 6
1 b 2 a 3 c 4 d 5 b 6 a

Unit 2
Exercise 1
1 stumbled 2 gravely 3 neck 4 share 5 hurdles
Exercise 2
1 a knock-on effect on 2 fidget 3 a breakthrough 4 drives me up the wall 5 brag 6 outlook
Exercise 3
1 Last year not only did we go to Spain, but we went to Portugal too. 2 So difficult was the test that she could not even get past the first three questions. 3 Only after I pass/have passed my driving test next year will I be able to drive without a passenger. 4 Under no circumstances are people allowed to open the train door while the train is moving. 5 Little did we know that an airport strike would delay our flight for four hours. 6 Such a big discount was it on my dream car that I immediately booked a test ride online.
Exercise 4
1 What 2 is 3 all 4 was 5 only 6 also 7 It 8 that 9 what 10 is 11 who/that
Exercise 5
1 did he become Formula 3 champion 2 long was the delay 3 did we know that 4 had been hoping to buy was 5 only then were we able 6 the future holds

Unit 3
Exercise 1
1 bespoke 2 entice 3 detrimental 4 impartial 5 shrewd 6 credulous
Exercise 2
1 cellar – basement 2 walls – mortar 3 beginning – end 4 top – bottom 5 mooning – mooching 6 plough through – plough on with
Exercise 3
1 He will be offered a refund. / A refund will be offered to him. 2 The purchases were sent to the customer. / The customer was sent the purchases. 3 This customer has been promised a refund. / A refund has been promised to this customer. 4 A new dish is being created from unusual ingredients. / Unusual ingredients are being used in a new dish.
Exercise 4
1 b 2 a 3 b 4 a
Exercise 5
1 branched out on her 2 knock something off 3 sweet-talked me into taking 4 meet halfway 5 was eventually prevailed upon
Exercise 6
1 d 2 b 3 c 4 a 5 c 6 b

Unit 4
Exercise 1
1 soggy 2 drops 3 board 4 devoured 5 yearned
Exercise 2
1 sucker 2 lurch 3 rustle 4 slurping 5 wafted 6 mouldy
Exercise 3
1 weren't, wouldn't be studying 2 would never have entered, hadn't been 3 Had you not studied, wouldn't have got 4 Should you need / If you need 5 I liked, would have gone for 6 hadn't bought, wouldn't be
Exercise 4
1 supposing 2 unless 3 provided 4 Without 5 would 6 long as
Exercise 5
1 been 2 would/could 3 otherwise 4 But 5 have 6 were
Exercise 6
1 Had it not been for 2 let your dinner go down before 3 the meal on condition that 4 brings it home (to you) 5 it would not be closed 6 rustle up

Unit 5
Exercise 1
1 debatable 2 valiant 3 atrophy 4 futile 5 leaped 6 deflect
Exercise 2
1 movement – motion 2 in – at 3 into – for 4 went – came 5 to – on 6 determinated – determined
Exercise 3
1 was supposed 2 could 3 ought to 4 from coming 5 managed to sleep
Exercise 4
1 can't have 2 managed to 3 must have 4 supposed to 5 didn't need to 6 might have
Exercise 5
1 run 2 comfort 3 head 4 came
Exercise 6
1 aptitude 2 Perseverance 3 misguided 4 destructive 5 tenacity 6 simplicity 7 mediocrity

Unit 6
Exercise 1
1 c 2 b 3 b 4 a 5 c
Exercise 2
1 apprehension 2 suppress 3 anticipation 4 serenity 5 life-enhancing 6 nerve-wracking
Exercise 3
1 getting 2 to spend 3 visit 4 they were given 5 to have researched
Exercise 4
1 It was rumoured that a famous astronaut would give / was going to give 2 The first computer is thought to have been designed 3 Body language is known to reflect 4 it was believed that health issues could be treated 5 Charlie Chaplin is said to have believed that laughter was/is
Exercise 5
1 freely 2 being 3 It 4 them 5 Off 6 have
Exercise 6
1 gave me the thumbs up 2 has been announced that there will 3 maintained that we should 4 have been inundated with offers from 5 criticised me for not paying enough/more 6 a half-baked plan

Unit 7
Exercise 1
1 garish 2 serendipity 3 take 4 rat 5 away
Exercise 2
1 tongue-in-cheek 2 jaw-dropping 3 finishing touches 4 with a twist 5 well-rounded 6 one-trick pony
Exercise 3
1 which 2 of whom 3 in which 4 – 5 who 6 who

Exercise 4
1 which 2 what 3 that success 4 whom the artist relied 5 both
Exercise 5
1 impenetrable 2 psychological 3 eye-catching 4 melodious 5 advantageous 6 vivacious
Exercise 6
1 lion's 2 whom 3 par 4 which/that 5 period 6 contrary

Unit 8
Exercise 1
1 come 2 hold 3 enjoy 4 hold 5 put 6 set
Exercise 2
1 sparkling 2 lean 3 antisocial 4 standoffish 5 social
Exercise 3
1 weedy 2 arched 3 muscular 4 glossy 5 athletic 6 glowing
Exercise 4
1 ø 2 the 3 ø 4 ø, 5 the, an
Exercise 5
1 b 2 c 3 d 4 d 5 b
Exercise 6
1 to take in what 2 the baby hummingbird that had (just) 3 Jacquie is doing the same 4 clamp down on people using / who use 5 is usually the life and soul 6 animal abuse can't be condoned

Unit 9
Exercise 1
1 boggling 2 light 3 fetched 4 eyebrows 5 stopping 6 riveting
Exercise 2
1 e 2 c 3 d 4 b 5 a
Exercise 3
1 put 2 conclusively 3 lay 4 far-fetched 5 definitive 6 inexplicable
Exercise 4
1 will be 2 will have been waiting 3 won't wake up 4 would be 5 would be waiting 6 will look
Exercise 5
1 bowled me over when my name 2 will leave her books all over 3 would give him some time to 4 never raises her voice at 5 you will watch TV so late 6 raised a few eyebrows
Exercise 6
1 recurring 2 prophetic 3 disregard 4 reputable 5 ridiculed 6 definitive

Unit 10
Exercise 1
1 fuse 2 back 3 mince 4 seat 5 mind 6 have
Exercise 2
1 upfront 2 resolute 3 supportive 4 defensive 5 confrontational 6 loudmouthed
Exercise 3
1 to give 2 to see 3 setting 4 confronting 5 wondering
Exercise 4
1 being held up 2 having been asked / being asked 3 to have been working 4 being taught 5 not to have been given 6 not being
Exercise 5
1 c 2 b 3 d 4 a 5 d
Exercise 6
1 can't bear not being included 2 speak your mind 3 up being ignored 4 to strike the right balance 5 is cut out to follow 6 covets my